The Encyclopedia of NORTH AMERICAN WILD FLOWERS

The Encyclopedia of NORTH AMERICAN WILD FLOWERS

JOAN BARKER

This is a Parragon Publishing Book
First published in 2004

Parragon Publishing
Queen Street House
4 Queen Street
Bath, BA1 1HE, UK

For details of photographs see pages 382/383

Produced by Atlantic Publishing
Designed by Judy Linard

ISBN 1 40543 035 4 (Hardback)
ISBN 1 40543 037 0 (Dutchbound)

Printed in China

CONTENTS

Introduction

There is a fine line between weed and wildflower, and it is by no means a universally accepted division – one person's attractive plant can quite easily be another person's troublesome weed. Wildflowers are flowering plants that grow naturally in the wild – and not just in the open countryside but also in the most urban areas, on vacant lots and cracks in the sidewalk. It is often amazing how such plants will thrive, when all the odds may seem to be stacked against them. In general, this book avoids those species that are widely considered to be invasive weeds, and concentrates mainly on native North American wildflowers. However, there are also many plants commonly seen across North America that are usually thought of as American wildflowers, but which were actually introduced from other areas of the world and have since run wild. Although many of these have been excluded from this book, a few of the most well-loved and widespread are included, along with a note of where they originate from.

The importance of wildflowers

At one time wildflowers were thought to be of little practical importance, and they were picked or dug up at will, wiped out in land development schemes or sprayed out of existence on agricultural land. As a result, some have vanished forever, and others are now endangered species. Luckily we are much wiser now, and plants that are considered to be at risk are usually protected by Congress or local state laws. These days it is recognized that many old herbal remedies do have some value – and who knows what valuable natural assets and cures for disease will be discovered as we continue to examine the wildflowers of our planet? It is therefore important to be responsible in the field – make sure to check local laws and never pick a flower or remove a plant from its environment unless you are quite sure it is acceptable to do so.

Plant types

Plants come in three basic types: annuals, biennials and perennials. Annuals flower and die in one season, biennials flower and die in their second year, and perennials live and flower for three or more years. Some biennials and perennials may retain their leaves over the winter; others lose their leaves in the fall, and are classified as herbaceous or deciduous. Some types keep a few leaves over winter and are described as being semi-evergreen. There is no hard and fast rule as to why some are herbaceous and others evergreen, as both categories can usually be found in members of the same genus.

Plant names

The plant world as a whole is classified into flowering plants (Angiospermae), cone-bearers (Gymnospermae), and ferns (Pteridophytae). Beyond that plants are divided into families, such as Liliaceae or Fabaceae. Within any given family are to be found genera, such as the genus *Primula* or the genus *Drosera* – the title of the genus is placed in italics, and given a capital letter. Finally, within any given genus are to be found the species, which have a lot in common, can interbreed (hybridize) and often have a limited geographical range; an example is *Drosera rotundifolia* (sundew with round leaves) or *Lilium canadense* (lily from Canada). The specific name is not given a capital letter, but is placed in italics, and it usually has some meaning with regard to the nature or the origin of the plant. Further subdivisions within a given species are indicated by "ssp." meaning "subspecies" or "var." meaning "variety," in that descending order. These abbreviations are not put in italics, so there are some plants with quite complex scientific names, such as *Dichelostemma capitatum* ssp. *capitatum*, or *Thalictrum fendleri* var. *polycarpum*. Wildflowers are often more usually known by their common name, for instance *Lilium canadense* is known as the Canada Lily or Meadow Lily. The plants in this book are listed by the most widely accepted common name for ease of reference, but alternative common names, the scientific name and family of each is also given, to aid in a firm identification. Across the world, the same plant may have many different common names, but the scientific name remains constant. The index covers both common and scientific names.

Identifying a wildflower

North America has a wide range of habitats, from semi-tropical to windswept tundra, from desert and arid grassland to lush and moist woodlands. Although some wildflowers will grow in a variety of places, most will grow best under a particular set of circumstances. Forest plants tend to like shade, so will not usually thrive in open meadows; bog plants need a constant supply of water, so will not like areas that dry out on a regular basis. The plants in this book have been placed into groups, depending on the location in which you might most expect to find them growing happily. There are a few that will grow in several types of location, or you may come upon an area that varies in environmental factors in different seasons, so if you can't find a particular plant in one section, try some of the related ones.

Having established the general habitat of a particular wildflower, look at the flower. Whereas cultivated flowers quite often come in a range of colors, each species of wildflower tends to have flowers in only one color, or in a limited range within the color spectrum. The flower can therefore be a very good identifying clue so, within their habitat, plants are arranged here in color groups.

After color you can also consider the general look of the plant. The type of flower is important – single, spike, cluster. See page 22 for illustrations of each flower type. The shape of the leaves and how they are arranged on the stem can also be a great help in narrowing the choice of potential species. Details of these are given in each entry – see the drawings on pages 23-25 for a visual reference for each type.

Finally, when you have a general idea of which plant you are looking at, check the further information on range and the general description to confirm your identification.

THE HABITATS

Rocky, Stony, Dry and Sandy Habitat

Rocky, stony, dry and sandy habitat covers areas with rocky outcrops or cliffs, stones or thick sand on the ground, and a lack of any obvious surface water. Such areas tend to have soil with very little organic material, so it is generally poor in nutrients and will dry out quickly. The soil may also be chalky and alkaline, so acid-loving plants will not choose to grow here. The plants in this section actually prefer poorer soil, and may have developed other ways of picking up the sustenance they need, such as having sticky, insect-catching hairs or fleshy leaves to retain moisture. There may be some crossover with the desert habitat and with the roadside and waste ground habitat, so if the plant you are looking for is not in this section, try those as alternatives.

Water Plants

Water habitat refers to an appreciable depth of fresh water, whether moving or still, such as ponds, lakes, streams and rivers. The plants that grow here are those that either float on the surface of the water or root deep below it and don't mind their base being continually waterlogged. They may have developed special features to cope with the conditions, such as inflated or large, flat leaves to enable the top of the plant to stay on the surface of the water. In areas where flooding is intermittent, or as the water becomes shallower near the shore, the conditions may become boggy or swampy, so if you cannot find what you are looking for in this section, try the boggy, swampy and damp section as an alternative.

Boggy, Swampy and Damp Habitat

Boggy, swampy and damp ground has a great deal of moisture absorbed within it - this may not be immediately evident, but if you tread on the ground your feet will sink and water will come up around them. Although there may be some surface water in scattered areas, this water will not be very deep. Plants in this section like a great deal of water, but do not like their roots or tops being continuously submerged. Most swampy areas inland will be fresh-water, but near the coast or along tidal estuaries the water may be brackish or salty, so if the plant you are looking for is not in this section, try the coastal as well as the water section.

Woodland and Forest Habitat

Woodland and forest habitat covers both deciduous and coniferous forests, and mixtures of the two. The trees may be set very close together - which limits the amount of undergrowth due to restricted light and nutrients – or further apart, which tends to encourage lush undergrowth. Plants that thrive in woodland and forest habitats prefer the shade and shelter that trees offer, and may not like direct sunlight. However, clearings within the wood will offer more open conditions, but with the shelter of surrounding trees. Plants growing in clearings may not be true woodland plants, so if you cannot find what you are looking for, assess other conditions and try the sections covering more open habitats.

Roadside and Waste Ground Habitat

Roadside and waste ground covers all the habitats alongside roads, pathways and other thoroughfares, and ground that has been disturbed or cultivated but now runs wild. Some of the most easily-recognizable wildflowers live in this habitat, plants that you see every day and may have dismissed as weeds. These plants will often grow nearly everywhere else as well, as they are very adaptable and able to take advantage of changing conditions. You may also find quite unexpected plants in this habitat, which have been introduced in seed mixes sown by highway agencies. If you cannot find what you are looking for in here assess the specific conditions, which may point you in the right direction. For instance, if the plant is growing in a flooded ditch, try the boggy, swampy and damp or water habitats.

Desert Habitat

There are many different kinds of desert, but all tend to be generally barren, open habitats with little water, and vegetation that is usually low-growing. The desert can be an inhospitable place, but many plants still manage to thrive there. These areas are rarely totally without water, because there may be streams deep underground, and temperature changes between day and night also cause the natural moisture in the air to condense into morning dew, which can be enough for many plants. Plants living in these regions have adapted to poor nutrients and lack of moisture by either storing water or having limited surface area through which to lose it by evaporation, or a combination of the two. If you cannot find what you are looking for in this section, try the rocky, stony, dry and sandy habitat, or even roadside and waste ground.

Mountain and Hillside Habitat

One of the main factors that comes into play in this section is altitude, as there are not that many plants that will survive happily above a certain height due to the generally lower temperatures and thinner air. If you are high in the mountains, there will not be such a variety of wildflowers around as there may be lower down. However, on hillsides and at lower elevations, the climate may be much less defined. On the leeward side of the slope the conditions will be more sheltered and may habitually be some degrees warmer than on the other, more exposed side, so this is something to take into consideration. Sometimes the ground on mountains and hills is rocky or stony due to soil erosion, in which case you could also try the rocky, stony, dry and sandy habitat if you cannot find the plant you want. If the soil seems rich and you are in an open meadow, try the meadow and field section.

Coastal Habitat

Coastal habitat covers areas that are next to the ocean, or within a few miles of it and subject to maritime conditions. The ground here may be both windswept and affected by salt, so plants have to be

able to tolerate such factors. Coastlines also often have cliffs or sandy soil, so if such conditions apply and the plant you are looking for is not in this section, try the rocky, stony, dry and sandy habitat. Wetlands near the coast tend to have brackish or salty water, but if there is an estuary nearby the fresh water coming off the land may overwhelm the salty water from the sea, creating a swampy area that is more freshwater than salt. If this is the case, you could also try the boggy, swampy, and damp section.

Meadow and Field Habitat

The meadow and fields section covers habitats that are, or have been cultivated in the recent past. The soil in them has been disturbed, and some plants that are not original may have been introduced by birds or in seed mixes. Meadows and fields are in some ways similar to plains and prairies, but they are areas smaller in scale, with hedges, fences and other barriers providing shelter at regular intervals. Regular grazing or harvesting of crops may wipe out some wildflowers in this habitat, but others will merely re-seed and start again. If you cannot find what you are looking for in this section, try plains and prairies, or roadside and waste ground as alternatives.

Plains and Prairie Habitat

In contrast to meadows and fields, the plains and prairies habitat covers areas where the grassland spreads for miles and may have been undisturbed for many years - although it also covers large areas that are commercially cultivated. Regular grazing or harvesting of crops may wipe out some native wildflowers in this habitat, but others will merely continually re-seed and start again. Since they stretch for miles, plains and prairies have little shelter to break the wind and moderate the weather, so plants in these areas tend to be low-growing or able to cope in other ways with such conditions. If you cannot find what you are looking for in this section, try meadow and field, or roadside and waste ground as alternatives.

Items of interest

The general text on each plant gives a clear description, information on its uses – both practical and in folklore – and any legends or facts associated with it. **Some are noted as poisonous, but this is not an infallible guide – do not eat any wild plant unless an expert has confirmed it is safe to do so. Likewise, traditional potions and recipes are referred to throughout the text but readers should consult an expert before experimenting with these.** If a plant is rare, protected or endangered, this is also noted in the text. In general, scientific terms have been avoided, but an explanation of the more common botanical terms is given in the Glossary on pages 18-21.

Good conservation practice

Wildflowers are an essential part of nature, and they also beautify and enrich our environment. Studying them and being able to identify them gives a great deal of pleasure to many people all around the globe. If you do find something in the wild that you cannot identify, or which you think may be rare, draw or photograph it to take for expert identification. Respect each plant's right to grow where it will, and our world will be a better place for it.

Glossary and Illustrations

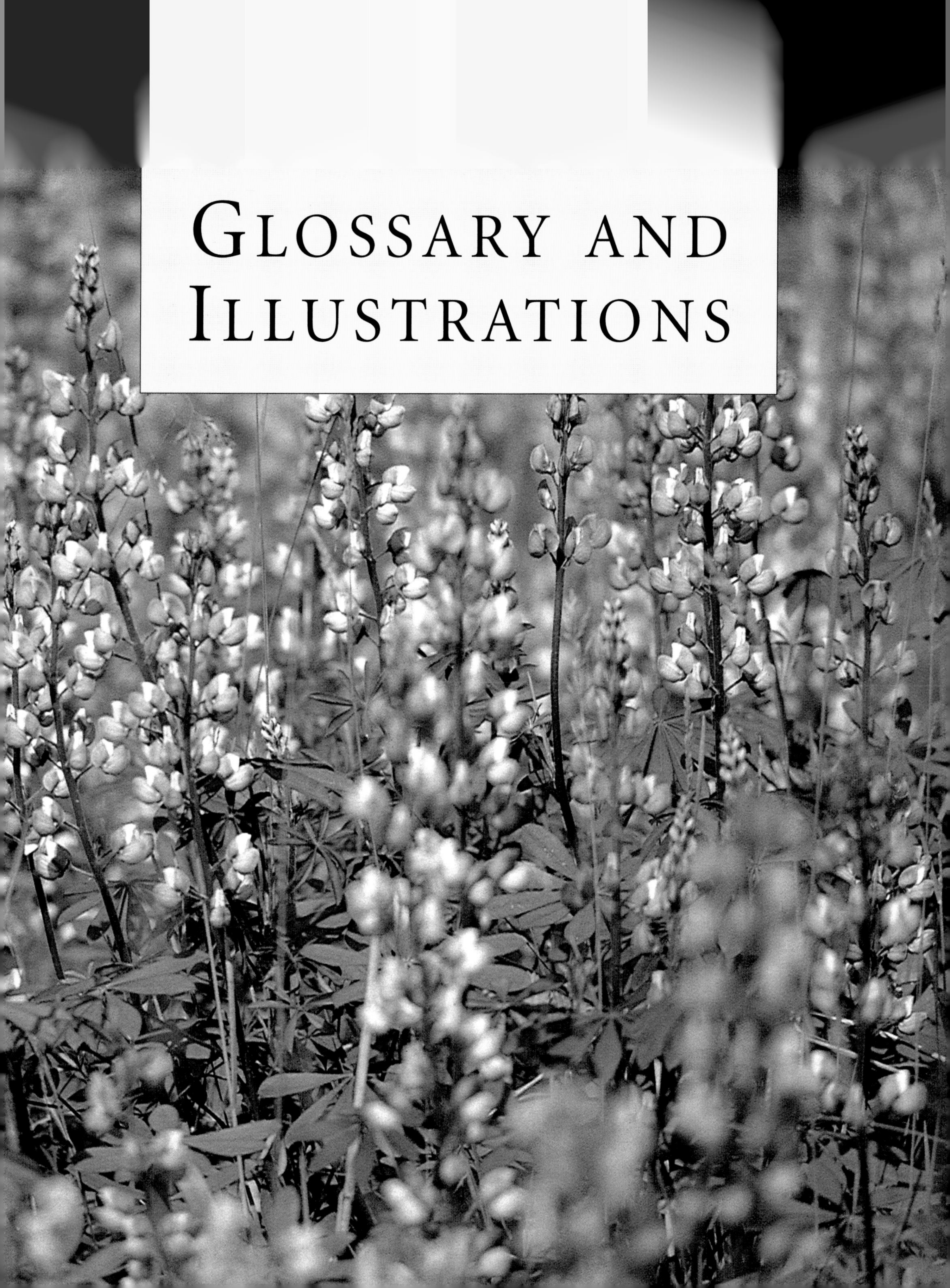

alternate leaf* - leaves arranged alternately up the stem.

anemoniform - flower similar to an anemone.

annual - a plant that flowers and dies in one season.

arrow-shaped leaf* - a leaf with a pointed apex and two pointed lower lobes.

basal - forming or belonging to the bottom layer or base.

basal rosette* - leaves arranged around the base of the stem, to form a rosette.

biennial - a plant that flowers and dies in its second year.

bipinnate leaf* - a compound leaf made up of several pinnate units.

blade - expanded area on either side of the midrib of a leaf.

bracts - specialized leaves that are often brightly colored and resemble a flower.

bulb - swollen underground stem, in which energy is stored to help survive the winter.

calyx - the set of sepals on the base of the flower that protect the flower bud.

carpel - the female reproductive organ of a flower.

clasping leaf*- leaf with its base partly surrounding the stem.

compound leaf - leaf composed of several separate leaflets arising from the same petiole.

compound palmate leaf* - leaf composed of several leaflets to create a palmate shape.

compound pinnate leaf* - leaf composed of several leaflets to create a pinnate shape.

cordate leaf* - a heart-shaped leaf, broadly ovate but with a pointed apex and the base turning in to form a notch for the petiole.

corm - a swollen underground stem, in which energy is stored to help survive the winter.

corymb* - a cluster of florets in which the stalks are arranged at random along the peduncle, but the florets are at one level creating a flat, round top.

cyme* - a cluster of florets in which the inner or top florets open first, blooming downwards along the peduncle.

dicotyledon - flowering plant in which the seedling has two leaflets.

dioecious - species in which the stamens and pistils are on separate plants, so plants of both sexes are required before fruit can form.

disk florets - a small, tubular floret, that combines with many others in a disk shape in a composite flower such as a tansy.

elliptical leaf* - a leaf two or three times longer than wide, and tapering to an acute or rounded base.

entire leaf* - leaf with smooth edges.

epiphyte - a plant that grows on another plant.

evergreen - a plant that retains its leaves all year round.

fibrous-rooted - root system made up of main roots branching off into smaller rootlets.

floret - small flower making up a composite flower head.

helicoid cyme* - a cluster of florets, which are all on one side of the peduncle.

herbaceous - a plant that loses its leaves or dies back in the fall.

hermaphroditic - a plant having stamens and pistils in the same flower.

incised leaf* - leaf with deep notches.

indusium - a thin membranous covering.

inflorescence - a cluster of flowers on a floral stem.

involucre - a whorl or rosette of bracts surrounding an inflorescence or at the base of an umbel.

keel - a prow-shaped pair of petals.

lanceolate leaf* - a leaf longer than wide, tapering towards the apex and rounded at the base.

lance-shaped leaf* - a long, pointed leaf, slightly wider at the base but tapering sharply.

linear leaf* - a narrow leaf, several times longer than wide and approximately the same width down its length.

lobed leaf*- leaf with indented edges, with the indents not reaching the center of the blade.

monocarpic - a plant that dies after flowering.

monocotyledon - flowering plant in which the seedling has one leaflet.

monoecious - plants that have male and female flowers on one plant.

net-veined leaf* - leaf in which the veins branch from the main midrib(s) and then subdivide into smaller veinlets.

oblanceolate leaf* - a leaf longer than wide, tapering towards the apex and base.

oblong leaf* - a leaf that is longer than it is wide, with a roughly even width along most of its length and rounded at both base and apex.

obvate leaf* - an egg-shaped leaf, wide at the apex and tapering towards the base.

opposite leaf* - leaves arrange opposite each other along the stem.

orbicular leaf* - a rounded, circular leaf.

ovate leaf* - an egg-shaped leaf, wide at the base and tapering towards the apex.

palmate leaf* - leaf with five or more lobes whose midribs all radiate from one point.

panicle - a loose, branching cluster of flowers.

parallel-veined leaf* - leaf in which the veins run essentially parallel to each other, connected by minute, straight veinlets.

peduncle - an elongated flower stem.

pendent - hanging down.

perennials - a plant that lives and flowers for three or more years.

perfect flower - a flower that contains functional stamens and pistils.

perfoliate leaf* - leaf with the stem piercing it.

petals - the highly colored portions of a flower.

petiole - stalk that supports the leaf blade.

pinna - primary division of a pinnate leaf, especially a fern (plural pinnae).

pinnate leaf* - compound leaf with pairs of leaflets arranged alternately on either side of the stem.

pinnatifid - divided pinnately, but not all the way to the central axis.

pseudoumbels - looking like umbels.

raceme* - flower cluster with separate flowers attached by short, equal stalks at equal distances along a central stem.

ray florets - a strap-shaped floret, that combines with many others in a ray formation in a composite flower such as a dandelion.

remontant - plant that will flower a second time if dead-headed.

reniform - kidney-shaped.

rhizomes - swollen underground stem, in which energy is stored to help survive the winter.

rhomboidal leaf* - a leaf in a rhomboid shape, wide in the center and tapering sharply at apex and base.

scandent - having a climbing habit.

scorpioid cyme* - a cluster of florets, which are alternate to each other along the peduncle.

semi-evergreen - a plant that retains a few leaves over the winter.

sepals - small, green, leaf-like structures on the base of the flower that protect the flower bud.

serrated leaf* - leaf with saw teeth pointing towards the apex.

sessile - attached directly by its base, without a stalk or peduncle.

simple leaf - leaf in which the blade is a single continuous unit.

solitary flower - a single flower on a stem.

sorus - spore-producing receptacle on the underside of a fern frond (plural sori).

spadix - a spike of minute flowers closely arranged round a fleshy axis, and typically enclosed in a spathe.

spathe - large sheathing bract enclosing the flower cluster.

spatulate leaf* - a rounded leaf, tapering towards the base.

spike* - flower cluster with separate sessile flowers, at equal distances along a central stem.

sporangium - receptacle in which asexual spores are formed (plural sporangia).

spore - a reproductive cell.

spur - a slender, tubular projection from the base of a flower.

stipule - a small, leaf-like appendage to a leaf, typically in pairs at the base of the leaf stalk.

stolon - a creeping horizontal plant stem or runner, that takes root along its length to form new plants.

tepal - a segment of the outer whorl of a flower that has no difference between petals and sepals.

terrestrial - on the ground.

toothed leaf* - leaf with notched edges.

tripalmate leaf* - leaf formed of three leaflets in a palmate shape.

tuber - swollen underground stem, in which energy is stored to help survive the winter.

twining - twisting around.

umbel* - a cluster of florets in which the stalks arise from one point, but the florets are at one level creating a flat, round top.

whorled leaf* - leaves arranged in circles along the stem.

FLOWERS

LEAVES

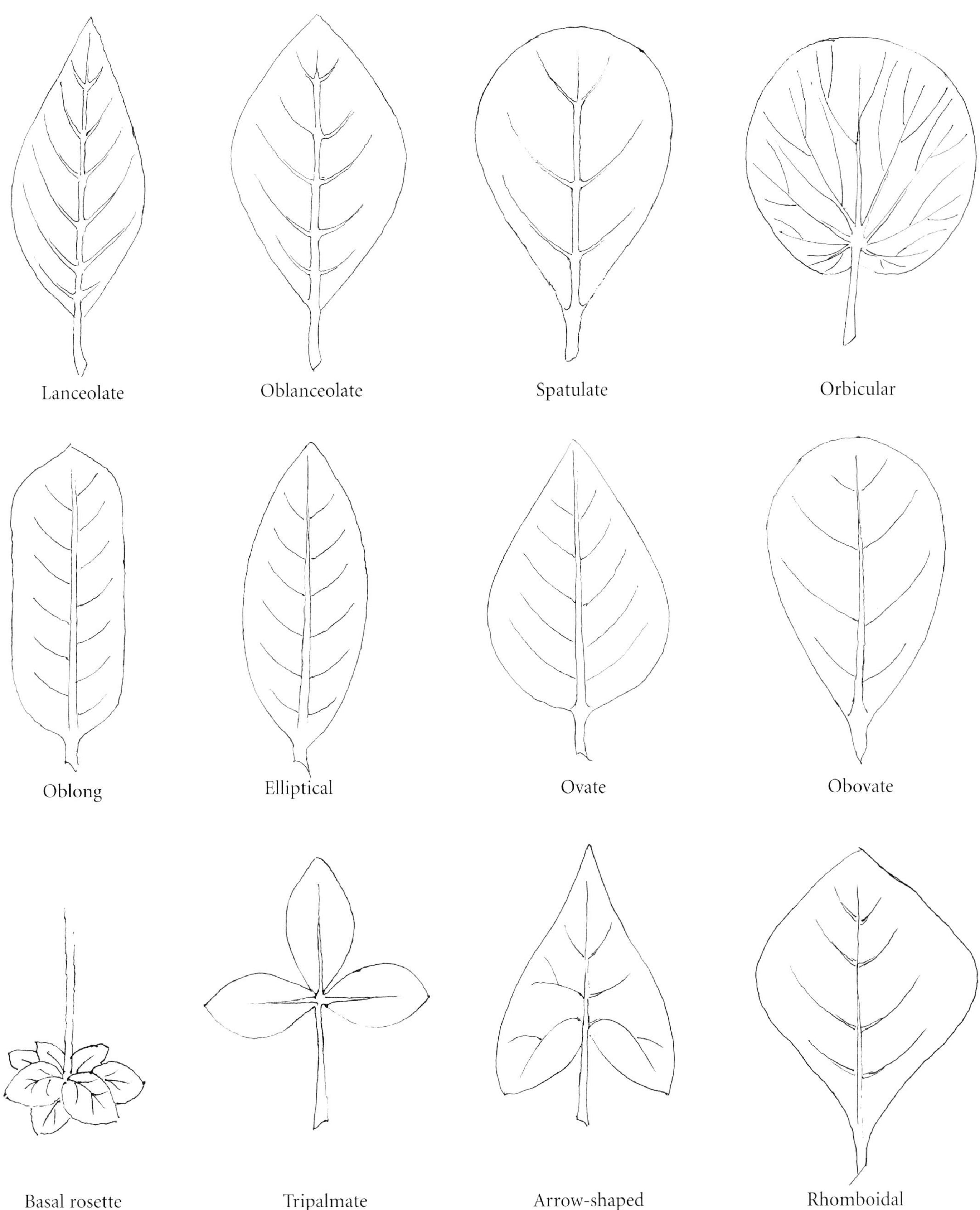
Lanceolate
Oblanceolate
Spatulate
Orbicular
Oblong
Elliptical
Ovate
Obovate
Basal rosette
Tripalmate
Arrow-shaped
Rhomboidal

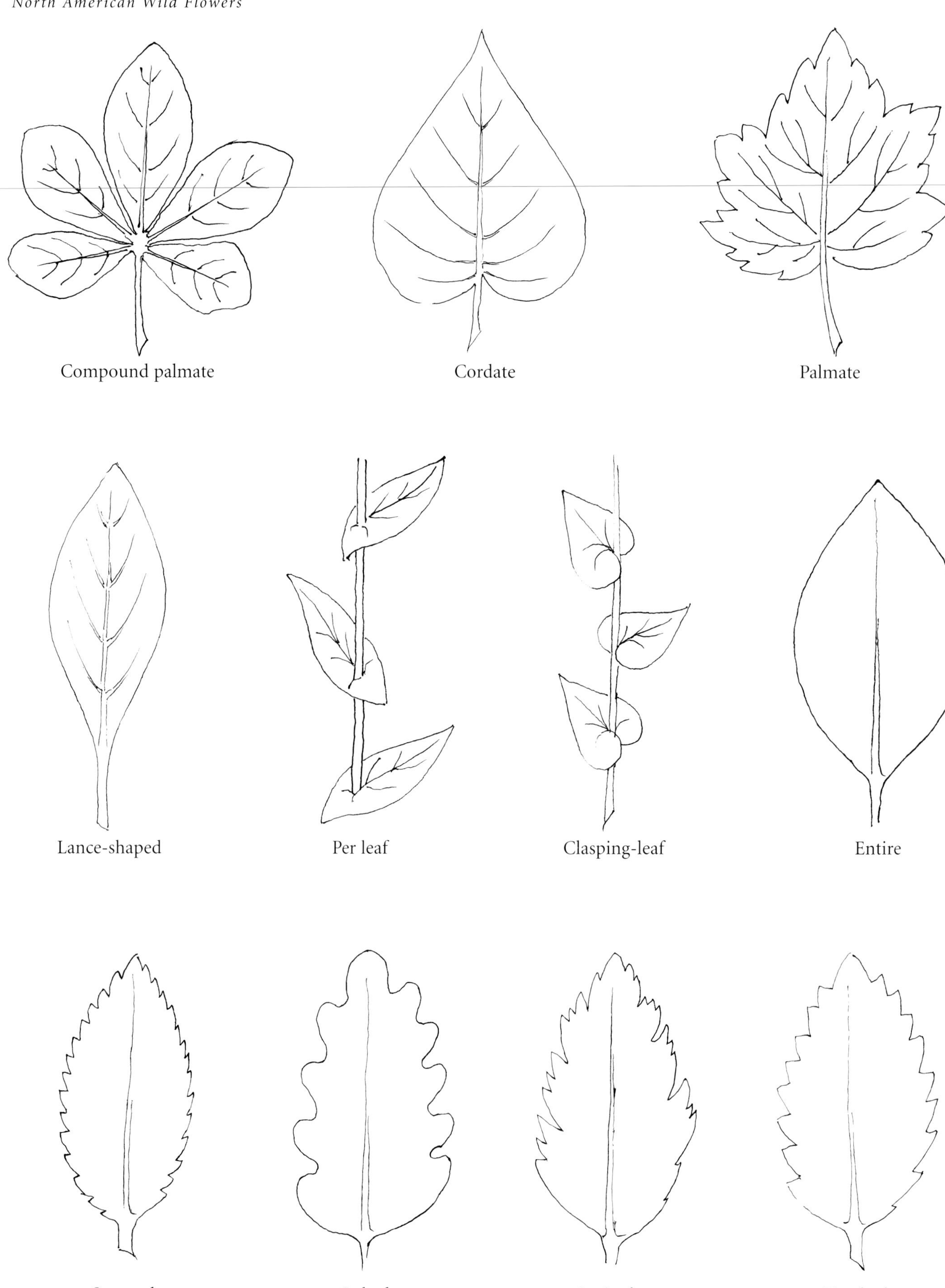
Compound palmate
Cordate
Palmate
Lance-shaped
Per leaf
Clasping-leaf
Entire
Serrated
Lobed
Incised
Toothed

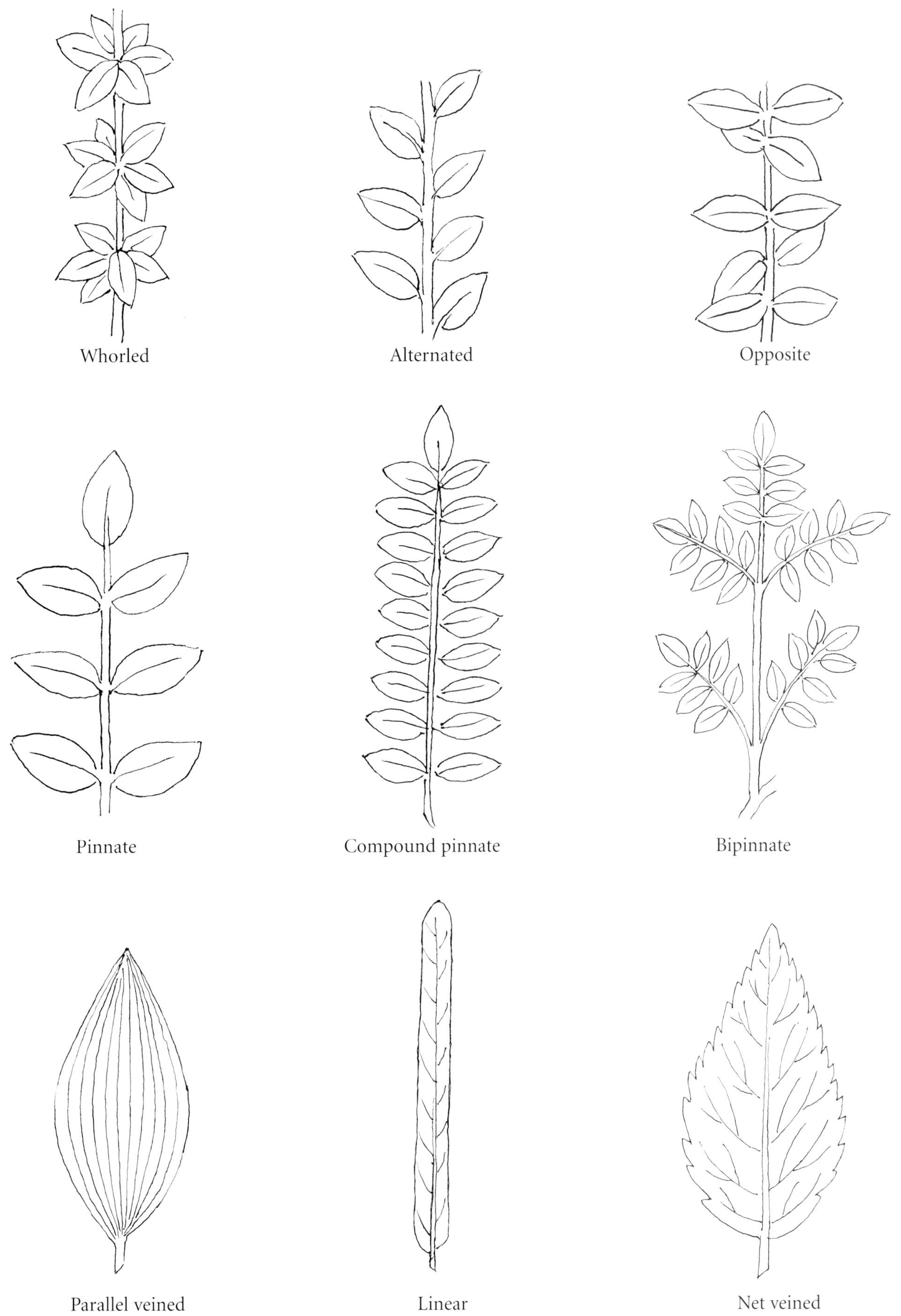
Whorled
Alternated
Opposite
Pinnate
Compound pinnate
Bipinnate
Parallel veined
Linear
Net veined

Boggy, Swampy and Damp Habitats

Red Baneberry

Scientific name:	*Actaea rubra*
Family:	Buttercup
Flower type:	Cone-shaped clusters, each flower $\frac{1}{4}$ inch (0.62cm) in diameter
Flowering period:	May–June
Flower color:	White
Leaf type:	Compound and pinnately divided, with ovate, toothed leaflets
Height:	14–30 inches (35–75cm)
Habitat:	Damp woodland and overgrown waste ground
Range:	Most of western North America, northern parts of the east

Red Baneberry has a smooth, many-branched stem, which bears compound leaves that are pinnately divided several times into ovate and toothed leaflets. The flowers are borne on short stalks that spring from the leaf axils, or at the ends of the stems, in small, cone-shaped raceme clusters. The individual small white flowers have sepals and petals that fall off as the flower opens, leaving behind the many feathery stamens. The common name of Red Baneberry comes from the bright red berries, which are very poisonous, and may cause vomiting and delirium – or even be fatal in young children. American Indians made a tea from the roots for use as a purgative after childbirth, for menstrual irregularity and to treat coughs and colds.

COLIC-ROOT; STARGRASS ▶

Scientific name:	*Aletris farinosa*
Family:	Lily
Flower type:	Elongated cluster, each flower $\frac{1}{4}$–$\frac{1}{2}$ inch (0.62–1.25cm) in length
Flowering period:	May-August
Flower color:	White
Leaf type:	Basal rosette has long, lanceolate leaves; stem leaves very small
Height:	18–36 inches (45–90cm)
Habitat:	Wet fields, bog edges, damp open woods
Range:	Ontario, east coast United States, Tennessee to Wisconsin

The flowers of Colic-root are arranged in a spike-like elongated cluster, at the top of a sturdy stem. At the bottom of the stem is a rosette of long, lanceolate, rather pale green leaves. The individual flowers are urn-shaped, and distinctly mealy on the outside. The unusual common name of Colic-root comes from when the bitter-tasting root was used to treat colic, as well as indigestion, diarrhea and rheumatism. The plant has been scientifically proven to have anti-inflammatory properties.

FLY POISON

Scientific name:	*Amianthium muscitoxicum*
Family:	Lily
Flower type:	Raceme spike, each flower $\frac{1}{2}$ inch (1.25cm) in diameter
Flowering period:	May-July
Flower color:	White
Leaf type:	Basal, linear, grass-like; upper smaller, linear, clasping
Height:	14–48 inches (35–120cm)
Habitat:	Bogs, open woodland
Range:	East and southeast United States

Fly Poison is a perennial growing from a bulb, with a single stem and mostly basal, long, linear leaves that are rather grass-like. The stem has a few much smaller, clasping leaves higher up, arranged alternately, and terminates in a showy spike of white flowers, which become greenish or purplish as they age. It gets its common name because the bulbs were once crushed and mixed with sugar to make a paste to attract and poison flies – the plant is also very poisonous to livestock. There is only one species in this genus in North America.

Yerba Mansa

Scientific name:	*Anemopsis californica*
Family:	Lizard's-tail
Flower type:	Cone-shaped spikes, each 1–2 inches (2.5–5cm) in length
Flowering period:	May–August
Flower color:	White
Leaf type:	Long, oblong
Height:	1 foot (30cm)
Habitat:	Damp areas, particularly with salty or alkaline water
Range:	Oregon and southwest United States, into Mexico

The flower of Yerba Mansa is not what it seems. At first glance it looks as if it has a cone-shaped centre and long white petals, but in fact the cone is a cluster of tiny, yellow flowers and the white "petals" are bracts. This flower head is held at the end of a long stalk, which springs from a cluster of oblong leaves on long stalks. There is only one species found in North America, and only in the southwest. Its root is quite pleasant-smelling, and has been used to treat cuts and burns and as a poultice for rheumatism.

White Turtlehead; Snakehead ▲

Scientific name:	*Chelone glabra*
Family:	Figwort
Flower type:	Spike, each flower 1–1½ inches (2.5–3.75cm) in length
Flowering period:	July–September
Flower color:	White
Leaf type:	Long, lanceolate, toothed
Height:	1–3 feet (30–60cm)
Habitat:	Wet thickets, along streams
Range:	North and eastern Canada, eastern United States

Turtlehead is a smooth-stemmed plant, with long, lanceolate toothed leaves arranged in opposite pairs along the stem, and terminal spikes of tightly clustered flowers on very short stalks. The flowers have an upper lip that arches over the lower petals, giving them a striking resemblance to the head of a turtle or snake – hence the species common names. They are usually white, or sometimes white tipped with pink or a very pale lavender. There are only four species in this genus across North America.

Swamplily ▲

Scientific name:	*Crinum americanum*
Family:	Amaryllis
Flower type:	Loose cluster, each flower 4 inches (10cm) in diameter
Flowering period:	Spring and fall
Flower color:	White
Leaf type:	Long, linear
Height:	3 feet (90cm)
Habitat:	Boggy areas, marshes, along streams
Range:	East coast United States

Despite its common name, the Swamplily is not really a true lily – it actually belongs to the Amaryllis family. It has a long, smooth, leafless stalk, which springs from the neck of an underground bulb and can extend up to three feet (90cm). Around the base of the stalk is a thick cluster of long, linear, strap-like leaves, and at the tip of the stalk there is a loose umbel cluster of very sweet-smelling, rather spidery-looking white flowers. Each flower has six petal-like segments and six long stamens, and is held at the end of its own short stalk. The underground bulb means that Swamplilies are perennials, springing up again every year. There are four species in this genus found across North America, all of them in the southeast.

Goldthread; Canker Root

Scientific name:	*Coptis trifolia (Coptis groenlandica)*
Family:	Buttercup
Flower type:	Radially symmetrical, ½ inch (1.25cm) in diameter
Flowering period:	May-July
Flower color:	White
Leaf type:	Basal, palmately divided, leaflets are scalloped, toothed
Height:	3–8 inches (8–20cm)
Habitat:	Swamps, bogs, damp woodland
Range:	Northeast North America

A very small perennial, Goldthread has a very thin, bright yellow underground stem, which is the basis for its common name. The alternative name of Canker Root comes from American Indians and early settlers chewing the root to cure mouth ulcers, although they also used it to treat nausea, jaundice, sore throats and stomach cramps. Above ground the plant has basal leaves that are palmately divided into three leaflets, each of which has scalloped and toothed edges. The single flower is borne at the end of a bare stalk, and has white sepals that look like petals, and green petals with a bulbous tip on a short stalk.

Roundleaf Sundew

Scientific name:	*Drosera rotundifolia*
Family:	Sundew
Flower type:	Radially symmetrical, $\frac{1}{4}$ inch (0.62cm) in diameter
Flowering period:	June–August
Flower color:	White
Leaf type:	Circular and covered in sticky hairs
Height:	4–9 inches (10–22cm)
Habitat:	Boggy ground
Range:	Across North America

Roundleaf Sundew is a perennial carnivorous plant, with a basal rosette of small, round leaves that are somewhat reddish due to colored hairs that exude small drops of sticky sap to catch small insects. When an insect is trapped, the leaf folds over to digest them. The flowers are small and arranged along one side of a leafless stalk in an elongated raceme – they are usually white, but are sometimes pink or red. The plant is able to survive in particularly poor soil because it gets much of the nutrients it requires from the insects it catches. There are eight species within this genus found across North America.

Boneset

Scientific name:	*Eupatorium perfoliatum*
Family:	Aster
Flower type:	Flat-topped clusters, each flower $\frac{1}{4}$ inch (0.62cm) in diameter
Flowering period:	July–October
Flower color:	White
Leaf type:	Lanceolate, toothed, wrinkled, sessile, perfoliate
Height:	1–4 feet (30–120cm)
Habitat:	Wet meadows and damp woodland
Range:	Most of eastern North America, except the very far north

Boneset is a hairy plant, with dense, flat-topped clusters of white to pale purple flowers and long, lanceolate and wrinkled leaves in pairs that completely surround the stem. The name Boneset originated because the leaves were used to treat dengue fever, in which the bones ache as if they were broken. Boneset was used in many home remedies by early settlers, particularly to treat influenza. Recent scientific research suggests the plant has immune system enhancing properties, but large doses are very dangerous as they may damage the liver.

Northern Bedstraw

Scientific name:	*Galium boreale (Galium septentrionale)*
Family:	Madder
Flower type:	Elongated cluster, each flower $\frac{1}{4}$ inch (0.62cm) in width
Flowering period:	July–August
Flower color:	White
Leaf type:	Long, narrowly lanceolate whorled
Height:	9–34 inches (22–85cm)
Habitat:	Stream edges, coastal areas, stony soil
Range:	Northeast North America

Northern Bedstraw is unlike other species in its genus as it is smooth-stemmed rather than bristly. The stem is often branched and very leafy, bearing many whorls of four bright green, long, narrowly lanceolate leaves, with three main ribs. The white flowers are in loose, elongated clusters at the top of the stem. The young leaves can be steamed and added to salads, or eaten as greens, and the round fruits can be dried and crushed to make a coffee substitute. There are around 78 species of Galium across North America.

Bloodroot

Scientific name:	*Sanguinaria canadensis*
Family:	Poppy
Flower type:	Radially symmetrical, 2 inches (5cm) in diameter
Flowering period:	March-June
Flower color:	White
Leaf type:	Palmately scalloped
Height:	11 inches (28cm)
Habitat:	Stream edges, damp woods
Range:	Eastern North America

One of the unusual things about Bloodroot is that the flower often appears before the leaf. It has just one basal leaf, which is deeply palmately lobed and curves around the single flower stalk. The flower has many long, narrowly pointed petals and a yellow center, and looks rather like that of a water lily. The sap of this plant is bright red-orange – hence its common name – and it was used by American Indians as a dye for craftwork and as war paint. It inhibits plaque on teeth, and is used commercially in toothpastes and mouthwashes. American Indians also made a root tea for lung ailments and rheumatism. Despite this, the plant is considered toxic in quantity and should not be eaten.

Sanguinaria canadensis

Oconee Bells

Scientific name:	*Shortia galacifolia*
Family:	Diapensia
Flower type:	Bell-shaped, 1 inch (2.5cm) in diameter
Flowering period:	March–April
Flower color:	White
Leaf type:	Basal, orbicular, bluntly toothed
Height:	3–9 inches (8–22cm)
Habitat:	Damp woodland, along streams
Range:	Southeast United States

Oconee Bells was first discovered in 1788, but was then lost for nearly 100 years. It is extremely rare, and only found in the mountains of Virginia and from Tennessee into Georgia – although it is also now grown in gardens. It has basal, rounded and shiny evergreen leaves, which are bluntly toothed; older leaves are often tinged with a rusty-red color near the edges. The single bell-shaped flower is white and hangs down from a bare stalk. Because of its rarity, Oconee Bells should never be picked or dug up if found in the wild.

TALL MEADOW-RUE

Scientific name:	*Thalictrum pubescens (Thalictrum polygamum)*
Family:	Buttercup
Flower type:	Panicle cluster, each flower ½ inch (1.25cm) in diameter
Flowering period:	July–August
Flower color:	White
Leaf type:	Pinnate, roundish 3-lobed leaflets
Height:	3–8 feet (90–250cm)
Habitat:	Swamps, stream edges, wet meadows
Range:	Northeast North America

The species of Meadow-rue found in the east of North America tend to be taller than those in the west, and Tall Meadow-rue can reach a height of 8 feet (250cm). It has compound pinnate pale blue-green leaves, with roundish three-lobed leaflets, the lower ones with short stalks and the upper sessile. The star-like flowers are borne in a loose branching cluster, and both male and female are found on the same plant. They are very attractive to butterflies and bees. There are at least ten species of this genus in eastern North America alone, and 15 across North America as a whole.

WESTERN FOAMFLOWER; FALSE MITREWORT; LACE FLOWER

Scientific name:	*Tiarella trifoliata (Tiarella unifoliata)*
Family:	Saxifrage
Flower type:	Raceme cluster, 4–8 inches (10–20cm) in length
Flowering period:	May–August
Flower color:	White
Leaf type:	Triangular, deeply indented into three leaflets, toothed
Height:	9–15 inches (22–38cm)
Habitat:	Damp woodland, along streams
Range:	Northwest North America

Above: Detail of the flower of Western Foamflower, peeping between the leaves of another plant.

There are several very similar species of this genus in the same general area, and they are sometimes known by the same common names. The variety with leaves indented right to the leafstalk is *T. trifoliata*, that with lobed leaves is *T. unifoliata. T. cordifolia* has much less indented leaves than the other two. The leaves in all three varieties are roughly triangular, with the base indented to take the stalk; the lower leaves have a long stalk and the upper a much shorter one. Western Foamflower has a raceme cluster of tiny, white hanging flowers.

Nodding Trillium ▲

Scientific name:	*Trillium cernuum*
Family:	Lily
Flower type:	Radially symmetrical, 1–2 inches (1.25–2.5cm) in diameter
Flowering period:	May–July
Flower color:	White
Leaf type:	Rhomboidal to orbicular, whorled
Height:	5–22 inches (12–55cm)
Habitat:	Swamps, moist woods
Range:	North and northeast North America

Nodding Trillium has many of its parts in threes – as is suggested by its name. The three whorled leaves are rhomboidal to orbicular in shape and have very short stalks. The flower has three sepals and three petals and nods at the end of a short, downward-curved stalk, so that the flower hangs beneath the leaves. The flower is white – or sometimes very pale pink – with the petals curved back at the tips, and with pink anthers. There are around 42 species of this genus in North America, most of them concentrated in the eastern half of the continent.

Giant Wakerobin; Giant Trillium

Scientific name:	*Trillium chloropetalum*
Family:	Lily
Flower type:	Radially symmetrical, 1–2 inches (1.25–2.5cm) in diameter
Flowering period:	February–June
Flower color:	White to maroon
Leaf type:	Rhomboidal to orbicular, whorled
Height:	5–22 inches (12–55cm)
Habitat:	Wet woodland
Range:	West North America

Like Nodding Trillium (*T. cernuum*) Giant Wakerobin is arranged in threes, with three whorled, rhomboidal leaves on a stout stem and a flower with three sepals and three petals. However, the leaves are mottled and have no stalks, while the flower is held erect, above the leaves, and the petals are only slightly curved backwards. The color of the flower ranges from white, through shades of pink to deep maroon, with yellow anthers. The deeper colors often have a touch of white at the base of the petals.

Painted Trillium

Scientific name:	*Trillium undulatum*
Family:	Lily
Flower type:	Radially symmetrical, 2–2½ inches (5–6.25cm) in diameter
Flowering period:	April–June
Flower color:	White and pink
Leaf type:	Rhomboidal to ovate, whorled
Height:	8–20 inches (20–50cm)
Habitat:	Wet woodland, acidic swamps
Range:	Northeast North America

Painted Trillium is one of the most attractive of the Trilliums to be found in North America. It has the usual three, large whorled leaves of the species, which are blue-green and have very pointed tips and short stalks. The flowers have green sepals and white, wavy-edged petals, with each petal having an inverted V in pink at the base; the stamens are also tipped in pink. This two-tone effect, as if the flower has been delicately colored with a fine paintbrush, makes it one of the most easily identified trilliums.

California Corn Lily

Scientific name:	*Veratrum californicum*
Family:	Lily
Flower type:	Panicle cluster, 8–20 inches (20–50cm) in length
Flowering period:	June–August
Flower color:	White
Leaf type:	Broadly ovate, pleated, sessile
Height:	4–8 feet (120–250cm)
Habitat:	Swamps, wet meadows, damp woodland
Range:	Southeast United States

The California Corn Lily looks spectacular, with a very tall, stout stem that has broadly ovate, pleated, sessile and clasping leaves along the lower half, and terminates in a long, very showy, dense panicle of small white flowers. The flowers are star-shaped, with a green center. The plant can reach a total height of 8 feet (250cm), so it is extremely noticeable. Unfortunately it is also extremely toxic – even the flowers are poisonous to bees and other insects, and if any part of the plant is eaten by grazing livestock it will cause very serious birth deformities.

Culver's Root; Culver's Physic

Scientific name:	*Veronicastrum virginicum*
Family:	Figwort
Flower type:	Spike, 4–8 inches (10–20cm) in length
Flowering period:	June–September
Flower color:	White
Leaf type:	Lanceolate to ovate, toothed, whorled
Height:	2–7 feet (60–210cm)
Habitat:	Damp woodland, wet fields
Range:	Central Canada, southeast United States

There are only two species in this genus, and the other grows in Siberia. Culver's Root is a medium-tall perennial with many branching, dense, feathery spikes of white, or sometimes pale purple, tubular flowers. The leaves are lanceolate to ovate in shape, with the edges sharply toothed, and they are arranged in whorls of between three and five at intervals on the stem. American Indians and nineteenth-century doctors used a tea made of the dried root as a laxative, to induce sweating or vomiting and as a diuretic. The fresh root is violently laxative and potentially toxic.

Western Monkshood; Aconite

Scientific name:	*Aconitum columbianum*
Family:	Buttercup
Flower type:	Elongated raceme cluster, each flower 1 inch (2.5cm) in length
Flowering period:	June–August
Flower color:	Blue
Leaf type:	Palmately lobed, toothed
Height:	1–7 feet (30–210cm)
Habitat:	Moist woods, meadows at higher altitude
Range:	Northwest and southern North America

Western Monkshood is very tall plant that has a very straight stem, with many large, palmately lobed and deeply toothed leaves arranged alternately along its length. The deep blue to blue-violet flowers are rather unusual in shape, with the upper sepals forming a hooded arch over the lower sepals and the rather small petals. The flowers are borne in a terminal and elongated raceme cluster. There are eight species of this genus found in North America, and most are poisonous to both people and livestock – although some have been used medicinally.

Eastern Bluestar; Blue Dogbane ▼

Scientific name:	*Amsonia tabernaemontana*
Family:	Dogbane
Flower type:	Radially symmetrical, $\frac{1}{2}$–1 inch (1.25–2.5cm) in diameter
Flowering period:	April–July
Flower color:	Blue
Leaf type:	Lanceolate to elliptical
Height:	12–40 inches (30–100cm)
Habitat:	Damp woodland, along streams
Range:	East and southeast United States

A fairly tall plant, Eastern Bluestar has a stem with many long, broad, lanceolate to elliptical leaves, and flowers borne in a showy terminal panicled cyme. The leaves have very short stalks and are so close together on the stem that they can appear to be opposite, rather than alternate. The flowers are a very pale blue, with a long tube opening out into star-shaped petals. A very similar-looking species, the Ozark Bluestar (*A. illustris*), is found in the western part of the same general area – it has narrow leaves that are set further apart along the stem.

Common Camas

Scientific name:	*Camassia quamash*
Family:	Lily
Flower type:	Elongated raceme cluster, each flower 1–2 inches (2.5–5cm) in width
Flowering period:	April–June
Flower color:	Blue
Leaf type:	Long, linear
Height:	6–32 inches (15–80cm)
Habitat:	Wet meadows
Range:	Western North America

A perennial that grows from a bulb, Common Camas has a single stem with several long, linear, grass-like leaves that spring from the base. The star-shaped flowers grow in an elongated raceme cluster, and are blue to blue-lavender in color. A species with radially symmetrical flowers that is only found west of the Cascade Range was once classed separately as *C. leichtlinii*, but is now included in the main species. Common Camas can be very abundant, covering an entire field with blue. The bulbs can be cooked and eaten, but only if identification is certain as the Death Camas (*Zigadenus venenosus*), which has white or bronze flowers but is otherwise very similar, is extremely poisonous.

Closed Bottle Gentian

Scientific name:	*Gentiana andrewsii*
Family:	Gentian
Flower type:	Tight, rounded cluster, each flower 1–1½ inches (2.5–3.75cm) in length
Flowering period:	August–October
Flower color:	Blue
Leaf type:	Ovate to lanceolate, opposite; whorled below flower cluster
Height:	1–2 feet (30–60cm)
Habitat:	Damp meadows, wet thickets
Range:	Eastern Canada, northeastern United States

The Closed Bottle Gentian has rather unusual, bottle-shaped, bright blue flowers that are arranged in a tight, rounded cluster on its stem – usually in the axil of a whorl of smooth, ovate to lanceolate leaves. At the tip of the flower the petals are very slightly open, showing fringed edges between the lobes. As well as the whorled leaves towards the top, the stem has further leaves that are arranged in opposite pairs lower down. The roots of the Gentian were once used to make a tonic. Closed Bottle Gentian is one of the easiest of the Gentian species to grow, so it is often included in cultivated wildflower gardens.

Blind Gentian; Bottle Gentian

Scientific name:	*Gentiana clausa*
Family:	Gentian
Flower type:	Tight, rounded cluster, each flower 1–1½ inches (2.5–3.75cm) in length
Flowering period:	August–October
Flower color:	Blue
Leaf type:	Ovate to lanceolate, opposite; whorled below flower cluster
Height:	1–2 feet (30–60cm)
Habitat:	Damp meadows, wet thickets
Range:	Eastern Canada, northeastern United States

The Blind Gentian is very similar to the Closed Bottle Gentian, and it can be difficult to tell the two species apart. The Blind Gentian also has bottle-shaped flowers arranged in a tight, rounded cluster on its stem, usually in the axil of a whorl of smooth, ovate to lanceolate leaves. However, the tip of the flower is tightly closed, so the fringed lobes are concealed unless the petals are forced open. The stem has further leaves arranged in opposite pairs lower down. There are around 56 species of Gentian across North America.

Harvestbells; Soapwort Gentian ▶

Scientific name:	*Gentiana saponaria*
Family:	Gentian
Flower type:	Tight, rounded cluster, each flower 1–1½ inches (2.5–3.75cm) in length
Flowering period:	August–October
Flower color:	Blue
Leaf type:	Ovate to lanceolate, opposite; whorled below flower cluster
Height:	1–2 feet (30–60cm)
Habitat:	Damp meadows, wet thickets
Range:	Midwest United States

Although otherwise it is similar to the Closed Bottle Gentian (*G. andrewsii*) and the Blind Gentian (*G. clausa*) Harvestbells has pale blue flowers. These are bottle-shaped, with the tip slightly open, and arranged in a tight, rounded cluster on the stem, usually in the axil of a whorl of smooth, ovate to lanceolate leaves. The stem also has further leaves arranged in opposite pairs lower down. The Soapwort Gentian has soapy-looking sap, and is found further west than the other two common species.

Fringed Gentian

Scientific name:	*Gentianopsis crinita*
Family:	Gentian
Flower type:	Urn-shaped, 2 inches (5cm) in length
Flowering period:	September–November
Flower color:	Blue
Leaf type:	Lanceolate, opposite
Height:	4–36 inches (10–90cm)
Habitat:	Wet meadows and thickets
Range:	Northeast and east North America

Fringed Gentian is a biennial that is becoming increasingly rare in the wild, so it should never be picked, dug up or otherwise removed from its natural habitat. It is a medium size, branching plant, with broad, light green lanceolate leaves and a bright blue, urn-shaped flower with fringed petals, which only opens in sunlight. There is a very similar species, Smaller Fringed Gentian (*G. procera*), which has narrower leaves and shorter fringes, and which is found across the Midwest. Both these species are quite late-flowering wildflowers, appearing in late summer to fall.

Great Lobelia; Blue Cardinal Flower ▶

Scientific name:	*Lobelia siphilitica*
Family:	Bellflower
Flower type:	Spike, each flower 1 inch (2.5cm) long
Flowering period:	August–October
Flower color:	Blue
Leaf type:	Long, oval to lanceolate, sometimes toothed
Height:	2–5 feet (60–150cm)
Habitat:	Damp woodland, swamps, moist meadows
Range:	Northeast and eastern North America

The Great Lobelia is very similar in appearance to the Cardinal Flower, except that its flowers are bright blue, not red. It is a quite tall perennial, with a spike of flowers 1-2 feet (30–60cm) long at the top of a leafy stem. The flowers are unusual, with three lobes at the bottom and two above, and with the underneath of the lower part striped in white. The leaves are long, oval or lanceolate and sometimes coarsely toothed. American Indians used a tea made from the roots to treat syphilis – hence its scientific name – and a tea of the leaves for colds, fevers and stomach problems. A poultice of the leaves was also applied to hard-to-heal sores. However, the plant is potentially poisonous.

Mountain Bluebells

Scientific name:	*Mertensia ciliata*
Family:	Borage
Flower type:	Loose, cyme cluster, each flower $\frac{1}{2}$–$\frac{3}{4}$ inch (1.25–1.88cm) in width
Flowering period:	May–July
Flower color:	Blue
Leaf type:	Long, elliptical
Height:	8-40 inches (20–100cm)
Habitat:	Wet meadows, seeps, along streams
Range:	Midwest states

Despite its name, the Mountain Bluebell is not necessarily found at high altitudes – it prefers wet and boggy ground and is often found along streams. It tends to grow in clumps, with leafy stems and loose cyme clusters of blue, bell-shaped flowers. As they age, the flowers turn pink-red, so there are often two colors in the same cluster at one time. The leaves are elliptical, with long stalks, and are arranged alternately on the stem. Plants in this genus are often also known as lungwort, as in Europe there is a species that was once believed to be a cure for diseases of the lung.

Above: Dipsacus fullonum viewed close up.

WILD TEASEL

Scientific name:	*Dipsacus fullonum*
Family:	Teasel
Flower type:	Egg-shaped flower head, $1\frac{1}{4}$–2 inches (3.12–5cm) in width
Flowering period:	April–August
Flower color:	Purple
Leaf type:	Long, lanceolate, opposite
Height:	2–7 feet (60–210cm)
Habitat:	Damp ground
Range:	Western North America

Wild Teasel was introduced from its native Europe and is now found across much of the west. The common name of teasel comes from cloth weavers using the dried flower heads of the species to raise, or tease, the nap of a fabric. It is a fairly tall plant, with stout, prickly stems bearing long, lanceolate leaves in opposite pairs, with the bases of the leaves joining round the stem. At the top of the stem is the egg-shaped flower head, surrounded by long spiny bracts and covered in tiny purple florets. The florets open round the middle of the flower head first, with new ones opening above and below until eventually there are two separate bands of color.

JEWELED SHOOTINGSTAR; AMETHYST SHOOTINGSTAR

Scientific name:	*Dodecatheon amethystinum*
Family:	Primrose
Flower type:	Umbel cluster, 1 inch (2.5cm) long
Flowering period:	April–June
Flower color:	Purple
Leaf type:	Basal cluster, long lanceolate
Height:	4–12 inches (10–30cm)
Habitat:	Damp areas
Range:	Central eastern states

The drooping flowers of this plant have backward-facing petals, so they look like shooting stars heading for earth. The flowers grow in an umbel cluster at the tip of a long, bare stalk, which springs from a basal cluster of long, smooth, dark green, lanceolate leaves. There are 15 species across North America, with flowers ranging from red, through pink to pale lavender. As the flowers are so attractive they are also often cultivated, so the plant may be found outside its natural habitat area.

Showy Prairie Gentian; Catchfly Gentian

Scientific name:	*Eustoma exaltatum ssp. Russellianum (Eustoma grandiflorum)*
Family:	Gentian
Flower type:	Radially symmetrical, $1\frac{1}{2}$ inches (3.75cm) in diameter
Flowering period:	May–September
Flower color:	Purple
Leaf type:	Oblong, opposite, clasping
Height:	2 feet (60cm)
Habitat:	Damp areas of prairie, moist fields
Range:	Southern United States

There are two varieties known as Catchfly Gentian in North America, both found in the south and both very similar. Showy Prairie Gentian (*E. exaltatum* ssp. *Russellianum* or *E. grandiflorum*) is found in damp places and has flowers that can be purple, blue, pinkish or yellow, while Seaside Gentian (*E. exaltatum*) – despite its name – is found in coniferous areas as well as coastal sites, and has blue, lavender or white flowers. They are both erect plants of around the same size, with oblong, opposite and clasping leaves, and flowers at the end of a long stalk. The main difference between the two is that the petals of Seaside Gentian are flared outwards at the tips, which gives the flower a more open appearance, while Showy Prairie Gentian has petals curving inwards, giving more bowl-shaped flowers.

Blue-pod Lupine; Garden Lupine

Scientific name:	*Lupinus polyphyllus*
Family:	Pea
Flower type:	Raceme spike, each flower $\frac{1}{2}$ inch (1.25cm) in length
Flowering period:	June–August
Flower color:	Purple
Leaf type:	Compound palmate, with leaflets like wheel spokes
Height:	2–5 feet (60–150cm)
Habitat:	Damp meadows and forests, along streams
Range:	Western North America

This is one of the tallest western lupines, with several stout hollow stems, each bearing a dense raceme spike 6-18 inches (15-45cm) long of purple to blue-violet flowers. The flowers are rather like those of the pea, but the leaves are roughly round, but palmately divided into 9-17 leaflets, each radiating out like the spokes of a wheel from a common stalk. There are over 150 species of lupine across North America, most of them in the west of the continent, although a few do grow in the east. The seeds are a valuable food for wild birds, but the plants themselves are poisonous to cattle.

Common Butterwort

Scientific name:	*Pinguicula vulgaris*
Family:	Bladderwort
Flower type:	Irregular with two symmetrical halves, $\frac{1}{2}$ inch (1.25cm) in diameter
Flowering period:	April–July
Flower color:	Purple
Leaf type:	Basal, broadly ovate, shallow teeth
Height:	3–8 inches (8–20cm)
Habitat:	Boggy ground, wet areas
Range:	Northern and northwest North America

Like Yellow Butterwort, the yellow-green, ovate to oblong leaves of Common Butterwort are arranged in a basal rosette, and they have a very greasy, sticky surface that is designed to catch insects. The leaves roll inwards to digest the catch, which provides extra nourishment to the plant. The single wide-mouthed purple flower is borne at the end of a long, leafless stalk, and looks rather like a violet. Despite its name, this plant is very rare in the southern areas of its range and should never be picked or dug up. This species is also found in both Europe and Asia.

Western Polemonium; Jacob's Ladder

Scientific name:	*Polemonium occidentale*
Family:	Phlox
Flower type:	Cluster, each flower ½ inch (1.25cm) in diameter
Flowering period:	June–August
Flower color:	Purple
Leaf type:	Bipinnate, lanceolate leaflets
Height:	10–34 inches (25–85cm)
Habitat:	Wet areas
Range:	Northwest North America

As the leaves resemble long ladders, all the species in this genus can commonly be known as Jacob's Ladder. Western Polemonium is a leafy plant, with narrow, bipinnate alternate leaves that have sessile lanceolate leaflets. The flowers are purple to blue in color, and are borne in a branching corymb cluster near the top of the stem. There are 20 species in this genus across most of North America, most of which are in the west and prefer cooler regions. American Indians used the roots of some species to induce vomiting and sweating, and for pleurisy, fevers, snakebites, bowel complaints and bronchial problems.

New England Aster ▼

Scientific name:	*Symphyotrichum novae-angliae (Aster novae-angliae)*
Family:	Aster
Flower type:	Compound flower head, 1–2 inch (2.5–5cm) in diameter
Flowering period:	August–October
Flower color:	Purple
Leaf type:	Lanceolate, clasping
Height:	32–96 inches (80–250cm)
Habitat:	Wet meadows, swamps
Range:	Northeast, east and parts of western North America

A large plant, with a stout, bristly-hairy, branching stem, New England Aster has many long, lanceolate leaves that clasp the stem and are arranged alternately. The flower heads are borne mainly towards the ends of the branches, and they have 40-50 ray florets around the yellowish central disk florets. The rays are often purple-blue, but they can be white or lavender, and there is also a pink variety. The narrow bracts are hairy and sticky. New England Aster is one of the best-known American asters and is often cultivated in gardens. American Indians made a tea from the roots to treat diarrhea and fevers.

Blue Vervain

Scientific name:	*Verbena hastata*
Family:	Verbena
Flower type:	Spike, each flower $\frac{1}{8}$ inch (0.31cm) in diameter
Flowering period:	July–September
Flower color:	Purple
Leaf type:	Long, lanceolate, toothed
Height:	2-6 feet (60–180cm)
Habitat:	Wet woodland, damp fields
Range:	Across North America

A perennial, with long, thin multiple flower spikes that make it look rather like a candelabra, Blue Vervain is a very attractive plant. The stem is square and grooved, with long, lanceolate, sharply and coarsely toothed leaves that are arranged in opposite pairs and have a very rough surface texture. The individual flowers open in a circle round the spike, moving upwards in sequence, and are usually purple – although rarely they can be pink. American Indians and nineteenth-century doctors used a tea made from the leaves as a tonic specifically for women, and to cure fevers and stomach complaints.

New York Ironweed

Scientific name:	*Vernonia noveboracensis*
Family:	Aster
Flower type:	Cluster, 3–4 inches (8–10cm) in width
Flowering period:	August-October
Flower color:	Purple
Leaf type:	Long, lanceolate, finely toothed
Height:	3–6 feet (90–180cm)
Habitat:	Damp ground, along streams
Range:	East and southeast United States

New York Ironweed has a tall, straight stem, which branches towards the top and has long, lanceolate, and finely toothed leaves, with very pointed tips, that are arranged alternately along its length. Each separate branch has a cluster of disk flowers, which are usually lavender to violet in color – although there is also a white form. The flowers have no rays and look rather like those of a thistle; there are usually at least 15 in a head, sometimes as many as 50. This plant is very common across its range and is one of the best-known species of Ironweed.

Common Blue Violet ▼

Scientific name:	*Viola sororia (Viola papilionacea, Viola floridana)*
Family:	Violet
Flower type:	Irregular with two symmetrical halves, $\frac{1}{2}$–$\frac{3}{4}$ inch (1.25–1.88cm) in diameter
Flowering period:	March-May
Flower color:	Purple
Leaf type:	Cordate, scalloped
Height:	4–8 inches (10–20cm)
Habitat:	Damp woodland and meadows, wet roadsides
Range:	Eastern North America

Common Blue Violet is a low-growing plant, with quite broad, heart-shaped leaves that have scalloped edges and are borne on short stalks springing from the base of the plant. The flowers are the typical violet shape, and can be purple to blue to white. There is also a pale gray form, which is known as the Confederate Violet. There are usually many flowers on a plant, each with its own separate stalk that also springs from the base. Violet flowers can be candied, and the leaves are high in vitamins and can be used in salads.

Swamp Milkweed

Scientific name:	*Asclepias incarnata*
Family:	Milkweed
Flower type:	Umbel cluster, each flower $\frac{1}{2}$ inch (0.62cm) in diameter
Flowering period:	June–August
Flower color:	Pink
Leaf type:	Long, lanceolate, opposite
Height:	2–4 feet (60–120cm)
Habitat:	Swamps, damp thickets, coastal areas
Range:	Eastern Canada, eastern and central United States, Rockies

Swamp Milkweed is a perennial plant with a many branched and smooth stem, which bears many long, lanceolate leaves that are arranged in opposite pairs. The flowers are held in umbel clusters at the top of the stems, and are usually pink in color – although they may sometimes be white. Unlike many other milkweeds, Swamp Milkweed much prefers damp and swampy ground, but it looks very similar to the other species and has the same milky-white sap. Early American colonists used a tea made from the roots to treat asthma, rheumatism and as a heart tonic, but it is now believed that the plant is potentially toxic so it should be used with some caution.

Western Bleeding Heart; Bleeding-heart

Scientific name:	*Dicentra formosa*
Family:	Fumitory
Flower type:	Heart-shaped, each flower $\frac{3}{4}$ inch (1.88cm) in length
Flowering period:	March–June
Flower color:	Pink
Leaf type:	Compound pinnate
Height:	9–18 inches (22–45cm)
Habitat:	Damp, shady areas, moist open woods
Range:	Pacific coast states, southern British Columbia

An attractive looking plant, Western Bleeding Heart has compound pinnate leaves that are elaborate and rather fern-like, above which is a branched cluster of small flowers. The flowers are heart-shaped, and either pale pink or rose in color. There are nine species of this genus found in North America in the wild, all in the west, but there are also several cultivated varieties. The very similar Bleeding Heart (*D. spectabilis*) has been introduced from Japan but has escaped to the wild in some areas – it can be distinguished by its larger and redder, or sometimes white flowers.

Common Joe-Pye-Weed; Trumpetweed; Hollow Joe-Pye-Weed ▲

Scientific name:	*Eupatorium fistulosum*
Family:	Aster
Flower:	Flat-topped cluster, width 4–6 inches (10–15cm)
Flowering period:	July-September
Flower color:	Pink
Leaf type:	Lanceolate, toothed, whorled
Height:	2–6 feet (30–180cm)
Habitat:	Damp fields and meadows, coastal areas
Range:	Northern and eastern North America, scattered areas of the west

There are several very similar-looking species of Joe-Pye-Weed, which gets its very unusual common name from an old folklore tradition that a nineteenth-century American called Joe Pye used it to cure typhus fever. Common Joe-Pye-Weed has a sturdy hollow stem, which has a whitish bloom, bearing whorls of long, lanceolate and blunt-toothed leaves with a single main vein – unlike other species in the genus, which have three main veins. At the top of the stem is a flat-topped cluster of fuzzy-looking flowers.

Spotted Joe-Pye-weed

Scientific name:	*Eupatorium maculatum*
Family:	Aster
Flower type:	Flat-topped cluster, width 4–6 inches (10–15cm)
Flowering period:	July–September
Flower color:	Pink/purple
Leaf type:	Lanceolate, toothed, whorled
Height:	2–6 feet (30–180cm)
Habitat:	Damp fields and meadows, coastal areas
Range:	Northern and eastern North America, scattered areas of the west

Spotted Joe-Pye-weed has a sturdy, deep purple – or thickly purple-spotted on green – stem and this is its most distinctive feature; other species in the genus have generally green stems with only a little amount of purple. The stem bears whorls of long, lanceolate and sharply toothed leaves on short stalks, while the rather fuzzy-looking flowers are borne in a flat-topped, branching cluster at the tip of the stem. American Indians used a tea made from the whole plant as a diuretic, and a tea made from the root to treat a variety of ailments, including fevers, colds, diarrhea, liver and kidney ailments and rheumatism.

Sweet-scented Joe-Pye-Weed; Gravel Root; Queen-of-the-Meadow

Scientific name:	*Eupatorium purpureum*
Family:	Aster
Flower type:	Rounded cluster, width 4–6 inches (10–15cm)
Flowering period:	July–September
Flower color:	Pink
Leaf type:	Lanceolate, toothed, whorled
Height:	2–12 feet (30–400cm)
Habitat:	Damp fields and meadows, coastal areas
Range:	Northern and eastern North America, scattered areas of the west

Sweet-scented Joe-Pye-weed differs from Spotted Joe-Pye-weed in that its stem is mainly green in color and its leaves smell of vanilla when they are crushed – hence its main common name. It has a tall, sturdy green stem, with purple only at the leaf nodes, and whorls of long, lanceolate and toothed leaves. The rounded cluster of rather fuzzy-looking, dull pink-purple flowers is borne at the tip of the stem. Traditionally, a tea made from the leaves and roots was once used to destroy stones in the urinary tract, and to cure urinary incontinence in children. Homeopathically it is currently used for gallbladder and urinary problems – although this treatment should only be administered by trained experts.

Streambank Globe-mallow; Mountain Globe-mallow

Scientific name:	*Iliamna rivularis*
Family:	Mallow
Flower type:	Elongated raceme cluster, each flower 1–2 inches (2.5–5cm) in width
Flowering period:	June–August
Flower color:	Pink
Leaf type:	Orbicular, with triangular palmate lobes
Height:	3–7 feet (90–210cm)
Habitat:	Mountain stream edges, round springs
Range:	Northwest North America

Streambank Globe-mallow is a rather tall-growing and stout-stemmed plant, with large leaves that are generally rounded in shape but have triangular lobes, making them look rather like those of the maple. The flowers are held in elongated raceme clusters, which are quite long at the top of the stem, but with shorter versions in the leaf axils. The individual flowers are cup-shaped and pink or pinky-lavender in color. The branching stems mean there are usually many flower clusters on each plant. Streambank Globe-mallow tends to be found at higher altitudes. There are several species of Globe-mallow found in North America, but the particular species that are found in the west all tend to prefer damp locations.

Dense Blazing Star; Gay Feather

Scientific name:	*Liatris spicata*
Family:	Aster
Flower type:	Spike, each flower ¼ inch (0.62cm) in width
Flowering period:	July–September
Flower color:	Pink
Leaf type:	Very long, linear
Height:	1–6 feet (30–180cm)
Habitat:	Damp meadows and prairies
Range:	Eastern North America, from north to south

Dense Blazing Star has a tall flower spike, very densely covered in sessile, bright pink flowers that have a rather feathery look due to the long styles that extend well beyond the petals. The lower part of the stem has numerous alternate and very long, linear leaves, which get progressively shorter the higher up they are. Devil's Bit (*Chamaelirium luteum*) is also sometimes called Blazing Star, but it has white flowers, not pink. There are 34 species of Blazing Star across North America, all of them found in the east of the continent.

Twinflower

Scientific name:	*Linnaea borealis*
Family:	Honeysuckle
Flower type:	Trumpet-shaped, ½ inch (1.25cm) in length
Flowering period:	June–July
Flower color:	Pink
Leaf type:	Rounded elliptical, toothed
Height:	Creeper 4 inches (10cm)
Habitat:	Bogs, shady woodland
Range:	Most of North America, except the southeast

An evergreen creeper, Twinflower has delicate stems that trail along the ground, with upright stalks of 3-6 inches (8-15cm) that terminate in twin flowers. The flowers are trumpet-shaped and hairy inside; they are pale pinky-white and sweet-smelling. The bright green leaves are a rounded ellipse in shape, toothed and arranged in opposite pairs low down on the stem. Although there is also a European variety of this species, Twinflower is a native American plant. The Algonquin used a tea made from it as a tonic during pregnancy and to treat children's fevers, but it is now relatively rare so should not be picked or removed from its natural habitat.

Wild Mint; Field Mint

Scientific name:	*Mentha arvensis*
Family:	Mint
Flower type:	Rounded cluster, each flower $\frac{1}{4}$ inch (0.62cm) in length
Flowering period:	July–August
Flower color:	Pink
Leaf type:	Long, lanceolate, sharply toothed
Height:	6–30 inches (15–75cm)
Habitat:	Damp soil, stream sides
Range:	Most of North America, except the far southeast

This is a branching plant, with its flowers held in rounded clusters whorled around the square, hairy stem in the upper leaf axils. The flowers normally range from pale pink through to lavender, although they are occasionally white, and have long stamens, making them look rather feathery. The leaves are long and lanceolate, with sharply toothed edges and are arranged in opposite pairs. When it is crushed, the plant smells strongly of mint and can be used as a flavoring. This is the only species of mint that is native to North America.

Virginia Bluebells; Virginia Cowslip ▶

Scientific name:	*Mertensia virginica*
Family:	Borage
Flower type:	Loose, cyme cluster, each flower 1 inch (2.5cm) in length
Flowering period:	March–May
Flower color:	Pink
Leaf type:	Basal long, those higher up elliptical
Height:	8–30 inches (20–75cm)
Habitat:	Wet woods, flood plains
Range:	Northeast North America

A quite large, erect plant, Virginia Bluebells has long basal leaves and smaller, elliptical ones higher up the stem; both types are smooth but strongly veined and with a grayish bloom. The showy, trumpet-shaped flowers are borne in loose, nodding cyme clusters, and start off pink when in bud, becoming a very light blue as they open into flower. Virginia Bluebells tends to grow in massed clumps, forming great beds that can look spectacular when in bloom. It is also sometimes cultivated in gardens.

Elephant's Head; Little Red Elephants

Scientific name:	*Pedicularis groenlandica*
Family:	Figwort
Flower type:	Raceme spike, each flower $\frac{1}{2}$ inch (1.25cm) in length
Flowering period:	June–August
Flower color:	Pink
Leaf type:	Long, pinnately divided into lobes, sharp toothed
Height:	32 inches (80cm)
Habitat:	Wet meadows, along streams
Range:	Northern and western North America, south to New Mexico in mountains

This species gets its unusual name from the strange shape of the flowers, which have one long lip like a trunk and two side lobes like ears, and look just like tiny pink elephant's heads. Elephant's Head has one, or sometimes two, stems that spring from a woody base, with long-stalked basal leaves. These are pinnately divided into many lobes, each of which is sharply toothed along the edges. The flowers are usually a deep pink-red in color, and are quite large and thickly clustered in a terminal raceme spike. Although Elephant's Head likes to grow in wet ground it also prefers the cooler temperatures commonly found at higher altitudes, so along mountain ranges in the west its range extends right down into New Mexico.

Obedient Plant; False Dragonhead

Scientific name:	*Physostegia virginiana*
Family:	Mint
Flower type:	Elongated cluster, 4–8 inches (10–20cm) in length
Flowering period:	June–August
Flower color:	Pink
Leaf type:	Narrowly lanceolate, sharply toothed
Height:	1–4 feet (30–120cm)
Habitat:	Swamps, damp thickets and prairies
Range:	Eastern North America

Obedient Plant is a medium size plant with a square stem – a typical feature of species in the mint family – with long, narrowly lanceolate and sharply toothed leaves, which are arranged in opposite pairs along its length. The large, showy, tubular flowers are borne in a loose, elongated cluster at the top of the stem. They are usually pink or pale purple in color, spotted with a deeper purple. The common name of Obedient Plant comes from the flowers, which will stay in whatever position they are placed for a short time. There are also several cultivated varieties of this species, which will often escape to the wild from gardens if the surrounding area is very damp.

Pale Meadow Beauty; Maryland Meadow Beauty

Scientific name:	*Rhexia mariana*
Family:	Meadow Beauty
Flower type:	Radially symmetrical, 1 inch (2.5cm) in diameter
Flowering period:	July–September
Flower color:	Pinky–purple
Leaf type:	Elliptical, toothed
Height:	6–28 inches (15–70cm)
Habitat:	Sandy swamps
Range:	East North America

Pale Meadow Beauty is a small to medium size plant, with elliptical, toothed leaves arranged in opposite pairs along the rather oblong-shaped stem. The leaves are very rounded at the base and have three, very prominent linear veins. The delicate four-petaled flowers vary from pale pinky-purple, through rose to white. They have comparatively long, distinctive arched yellow stamens, and are borne in a loose terminal cluster. There are ten species of this genus across North America, all preferring to grow in damp ground and all found in the east of the continent. Despite its alternative common name of Maryland Meadow Beauty, Pale Meadow Beauty is found in many states other than Maryland.

Virginia Meadow Beauty; Deergrass

▶

Scientific name:	*Rhexia virginica*
Family:	Meadow Beauty
Flower type:	Radially symmetrical, 1–1½ inches (2.5–3.75cm) in diameter
Flowering period:	July–September
Flower color:	Pink
Leaf type:	Ovate to elliptical, toothed
Height:	6–28 inches (15–70cm)
Habitat:	Sandy swamps
Range:	From northeast to southeast North America

Virginia Meadow Beauty is very similar to Pale Meadow Beauty, but has darker flowers and a much larger range. It is a fairly tall plant, with ovate to elliptical, toothed leaves arranged in opposite pairs along the squarish, branching stem. The leaves are very rounded at the base and have three prominent linear veins. The flowers are bright deep pink, with long, arched yellow stamens, and are borne in a loose terminal cluster. All species in this genus have a distinctive four-pointed, urn-shaped fruit.

Leafy Aster

Scientific name:	*Symphyotrichum foliaceum (Aster foliaceus)*
Family:	Aster
Flower type:	Compound flower head, 1–2 inches (2.5–5cm) in diameter
Flowering period:	June–September
Flower color:	Pink to lavender
Leaf type:	Long, lanceolate
Height:	9–22 inches (22–55cm)
Habitat:	Moist woodland, damp meadows and roadsides
Range:	Western North America

Leafy Aster is an attractive perennial, with a branching stem and long, lanceolate leaves. It grows in moist woodland or damp meadows and often forms quite large clumps. The basal leaves become very narrow at the base where they join the stem, although they do not have true stalks, while the upper ones are smaller and partly clasping. The branches terminate in several flower heads, with narrow pink to lavender ray florets and a yellow central disk. Leafy Aster is now scientifically classified in the genus *Symphyotrichum*, but was previously in *Aster*.

Cardinal Flower

Scientific name:	*Lobelia cardinalis*
Family:	Bellflower
Flower type:	Spike, each flower $1\frac{1}{2}$ inch (3.75cm) in length
Flowering period:	July–September
Flower color:	Red
Leaf type:	Long, oval to lanceolate, toothed
Height:	2–4 feet (60–120cm)
Habitat:	Damp areas along streams
Range:	Most of North America, except the northwest

Although this species is quite common, its showy flowers mean they are often picked, which has made it scarce in some areas of its range. It is a tall, leafy perennial, with bright red, tubular flowers arranged along the stem in a tall spike. The length of the flowers and their red color means they are usually pollinated by hummingbirds. The alternate leaves are long, oval to lanceolate, and toothed. American Indians used a tea made from the roots for stomach-ache and typhoid, and a leaf tea for colds, headaches and rheumatism – however, Cardinal Flower is considered potentially poisonous.

Orange Jewelweed; Spotted Touch-me-not

Scientific name:	*Impatiens capensis*
Family:	Touch-me-not
Flower type:	Irregular with two symmetrical halves, 1 inch (2.5cm) in length
Flowering period:	June–September
Flowering color:	Orange
Leaf type:	Long, thinly ovate, bluntly toothed, lower opposite, upper alternate
Height:	3–5 feet (90–150cm)
Habitat:	Shaded wet ground
Range:	Most of North America, except the southwest

Widespread in wet areas, Orange Jewelweed is an annual with a branched stem, alternate, long, thinly ovate and bluntly toothed leaves, and bright orange flowers spotted with red-brown. The flowers are borne on drooping stems, and have a spur at the back that curls round and underneath. The name Touch-me-not comes from the ripe fruits, which explode when touched. There are 10 species of Jewelweed in North America, most of which prefer wet ground. The young shoots can be used as potherbs, and the plant's juice relieves the symptoms of poison ivy. The leaves have been scientifically proven to have antihistamine and anti-inflammatory properties.

Canada Lily; Wild Yellow Lily; Field Lily

Scientific name:	*Lilium canadense*
Family:	Lily
Flower type:	Bell-shaped, 2–3 inches (5–8cm) in width
Flowering period:	June-August
Flower color:	Orange
Leaf type:	Long, lanceolate, whorled
Height:	2–5 feet (60–150cm)
Habitat:	Wet meadows, damp woodland edges
Range:	Eastern and central North America

Despite its name, the Canada Lily is not only found in Canada, but also in the eastern states and across Arkansas, Kansas and Nebraska. It has a tall stem, with long, lanceolate leaves in whorls, and showy, nodding, bell-shaped, orange, red-orange or yellow flowers with dark spots. There are usually many flowers on each stem, either on long stalks springing from the leaf axils or in a cluster at the top. American Indians traditionally made a tea from the roots to treat stomach problems, dysentery and rheumatism, and applied a poultice of the roots to snakebites.

Leopard Lily; Panther Lily

Scientific name:	*Lilium pardalinum*
Family:	Lily
Flower type:	Bell-shaped, 2–3 inches (5–8cm) in diameter
Flowering period:	May–August
Flower color:	Orange
Leaf type:	Long, narrow, lanceolate, whorled
Height:	2–7 feet (60–210cm)
Habitat:	Along forest streams, near springs
Range:	Most of California

The Leopard Lily has large, showy, bright orange-red, nodding flowers, at the top of a tall, leafy stem. The flowers have long, petal-like segments that curve backwards almost to touch the base of the flower, which inside is heavily spotted with a darker red-brown. The leaves are long, very narrowly lanceolate, and mainly arranged in whorls of 9-15, although sometimes there are a few additional leaves higher up the stem. As the flowers are so attractive and showy they are often picked by visitors, or the plants are dug up to be transplanted into gardens, which may come to endanger their future in the wild.

Golden Columbine

Scientific name:	*Aquilegia chrysantha*
Family:	Buttercup
Flower type:	Radially symmetrical, $1\frac{1}{2}$–3 inches (3.75–8cm) in diameter
Flowering period:	July–August
Flower color:	Yellow
Leaf type:	Compound palmate, deeply cleft and lobed
Height:	16–48 inches (40–120cm)
Habitat:	Damp shade
Range:	Central south United States and into Mexico

Golden Columbine is a branching, bushy perennial with compound palmate leaves and very attractive, showy, bright yellow flowers on long stalks. The flower petals have a very long spur extending from the back, which makes them very distinctive. There are 23 species of wild Columbine to be found across North America, but many more have been developed as cultivated garden flowers. In the wild, many of the yellow-flowered varieties are quite rare.

Marsh Marigold; Cowslip

Scientific name:	*Caltha palustris*
Family:	Buttercup
Flower type:	Radially symmetrical, 1–1½ inches (2.5–3.75cm) in diameter
Flowering period:	May–June
Flower color:	Yellow
Leaf type:	Basal reniform to heart-shaped, upper sessile
Height:	8–24 inches (20–60cm)
Habitat:	Stream edges, roadside ditches, swamps
Range:	North and eastern North America

The Marsh Marigold is a showy perennial, with yellow-orange flowers that look far more like buttercups than marigolds. It has a thick, succulent, hollow and branching stem bearing many glossy-green kidney to heart-shaped leaves, the lower ones on stalks and the upper sessile. The Ojibwa Indians mixed a tea made from the leaves with maple syrup to make a cough syrup, which was also used as an antidote to snake venom. The raw buds and leaves are very poisonous. There is also another species known as Marsh Marigold in the west, *C. leptosepala*.

Sneezeweed

Scientific name:	*Helenium autumnale*
Family:	Aster
Flower type:	Compound flower head, 1–2 inches (2.5–5cm) in diameter
Flowering period:	August–November
Flower color:	Yellow
Leaf type:	Long, lanceolate, coarsely toothed, sessile
Height:	2–6 feet (60–180cm)
Habitat:	Swamps, wet fields and roadsides
Range:	Most of North America, except the Arctic

Sneezeweed gets its name from its dried leaves once having been used in snuff, to promote sneezing to rid the body of evil spirits. It was also a folk remedy for fevers. It is a tall plant, with a leafy stem ending in a yellow daisy-like flower head. The leaves are long lanceolate and toothed, and are arranged alternately, with their bases extending down the stem on either side like tiny wings. The flower heads have a distinctive ball of disk flowers at the center, surrounded by long, drooping ray petals. There are 20 species of Sneezeweed found across North America.

Giant Sunflower ▲

Scientific name:	*Helianthus giganteus*
Family:	Aster
Flower type:	Compound flower head, 2-3 inches (5-8cm) in diameter
Flowering period:	July–October
Flower color:	Yellow
Leaf type:	Long, lanceolate, finely toothed, rough
Height:	3–7 feet (90–210cm)
Habitat:	Swamps, wet open ground
Range:	Northeast North America

Despite its name, Giant Sunflower does not have a very large flower – giant refers to its height, which can be up to seven feet (210cm). It has a rough, reddish-purple stem, which bears long, lanceolate, finely toothed but rough-surfaced leaves, usually arranged alternately, but sometimes opposite. The flower head has bright yellow ray flowers, around a darker yellow central disk. There are around 50 species of sunflower across North America, most of which grow east of the Rockies. Wild sunflower seeds are very nutritious, and are an important winter food for songbirds and gamebirds.

Above: Lysimachia species

Swamp Candles; Yellow Loosestrife

Scientific name:	*Lysimachia terrestris*
Family:	Primrose
Flower type:	Raceme spike, each flower $\frac{1}{2}$–$\frac{3}{4}$ inch (1.25–1.88cm) in width
Flowering period:	June–August
Flower color:	Yellow
Leaf type:	Long, narrowly lanceolate
Height:	8–48 inches (20–120cm)
Habitat:	Swamps and bogs
Range:	Eastern North America, western Washington

A native of eastern North America, Swamp Candles was introduced to the cranberry bogs of western Washington by accident, and has now become established there, spreading quickly via underground stems. It is a slender plant, with an erect stem, that prefers to grow in damp and boggy places. Its lanceolate leaves can be 5 feet (150cm) long, and are arranged in opposite pairs along the stem. The raceme spike of attractive yellow flowers can be very showy. Each flower has a circle of dark red spots on the inner end of the pointed petals. There are 16 species of this genus, spread across the whole of North America.

Yellow Skunk Cabbage

Scientific name:	*Lysichiton americanus*
Family:	Arum
Flower type:	Spike, 8 inches (20cm) long
Flowering period:	March–July
Flower color:	Yellow
Leaf type:	Oval, upright, very long
Height:	12–22 inches (30–55cm)
Habitat:	Swamps
Range:	Western North America, from Alaska to California

The common name of Skunk Cabbage comes from the very fetid smell of the sap of this plant, which is designed to attract flies to pollinate the flowers. The flowers themselves are tiny, and are densely clustered in a long spike that is partly enclosed in a large, distinctive cream or yellow-colored bract. The bright green oval leaves can grow up to 5 feet (150cm) in length, and they spring from the base of the plant, standing erect in a cluster. This is the only species of this genus found in North America. American Indians once dug up and baked the rather fleshy underground stem to supplement their winter diet, and it is still often dug up and eaten by wild animals today.

Tufted Loosestrife

Scientific name:	*Lysimachia thyrsiflora*
Family:	Primrose
Flower type:	Cluster, each flower $\frac{1}{4}$ inch (0.62cm) in length
Flowering period:	May–June
Flower color:	Yellow
Leaf type:	Long, lanceolate, opposite
Height:	8–32 inches (20–80cm)
Habitat:	Swamps, ditches, lakes
Range:	Most of northern North America

Tufted Loosestrife is found across much of North America except the far south, and prefers to grow in very wet swamps. It has an erect stem with long, lanceolate leaves in opposite pairs, arranged at equal intervals. The bright yellow flowers have erect stamens, giving them a fuzzy appearance, and are borne in dense raceme clusters set around the middle of the stem, springing from the leaf axils. Tufted Loosestrife will easily hybridize with Swamp Candles, creating plants with flower clusters both in the middle and in elongated clusters at the top of the stem. Tufted Loosestrife also occurs in Europe and Asia.

Common Monkeyflower

Scientific name:	*Mimulus guttatus*
Family:	Figwort
Flower type:	Irregular with two symmetrical halves, each flower $\frac{1}{2}$–1 inch (1.25–2.5cm) in length
Flowering period:	July–August
Flower color:	Yellow
Leaf type:	Long, ovate, toothed, clasping
Height:	40 inches (100cm)
Habitat:	Wet areas
Range:	Most of North America, except the southeast

It can be difficult to identify Common Monkeyflower as plants can be quite variable. It may be tall and thin or short and bushy, and the smooth stem may stand erect, or trail over other plants. Its flowers may be solitary or borne in a short raceme, and the leaves are long and ovate, or rounded, toothed and clasping. There are also two other species in parts of the same range that are also known as Yellow Monkeyflower: *M. moschatus*, which is a hairy-stemmed plant with an open-throated yellow flower, and *M. glabratus*, which is smooth-stemmed, but also has an open-throated flower. Across the whole of North America there are 85 species, but over half are found only in California.

Yellow Butterwort

Scientific name:	*Pinguicula lutea*
Family:	Bladderwort
Flower type:	Irregular with two symmetrical halves, $\frac{3}{4}$–1 inch (1.88–2.5cm) in diameter
Flowering period:	March–May
Flower color:	Yellow
Leaf type:	Basal, broadly ovate
Height:	6–18 inches (15–45cm)
Habitat:	Damp, sandy ground
Range:	Southeast United States

The yellow-green, ovate to oblong leaves of Yellow Butterwort are arranged in a basal rosette, and they have a very sticky surface that is designed to catch unwary insects. The leaves roll inwards and use enzymes to digest the catch, which provides extra nourishment to the plant, allowing it to grow in very poor soil. The single wide-mouthed flower is borne at the end of a long, leafless stalk. The scientific genus name comes from the Latin word *pinguis*, meaning fat, as the upper surface of the leaves feels very greasy to the touch. There are eight species of this genus in North America.

Common Buttercup

Scientific name:	*Ranunculus acris*
Family:	Buttercup
Flower type:	Radially symmetrical, 1 inch (2.5cm) in diameter
Flowering period:	May–September
Flower color:	Yellow
Leaf type:	Long-stalked, deeply palmately incised into lanceolate, toothed segments
Height:	20–36 inches (50–90cm)
Habitat:	Damp areas, particularly meadows and disturbed soil
Range:	Most of North America, except the mid-southern states

Introduced from its native Europe, the Common Buttercup is now one of the most common North American buttercups. It is a tall, erect plant, with hairy, branching stems and long-stalked, alternate leaves that are deeply palmately incised into lanceolate, toothed segments. The basal leaves are quite large, the upper ones smaller. The flowers are the typical shiny buttercup yellow – the waxy nature of the petals is created by a special layer of cells. This species is rather poisonous to animals, and its unpleasant-tasting sap discourages them from grazing on the plant. American Indians made a poultice from the roots for boils and abscesses, using the irritant effect of the sap to burn them off. However, the plant can cause blistering of the skin.

Green Corn Lily; Green False Hellebore

Scientific name:	*Veratrum viride*
Family:	Lily
Flower type:	Elongated cluster, each flower $\frac{1}{2}$–1 inch (1.25–5cm) in length
Flowering period:	April–July
Flower color:	Greenish–yellow
Leaf type:	Elliptical, pleated, parallel-veined, clasping
Height:	2–8 feet (60–250cm)
Habitat:	Wet meadows at altitude, swamps, wet woods
Range:	Northwest and northeast United States

Green Corn Lily has a single, stout stem, with many large, elliptical, pleated and parallel-veined leaves that clasp the stem at lower levels, all pointing upwards. The stem terminates in a flower stalk that can be up to 4 feet (120cm) in length, with numerous branching clusters of star-shaped flowers. The flowers have hairy petals and are a greeny-yellow in color. Like the other *Veratrum* species this one is poisonous, and extracts from it have been used in insecticides. Even handling it is dangerous, as its poison can be absorbed through the skin. However, it is used pharmaceutically in drugs to slow heart rate and lower blood pressure, and to stimulate blood flow to the kidneys and liver.

Stream Violet; Pioneer Violet; Smooth Yellow Violet

▼

Scientific name:	*Viola glabella*
Family:	Violet
Flower type:	Irregular with two symmetrical halves, $\frac{1}{2}$–$\frac{3}{4}$ inch (1.25–1.88cm) in diameter
Flowering period:	March–June
Flower color:	Yellow
Leaf type:	Cordate, toothed
Height:	3–12 inches (8–30cm)
Habitat:	Damp woodland, along streams
Range:	Northeast North America

A very common species, the Stream Violet is often found in damp, shaded places in its range. It is fairly low-growing, although its heart-shaped leaves with their finely toothed edges are borne on quite long stalks. The small flower is bright yellow, although the lower three petals have very fine maroon lines radiating out from their bases. As in most other western violets, the lower central petal also acts as a landing place for insects coming to find the nectar and pollinate the flower. There are around 80 species of violet across North America.

Jack-in-the-pulpit; Indian turnip

Scientific name:	*Arisaema triphyllum*
Family:	Arum
Flower type:	Cluster, 2–3 inches (5–8cm) in length
Flowering period:	April–June
Flower color:	Brown
Leaf type:	Tripartite, each leaflet elliptical
Height:	12–30 inches (30–75cm)
Habitat:	Swamps, damp woodland
Range:	Eastern Canada, central and eastern United States

The name Jack-in-the-pulpit comes from the spadix enclosed in the spathe, rather like a person standing in a pulpit. The spathe curves over the top of the spadix and is green, streaked and mottled with brown-purple. The spadix has male and female flowers hidden away at its base. Jack-in-the-pulpit usually has only one or two leaves, which are divided into three parts, each elliptical in shape, and are set at the end of long stalks. A tea made from the dried root was traditionally used as a purgative and an expectorant for the treatment of asthma, bronchitis, colds and headaches.

Skunk Cabbage ▶

Scientific name:	*Symplocarpus foetidus*
Family:	Arum
Flower type:	Spike, 1 inch (2.5cm) in length
Flowering period:	February–May
Flower color:	Brown
Leaf type:	Large, oblanceolate
Height:	12–22 inches (30–55cm)
Habitat:	Swamps, marshes, wet woodland
Range:	Northeast North America

Skunk Cabbage has strongly fetid sap, particularly when the plant is bruised, which attracts flies to pollinate the flowers. These are tiny, and densely clustered in a long spike or spadix that is enclosed in a large, purple-brown spathe mottled with green. The flowers appear before the oval leaves, which spring direct from the soil in late spring. The leaves can be as long as 2 feet (60cm) and 1 foot (30cm) wide. American Indians used the root to treat whopping cough and toothache, and a leaf poultice to reduce swelling. However, eating the leaves is very dangerous and will cause burning and inflammation.

DESERT

Spreading Fleabane

Scientific name:	*Erigeron divergens*
Family:	Aster
Flower type:	Compound flower head, 1 inch (2.5cm) in diameter
Flowering period:	May–September
Flower color:	White
Leaf type:	Long, lanceolate
Height:	6–26 inches (15–65cm)
Habitat:	Sandy deserts, open foothills, plains
Range:	Western and southern North America

There are around 140 species in this genus found in North America, and a large number may be quite difficult to tell apart. Spreading Fleabane has a branching stem covered in short hairs, and with many small, lanceolate leaves arranged alternately. The base leaves are larger and longer, often arranged in tufts. The flower heads are held at the tips of the branches and usually have many, very narrow, white or pinkish ray flowers around a bright yellow, flat central disk. However, sometimes the ray florets are entirely missing, leaving only the disk florets.

Desert Trumpet; Indianpipe Weed ▶

Scientific name:	*Eriogonum inflatum*
Family:	Buckwheat
Flower type:	Rounded cluster, $\frac{1}{2}$ inch (1.25cm) in diameter
Flowering period:	March–July
Flower color:	White
Leaf type:	Basal rosette, long-stalked, oval
Height:	9–38 inches (22-95cm)
Habitat:	Sandy or rocky deserts
Range:	Southwest United States

Desert Trumpet is a rather odd-looking plant, with erect, slender, gray-green stems that are swollen toward the top, the stem branching out just above the inflated section. The bare stems spring from a basal rosette of long-stalked, small, oval to rounded leaves. The white to yellow flowers are very tiny, set in woolly cups, and grow at the tips of slender stalks in small, rounded clusters. Cups around the tiny flowers is a typical feature of species in this genus. The alternative common name of Indianpipe Weed comes from American Indians having once used the dried stems as smoking pipes.

Desert Lily

Scientific name:	*Hesperocallis undulata*
Family:	Lily
Flower type:	Radially symmetrical, 2–3 inches (5–8cm) in length
Flowering period:	March–May
Flower color:	White
Leaf type:	Basal, linear, undulating edges
Height:	15–48 inches (38–120cm)
Habitat:	Sandy desert
Range:	Central western United States

An unusual and particularly attractive plant in its very arid habitat, Desert Lily can grow very tall and so be quite conspicuous in flat, sandy desert areas. It has long, linear and strap-like basal leaves, which partly clasp the sturdy stem and have very undulating edges along the full length. The stem terminates in an open raceme cluster of funnel-shaped white flowers, which open out into six petal-like, pointed segments. The segments curve very gently outwards, but not far back on themselves. This is the only species in this genus found in North America.

Western Peppergrass

Scientific name:	*Lepidium montanum*
Family:	Mustard
Flower type:	Rounded cluster, 1½ inches (3.75cm) in diameter
Flowering period:	March–August
Flower color:	White
Leaf type:	Linear, pinnately lobed
Height:	14–18 inches (35–45cm)
Habitat:	Open desert, sagebrush, rangeland
Range:	Central western United States

The many slender branches of Western Peppergrass create a rounded, bushy shape. The basal leaves are long and deeply pinnately lobed, but those on the stem are rather smaller and may not be lobed. Each of the branches terminates in a small, rounded, densely packed raceme cluster of tiny white flowers, each of which has four minute petals. There are several species of peppergrass found in North America, many of them considered to be weeds. Some varieties, such as Fremont's Peppergrass (*L. fremontii*) and Virginia Peppergrass (*L. virginicum*) are edible, the leaves being added to salads or used as a pot herb, and the seeds sprinkled on soups and meats as a seasoning.

Above: The fruit of Virginia Peppergrass is edible.

Dune Evening-primrose; Birdcage Evening-primrose

Scientific name:	*Oenothera deltoides*
Family:	Evening-primrose
Flower type:	Radially symmetrical, 1–3 inches (2.5–8cm) in diameter
Flowering period:	April–June
Flower color:	White
Leaf type:	Ovate or elliptical, toothed
Height:	3–12 inches (8–30cm)
Habitat:	Sandy desert
Range:	Southwest United States

Dune Evening-primrose is a grayish plant, with a dense basal rosette of ovate or elliptical, toothed leaves. The stems spring from the rosette but lie along the ground; they have few leaves along their length but are leafy at the ends. The flowers are borne at the ends of the stems or on a short stalk. They are white, with four broad, papery petals, and they only open in the evening. The alternative common name of Birdcage Evening-primrose comes from the birdcage-like shape the dried stems of this plant make when it dies. Like other species in this genus, the roots of Dune Evening-primrose are edible and can be candied, boiled, fried or added to stews.

Nuttall's Larkspur

Scientific name:	*Delphinium nuttallianum*
Family:	Buttercup
Flower type:	Elongated cluster, each flower 1 inch (2.5cm) in diameter
Flowering period:	April–July
Flower color:	Blue
Leaf type:	Orbicular, pinnately dissected, lobes very narrow
Height:	4–15 inches (10–38cm)
Habitat:	Sagebrush desert, open coniferous woodland
Range:	Northwest to west North America

A medium-size plant, Nuttall's Larkspur has a single stem, with several leaves borne on long slender stalks springing from near the base. The leaves are roughly circular in overall shape, but are deeply pinnately dissected into very narrow lobes. The softly hairy blue flowers are irregular, with two symmetrical halves, and have five sepals and four petals. The sepals are blue, and the upper one has a long, backward-pointing spur. The petals can be either blue or white with blue streaks; the bottom two are deeply notched at the tip. The flowers are borne at the top of the stem, in one or more open raceme clusters. Nuttall's Larkspur is very similar to other species in the same genus, and it can be very difficult to tell them all apart.

Desert Bell ▶

Scientific name:	*Phacelia campanularia*
Family:	Waterleaf
Flower type:	Bell-shaped, 1–1½ inches (2.5–3.75cm) in length
Flowering period:	March–April
Flower color:	Blue
Leaf type:	Ovate, lobed, toothed
Height:	10–30 inches (25–75cm)
Habitat:	Sand or gravel desert
Range:	Southern California, west Arizona

A native of southern California, Desert Bell has now been introduced along roadsides in western Arizona, where it has acclimatized very well. It is a medium-height, erect plant, with very stiff and hairy stems that bear many long, broadly ovate leaves. The edges of the leaves are both slightly lobed and sharply toothed. The bell-shaped, deep blue flowers are borne in a loose branching cluster at the top of the plant. There are over 140 species in this genus found in North America, most of them native wildflowers in the western half of the continent.

CHIA

Scientific name:	*Salvia columbariae*
Family:	Mint
Flower type:	Rounded cluster, each flower ½ inch (1.25cm) in length
Flowering period:	April–June
Flower color:	Purple
Leaf type:	Basal, roughly oblong, irregularly divided
Height:	6–22 inches (15–55cm)
Habitat:	Open desert, chaparral
Range:	Southwest United States

Chia is a rather leggy, medium height plant, with long, square-section stems and leaves mainly borne at the base. The leaves are roughly oblong in shape, and are irregularly divided. The rather spiky-looking flowers are also irregular with two symmetrical halves, and are borne in dense rounded clusters set around the stem at spaced intervals. They range in color from deep blue to purple – sometimes rather tinged with red. Chia is also the common name of several other similar salvia species.

TAHOKA DAISY

Scientific name:	*Machaeranthera tanacetifolia*
Family:	Aster
Flower type:	Compound flower head, 2 inches (5cm) in diameter
Flowering period:	June–September
Flower color:	Purple
Leaf type:	Bipinnately lobed
Height:	6–15 inches (15–38cm)
Habitat:	Sandy deserts
Range:	Central western and south North America

A very attractive plant, Tahoka Daisy has slender branching stems, bearing feathery, fern-like bipinnately lobed leaves. The leaves are quite long and the main lobes are pointed at the tip. The compound flower heads are borne at the end of the branches, and consist of numerous, very narrow, bright purple ray florets around a yellow central disk. There are around 25 species in this genus found in North America, including False Tahoka Daisy (*M. parviflora*), which has small flower heads and less divided leaves.

Above: A close-up view of *Salvia columbariae.*

Desert Sand Verbena

Scientific name:	*Abronia villosa*
Family:	Four-o'clock
Flower type:	Rounded cluster, 2–3 inches (5–8cm) in diameter
Flowering period:	March–October
Flower color:	Pink
Leaf type:	Ovate, scalloped
Height:	Creeper, 6 inches (15cm)
Habitat:	Sandy desert
Range:	Southeastern United States

Desert Sand Verbena is a low-growing, creeping plant, with long, trailing, reddish stems that can extend up to 36 inches (90cm). The steams bear ovate, dark green leaves with slightly scalloped edges, which are arranged in opposite pairs, and both leaves and stems are fleshy and covered with a fine layer of soft, sticky hairs. The flower stalks spring from the leaf axils, and end in rounded, almost spherical clusters of bright pink to purple-red, trumpet-shaped flowers. Sweet Sand Verbena (*A. fragrans*) has sweet-smelling white flowers and is a more erect plant; it is found in a similar area, but its range extends further north and east. There are 23 species in this genus found in North America, mostly in the west.

Desert Four-o'clock

Scientific name:	*Mirabilis multiflora*
Family:	Four-o'clock
Flower type:	Rounded clusters, each flower 1 inch (2.5cm) in diameter
Flowering period:	May–September
Flower color:	Pink
Leaf type:	Ovate or cordate
Height:	16–20 inches (40–50cm)
Habitat:	Sandy deserts, open coniferous woodland
Range:	Southwest United States

The vivid, deep pink, trumpet-shaped flowers of Desert Four-o'clock open only in the evenings and remain closed during the heat of the day. The plant is quite bushy, with many stems bearing long, ovate or cordate leaves on short stalks. Several flowers are clustered together growing from a cup with five lobes, which is borne on the end of a short stalk that springs from a leaf axil. There are around 35 species in this genus found in North America, all of which are found in the west; they all prefer drier ground.

Desert Mallow

Scientific name:	*Sphaeralcea ambigua*
Family:	Mallow
Flower type:	Radially symmetrical, 1–1½ inches (2.5–3.75cm) in diameter
Flowering period:	May–August
Flower color:	Red/orange/purple/white
Leaf type:	Palmately-lobed, toothed
Height:	18–40 inches (45–100cm)
Habitat:	Arid, open ground
Range:	Southwest United States

Desert Mallow is a leafy, branching, softly hairy plant, with tripalmately lobed, toothed leaves. The flowers range in color depending on where the plant is growing in its range – in southwest Utah and Arizona they are orange to orange-red, but in northern California they are lavender or white. The flowers have five broad petals and are borne in narrow clusters that spring from the upper leaf axils. It may be difficult to identify Desert Mallow precisely, as there are other, very similar species within the same general area. Scaly Globe-mallow (*S. leptophylla*) shares the same range and has gray hairs that are more like scales; Scarlet Globe-mallow (*S. coccinea*) has palmately-dissected leaves with narrow segments and irregular teeth.

Above: Sphaeralcea species

Mexican Gold Poppy

Scientific name:	*Eschscholzia californica ssp. mexicana*
Family:	Poppy
Flower type:	Radially symmetrical, $\frac{3}{4}$–2 inches (1.88–5cm) in diameter
Flowering period:	March–June
Flower color:	Orange
Leaf type:	Bipinnate, finely dissected
Height:	10–18 inches (25–45cm)
Habitat:	Gravelly desert
Range:	Southeast and south United States

Mexican Gold Poppy was once thought to be a species in its own right, but is now generally considered to be a subspecies of California Poppy (*E. californica*). It has several blue-green stems and deeply dissected, rather fern-like leaves, with a bright flower on the end of a long, bare stalk. The flower has four broad petals in a shallow bowl shape and is orange-yellow, often grading in color from deep orange at the base of the petals to pale yellow or cream at the tips. The flowers only open in sunlight, closing at night and on very cloudy days. There are around ten species in this genus found in western North America.

Arizona Caltrop; Desert Poppy

Scientific name:	*Kallstroemia grandiflora*
Family:	Caltrop
Flower type:	Radially symmetrical, 2 inches (5cm) in diameter
Flowering period:	May–October
Flower color:	Orange
Leaf type:	Compound pinnate
Height:	Creeper, 6 inches (15cm)
Habitat:	Sandy ground in deserts
Range:	South United States, southeast California

Although the flower of Arizona Caltrop looks very like a poppy, the plant is not even a member of the same family. It is a creeper, with trailing, hairy, branching stems that can grow up to 36 inches (90cm) in length. The stems bear long, compound pinnate leaves, arranged in opposite pairs. The flowers are cup-shaped, with five broad, vivid orange petals, and they are held at the tops of erect stalks. There are seven species in this genus found in North America.

Desert Marigold

Scientific name:	*Baileya multiradiata*
Family:	Aster
Flower type:	Compound flower head, $1\frac{1}{2}$–2 inches (3.75–5cm) in diameter
Flowering period:	April–September
Flower color:	Yellow
Leaf type:	Ovate, deeply pinnately lobed, lobes toothed
Height:	12–22 inches (30–55cm)
Habitat:	Sandy or gravel desert
Range:	Southern United States

A branching, leafy plant, Desert Marigold prefers to grow in sandy or gravelly soil. It has gray, softly hairy stems, with most of the leaves borne on the lower half. The leaves are roughly ovate in overall shape, but are deeply pinnately lobed, with the lobes further toothed. The one or more compound flower heads are each borne at the tip of a long, bare flower stalk, and are made up of 20-50 oblong yellow ray florets with toothed tips, set round a yellow central disk. Desert Marigold spreads to form large patches, particularly along desert roads.

Yellow Bee Plant

Scientific name:	*Cleome lutea*
Family:	Caper
Flower type:	Rounded raceme cluster, 1–2 inches (2.5–5cm) in diameter
Flowering period:	June–September
Flower color:	Yellow
Leaf type:	Compound palmate; leaflets lanceolate
Height:	18–60 inches (45–150cm)
Habitat:	Desert plains near water
Range:	Central eastern United States

Yellow Bee Plant has small but attractive, rounded flower clusters, which are made up of many tiny yellow flowers with four open petals and six long stamens. These clusters are borne at the top of the plant, at the tips of branching stems. The light green leaves are compound palmate, with three to seven long, lanceolate leaflets. The long, narrow seed pods are held at the end of curving stalks that spring from the stems. There are 12 species in this genus found across North America.

Sulfur Buckwheat

Scientific name:	*Eriogonum umbellatum*
Family:	Buckwheat
Flower type:	Rounded cluster, 2–4 inches (5–10cm) in diameter
Flowering period:	May–August
Flower color:	Yellow
Leaf type:	Long, ovate, hairy
Height:	3–16 inches (8–40cm)
Habitat:	Sagebrush deserts, dry foothills
Range:	West and southwest United States

Sulfur Buckwheat has short, woody branches with the ends bearing clusters of long, ovate leaves on slender stalks. The leaves are gray-green and have very hairy undersides. The long, bare, erect flower stalks spring from the leaves, bearing tiny yellow-cream or yellow flowers in small, rounded clusters. The flowers grow from tiny cups, with several springing from each – a typical feature of the flowers of this species. There are 180 species in this genus in North America, most found in the western half of the continent.

Desert Rosemallow

Scientific name:	*Hibiscus coulteri*
Family:	Mallow
Flower type:	Radially symmetrical, 1–2 inches (2.5–5cm) in diameter
Flowering period:	April–October
Flower color:	Yellow
Leaf type:	Lower ovate; upper divided, three toothed lobes
Height:	30–48 inches (75–120cm)
Habitat:	Brushy desert
Range:	South United States

Desert Rosemallow is a medium size, roughly hairy plant that prefers to grow in brushy desert. It has lower leaves that are narrowly ovate, and upper ones that are divided into three narrow lobes with coarsely toothed edges. The large flowers are bowl-shaped, with five broad petals and many stamens. A characteristic of all mallow flowers is that the stamens are united to make a column in the center of the flower. The petals are usually yellow, but can be whitish or tinged with red.

Gordon's Bladderpod ▲

Scientific name:	*Lesquerella gordonii*
Family:	Mustard
Flower type:	Radially symmetrical, $\frac{1}{2}$ inch (1.25cm) in diameter
Flowering period:	April–June
Flower color:	Yellow
Leaf type:	Lanceolate
Height:	Trailing, 6 inches (15cm)
Habitat:	Sand or gravel ground in deserts
Range:	South United States

An annual plant, Gordon's Bladderpod grows in sandy or gravelly ground in desert areas. It has several long, trailing stems, which turn up at the ends, bearing long, lanceolate, strap-like leaves. The leaves nearest the base of the plant are sometimes slightly toothed. The bright yellow flowers have four rounded petals and are borne in loose raceme clusters at the ends of the stems. Fendler's Bladderpod (*L. fendleri*) is found in the same area, and has the same color flowers, but it is a tufted, more tightly packed, gray-green perennial without trailing stems.

Desert Prince's-plume

Scientific name:	*Stanleya pinnata*
Family:	Mustard
Flower type:	Elongated cluster, 6–25 inches (15–60cm) in length
Flowering period:	May–July
Flower color:	Yellow
Leaf type:	Lanceolate, pinnately divided
Height:	18–60 inches (45–150cm)
Habitat:	Desert, sagebrush
Range:	South and southeast United States

Its height makes Desert Prince's-plume quite conspicuous within its range. It has tall, rather stout, blue-green stems, bearing many broad, lanceolate leaves that are usually pinnately divided – although the smaller leaves higher up the stem may not be. The small yellow flowers are very hairy inside, and are borne in long, wand-like, raceme clusters. There are six species in this genus found in North America, all in the west, but Desert Prince's-plume has the widest range. White Desert Plume (*S. albescens*) has white hairy flowers, and is found in parts of Arizona, Colorado and New Mexico.

Woodland and Forest

Vanilla Leaf; Deer Foot

Scientific name:	*Achlys triphylla*
Family:	Barberry
Flower type:	Spike, 1–2 inches (2.5–5cm) in length
Flowering period:	April–June
Flower color:	White
Leaf type:	Orbicular, divided into three fan-shaped leaflets
Height:	12–22 inches (30–55cm)
Habitat:	Woodland
Range:	Western North America

Vanilla Leaf is an unusual plant, with what looks like twin stems – one of which is the stalk of the leaf and the other that of the flower. The leaf is round overall in shape, but deeply incised so it is divided into three fan-shaped leaflets, which are bluntly toothed at the ends. The leaves smell of vanilla when they are dried, hence the common name. The flower head is a dense spike of very small white flowers. There are only two species in this genus found in North America – the other is California Vanilla Leaf (*A. californica*), which is found nearer the coast.

White Baneberry; Doll's Eyes

Scientific name:	*Actaea pachypoda (Actaea alba)*
Family:	Buttercup
Flower type:	Raceme cluster, each flower $\frac{1}{4}$ inch (0.62cm) in width
Flowering period:	July–October
Flower color:	White
Leaf type:	Pinnate, leaflets ovate, toothed
Height:	12–26 inches (30–65cm)
Habitat:	Woodland and thickets
Range:	Eastern North America

An attractive-looking perennial, White Baneberry has a tall, straight stem with many large pinnate leaves, which have ovate and toothed leaflets. The stem terminates in an oblong-shaped raceme cluster of white, spindly flowers, which have numerous long, white stamens. The common name of Doll's Eyes comes from the berries, which are round and white with a purple-black dot at the tip, and look rather like old-fashioned china dolls' eyes. They are extremely poisonous, as are those of the similar red-berried species, Red Baneberry (*A. Rubra*).

Wild Leek; Ramp

Scientific name:	*Allium tricoccum*
Family:	Lily
Flower type:	Rounded cluster, 1–2 inches (2.5–5cm) in diameter
Flowering period:	June–July
Flower color:	White
Leaf type:	Wide, elliptical
Height:	6–18 inches (15–45cm)
Habitat:	Rich woodland
Range:	Northeast North America

Wild Leek is a perennial, with a bulb rather like that of an onion. The tall, wide, elliptical leaves spring from the bulb, but wither away before the flowers appear in June to July. They are quite fleshy, and smell strongly of onion or leek. The flowers are white, often with a creamy tint, and are borne at the end of a long, erect, bare stem, in a domed umbel cluster. American Indians once ate the leaves as a spring tonic, and to ward off colds, while the juice from the bulbs was used on stings, or warmed and used to relieve earache. The young leaves can also be added to salads, or cooked as a vegetable.

Wild Sarsaparilla

Scientific name:	*Aralia nudicaulis*
Family:	Ginseng
Flower type:	Globe-shaped umbel clusters, 1½–2 inches (3.75–5cm) in diameter
Flowering period:	May–August
Flower color:	White
Leaf type:	Three sets of 5–7 leaflets, each ovate, finely toothed
Height:	9–24 inches (22–60cm)
Habitat:	Woodland
Range:	Across northern and eastern North America, except the Arctic

Wild Sarsaparilla has unusual leaves with three separate stalks, each having five to seven ovate and finely toothed leaflets. The leaves are at the end of a long stem, shading the flowers like an umbrella. The flowers are borne at the end of a bare stalk, in globe-shaped umbel clusters, and are greenish-white in color. There are usually at least three separate clusters on each stalk, and sometimes as many as seven. The rhizomes are aromatic and can be dried and used as a substitute for sarsaparilla. American Indians made it into a pleasantly flavored drink, which was also used as a tonic. Fresh root was made into a poultice to relieve sores, burns and boils, and to reduce swelling and cure infections.

American Spikenard; Pretty Morrel

Scientific name:	*Aralia racemosa*
Family:	Ginseng
Flower type:	Umbel clusters, 1½–2 inches (3.75–5cm) in diameter
Flowering period:	June–August
Flower color:	White
Leaf type:	Compound, with heart-shaped, toothed leaflets
Height:	3–5 feet (90–150cm)
Habitat:	Rich woodland
Range:	Eastern North America

A perennial, American Spikenard is found in rich woodland across the east. It has a smooth, dark green or reddish stem, with compound leaves that have heart-shaped, toothed leaflets. The flowers are greenish-white, and are borne in small umbel clusters, forming a raceme spike. American Indians made the fresh root into a poultice to relieve sores, burns and boils, and to reduce swelling and cure infections. The root tea is pleasant-tasting and was used to treat coughs, asthma, lung illnesses, rheumatism and kidney ailments, and was also often used in cough syrups.

Goatsbeard ▲

Scientific name:	*Aruncus dioicus (Aruncus sylvester)*
Family:	Rose
Flower type:	Elongated cluster, $\frac{1}{8}$ inch (0.31cm) in width
Flowering period:	March–July
Flower color:	White
Leaf type:	Pinnate, with ovate, sharply toothed leaflets
Height:	4–7 feet (120–210cm)
Habitat:	Moist woodland
Range:	Northwest, west and much of eastern North America

Goatsbeard is a tall woodland plant, with many bipinnate leaves that have large, ovate and sharply toothed leaflets. The tiny white flowers are borne in many dense, narrow, arching, elongated clusters, which together form a very large, showy, pyramid-shaped and open panicle. Male and female flowers occur on separate plants, and there are only two species in this genus in North America. Cherokee Indians pounded the root of Goatsbeard to make a poultice to relieve bee stings, and a tea of the root was used to reduce bleeding after child-birth and to bathe swollen feet.

Crinkleroot; Twoleaf Toothwort; Pepper Root

Scientific name:	*Cardamine diphylla*
Family:	Mustard
Flower type:	Terminal cluster, each flower $\frac{3}{4}$ inch (1.88cm) in diameter
Flowering period:	April–June
Flower color:	White
Leaf type:	Tripalmate, sharply toothed, whorled
Height:	6–14 inches (15–35cm)
Habitat:	Moist woodland
Range:	Eastern central North America

Crinkleroot is very similar to Cutleaf Toothwort, but has only two tripalmate leaves that are lanceolate and sharply toothed, and arranged nearly opposite just above the midpoint of the stem. The basal leaves vanish before the plant comes into flower. The four-petaled flowers are borne in a terminal cluster and are either white or pinkish. The root was used as a folk remedy for toothache, and American Indians chewed it for colds and made it into a poultice for headaches. A tea made from the root was used as a gargle for sore throats. Crinkleroot was previously in a different genus, and had the scientific name of *Dentaria diphylla*.

White Bluebead Lily

Scientific name:	*Clintonia umbellulata*
Family:	Lily
Flower type:	Umbel cluster, each flower $\frac{3}{4}$–1 inch (1.88–2.5cm) in length
Flowering period:	May–August
Flower color:	White
Leaf type:	Basal, oblong
Height:	6–16 inches (15–40cm)
Habitat:	Damp woodland with acid soil
Range:	East United States

White Bluebead Lily is much less common than Bluebead Lily and is only found in a limited area from New York to Georgia, and west to Tennessee. Its berries are black, rather than blue and it has an upright umbel cluster of bell-shaped, white flowers at the end of a long, bare flower stalk. White Bluebead Lily also has a basal cluster of shiny bright green, broad, oblong leaves with pointed tips, which grow from an underground rhizome. The young and tender leaves of White Bluebead Lily can eaten in salads or as greens, but the older leaves are too tough.

Queen's Cup; Bride's Bonnet

Scientific name:	*Clintonia uniflora*
Family:	Lily
Flower type:	Radially symmetrical, 1–1$\frac{1}{2}$ inches (2.5–3.75cm) in diameter
Flowering period:	May–July
Flower color:	White
Leaf type:	Basal, oblong to elliptical
Height:	2–6 inches (5-15cm)
Habitat:	Damp coniferous woods
Range:	Northwest North America

Queen's Cup is a very low-growing woodland plant, with a basal cluster of oblong to elliptical leaves, which grow in patches in the same area from an extensive system of underground stems. Like Bluebead Lily (*C. borealis*) it has blue berries, but the flowers are very different as they are star-shaped rather than bell-shaped and are not borne in umbel clusters. The bare flower stalk of Queen's Cup rises up from the center of each patch of leaves and usually terminates in single white flower – sometimes there may be two but never more.

Bunchberry

Scientific name:	*Cornus canadensis*
Family:	Dogwood
Flower type:	Radially symmetrical, $1\frac{1}{2}$ inch (3.75cm) in diameter
Flowering period:	May–July
Flower color:	White
Leaf type:	Ovate, pointed, whorled
Height:	3–8 inches (8–20cm)
Habitat:	Cool woodland
Range:	Northern North America

A rather small plant, Bunchberry has an erect stem with a whorl of six long, ovate, pointed leaves, which have veins that curve in an arc from the central midrib. The flower head is held just above the leaves, and is made up of many tiny, yellowish-green central florets surrounded by four large white petal-like sepals, which together look like a large, white flower. American Indians made a tea from the leaves for aches, pains fevers and as an eyewash, and a root tea for infant colic. The scarlet berries were eaten as a snack, or stored as winter supplies.

Squirrel-corn ▶

Scientific name:	*Dicentra canadensis*
Family:	Fumitory
Flower type:	Elongated raceme cluster, each flower $\frac{1}{2}$ inch (1.25cm) in length
Flowering period:	April–May
Flower color:	White
Leaf type:	Basal, compound, deeply cleft, feathery
Height:	5–10 inches (12–25cm)
Habitat:	Rich woodland
Range:	Northeast North America

Squirrel-corn is very similar to Dutchman's Breeches (*D. cucullaria*) and occupies the same habitat and range, but its flowers lack the spurs and so are more heart-shaped. The flowers are white in color and are very fragrant. Since they are so long, few insects and bees have a proboscis long enough to reach the nectar so many merely snip a hole in the side of the flower to reach it. The gray-green leaves spring from the base of the plant on long stalks, and are compound, with deeply cleft leaflets, which makes them look quite feathery.

Dutchman's Breeches

Scientific name:	*Dicentra cucullaria*
Family:	Fumitory
Flower type:	Elongated raceme cluster, each flower $\frac{3}{4}$ inch (1.88cm) in length
Flowering period:	April–May
Flower color:	White
Leaf type:	Basal, compound, deeply cleft, feathery
Height:	5–10 inches (12–25cm)
Habitat:	Rich woodland
Range:	Northeast North America

The unusual common name of Dutchman's Breeches comes from the shape of the flowers, which have two long spurs and look like tiny pairs of trousers hanging upside down from the bare stem. The flowers are white in color, sometimes tipped with yellow, and as they are very long they have the same pollination problems as Squirrel-corn (*D. canadensis*). The gray-green leaves spring from the base of the plant on long stalks, and are compound, with deeply cleft leaflets, which makes them look quite feathery. Iroquois Indians used the leaves to make a rub for athletes, while for the Menomini the plant was a powerful love charm that could attract a woman even against her will. However, Dutchman's Breeches is considered potentially poisonous and may cause a skin rash.

White Trout Lily

Scientific name:	*Erythronium albidum*
Family:	Lily
Flower type:	Radially symmetrical, 1 inch (2.5cm) in diameter
Flowering period:	March–May
Flower color:	White
Leaf type:	Basal sheath, long, narrow, elliptical
Height:	4–12 inches (10–30cm)
Habitat:	Woodland and meadows
Range:	Northeast North America

White Trout Lily has a very similar range and habitat to the Trout Lily (*E. americanum*) but its two leaves are distinctly narrower and may not be mottled. The leaves are long and elliptical and sheath the base of the stem. The small bell-shaped flower is borne at the end of a bare stalk, and is white inside but often tinged with lavender outside. There may be several flowers on each plant. Traditionally, a poultice of the leaves of White Trout Lily was used to treat ulcers and to draw out splinters and reduce swelling. The leaves have been tested scientifically and proved to soften the skin, but they may also cause an allergic reaction so they should not be applied by unqualified practitioners.

Goldenseal ▼

Scientific name:	*Hydrastis canadensis*
Family:	Buttercup
Flower type:	Radially symmetrical, $\frac{1}{2}$ inch (1.25cm) in diameter
Flowering period:	April–May
Flower color:	White
Leaf type:	Palmate, wrinkled, toothed
Height:	8–12 inches (20–30cm)
Habitat:	Woodland
Range:	Northeast North America

The solitary flower of Goldenseal has no petals – it is actually made up of many prominent white stamens. It is borne at the end of a hairy stalk and is held above a pair of stem leaves and a single, large basal leaf. All the leaves are palmately lobed, with toothed edges, prominent veins and heavily wrinkled blades. The plant grows from a golden-yellow underground stem, which gives it its common name. Goldenseal is now becoming very rare in the wild, as it has been over-collected for medicinal use. It contains an antibacterial agent and was once used commercially in eyewash solutions, and has been proved to lower blood pressure and act as a sedative. It also may be useful to treat drug-resistant tuberculosis.

TWINLEAF

Scientific name:	*Jeffersonia diphylla*
Family:	Barberry
Flower type:	Radially symmetrical, 1 inch (2.5cm) in diameter
Flowering period:	April–May
Flower color:	White
Leaf type:	Basal, long-stemmed, two symmetrical lobed halves
Height:	6–10 inches (15–25cm)
Habitat:	Damp, open woodland
Range:	Northeast North America

The common name of this plant comes from its leaves, which are in two separate mirror-image halves. They are basal, but with long stalks, and the individual halves are roughly kidney-shaped and with rather pointed lobes. The single white flower has six to nine petals arranged in a very open bowl shape. These days Twinleaf is too rare to harvest, but Native Americans used its root extensively, making it into a tea that was drunk to treat cramps, spasms, kidney stones and urinary infections, and applied externally for rheumatism, sores and ulcers.

Canada Mayflower; Two-leaved Solomon's Seal

Scientific name:	*Maianthemum canadense*
Family:	Lily
Flower type:	Elongated raceme cluster, each flower $\frac{1}{8}$ inch (0.31cm) in length
Flowering period:	May–June
Flower color:	White
Leaf type:	Cordate, alternate clasping
Height:	4–8 inches (10–20cm)
Habitat:	Forest clearings, open woodland
Range:	Canada, eastern United States

Canada Mayflower is an attractive woodland perennial that grows from a rhizome, so it often spreads easily across quite large areas. Its rather short stem looks as if it is zigzagging at each leaf joint and ends in a small dense raceme of white flowers, each of which has two petals, two sepals, and four stamens. The parallel-veined leaves are alternate, cordate and clasping and there are usually only two on the stem, hence its alternate common name of Two-leaved Solomon's Seal. The similar-looking Three-leaved Solomon's Seal (*Smilacina trifolia*) has three leaves that taper at the base and star-shaped flowers with six points.

False Lily-of-the-valley

Scientific name:	*Maianthemum dilatatum*
Family:	Lily
Flower type:	Elongated raceme cluster, 1-2 inches (2.5-5cm) in length
Flowering period:	May–June
Flower color:	White
Leaf type:	Long, cordate
Height:	6–16 inches (15–40cm)
Habitat:	Damp, shady woods
Range:	Western North America, from Alaska to northern California

The common name of False Lily-of-the-valley comes from its resemblance to the European plant Lily-of-the-valley (*Convallaria majalis*). False Lily-of-the-valley is an attractive woodland perennial that grows from a rhizome, so it is a useful and attractive ground cover across shaded areas. It has heart-shaped leaves, usually two on each stem, and slender racemes of sweet-scented white flowers on long, erect stems. These open into a star-shape with four segments, which is unlike the bell-shaped flowers of true Lily-of-the-valley.

Partridgeberry; Squaw-vine

Scientific name:	*Mitchella repens*
Family:	Madder
Flower type:	Radially symmetrical, $\frac{1}{2}$–$\frac{3}{4}$ inch (1.25–1.88cm) in length
Flowering period:	May–July
Flower color:	White
Leaf type:	Broadly ovate, green with white veins
Height:	Creeper, 6 inches (15cm)
Habitat:	Woodland
Range:	Eastern North America

Although the bright red berries of Partridgeberry are very eye-catching and edible, they are not a staple food of the partridge. The plant is a trailing creeper and is a useful ornamental ground cover for shady areas, because its shiny evergreen leaves have attractive white veining. The white, tubular flowers are very fragrant, and are borne in pairs on a single short stem. The alternative common name of Squaw-vine comes from its historical use to treat irregular and painful menses, and for pain during childbirth. It can also be made into a wash for arthritis, rheumatism and sore nipples. There is only one species of this genus in North America.

Miterwort; Bishop's Cap

Scientific name:	*Mitella diphylla*
Family:	Saxifrage
Flower type:	Elongated cluster, each flower $\frac{1}{8}$ inch (0.31cm) in length
Flowering period:	April–June
Flower color:	White
Leaf type:	Basal long, cordate, lobed; stem sessile, opposite
Height:	8–18 inches (20–45cm)
Habitat:	Woodland
Range:	Northeast North America

Miterwort has an unusual snowflake-like flower with five curving, fringed petals. There are several on each stem, borne in a very elongated cluster. The stem has two opposite, sessile leaves that are set around halfway up, which are elliptical with three lobes. The other leaves on the plant are basal with long stems, and are broader and generally heart-shaped, but also lobed. The alternative common name of Bishop's Cap comes from the fruit, which is shaped like a bishop's hat. Naked Miterwort (*M. Nuda*) is very similar to Miterwort but is smaller, and has yellowish flowers and no mid-stem leaves. It is found in the same general area, but also spreads much further west.

Wood Nymph; Waxflower; One-flowered Pyrola

Scientific name:	*Moneses uniflora*
Family:	Wintergreen
Flower type:	Radially symmetrical, $\frac{3}{4}$ inch (1.88cm) in diameter
Flowering period:	June–July
Flower color:	White
Leaf type:	Orbicular, whorled, toothed
Height:	3–6 inches (8–15cm)
Habitat:	Coniferous forests
Range:	Canada, western and northeastern United States

Although it is a rather small plant, Wood Nymph has a comparatively large and attractive flower, which hangs downwards from the top of the stem. The five waxy petals are white or pinkish in color and concavely curved, with a conspicuous pistil and a bright green ovary. The evergreen leaves are generally basal, orbicular and whorled, with small teeth, but they can sometimes be seen in opposite pairs, and rather longer. This species was once placed in the genus *Pyrola*, and it also occurs in both Europe and Asia.

Indian Pipe; Ice Plant

Scientific name:	*Monotropa uniflora*
Family:	Indian Pipe
Flower type:	Bell-shaped, $\frac{3}{4}$ inch (1.88cm) in length
Flowering period:	June–August
Flower color:	White
Leaf type:	Scales on stem
Height:	3–10 inches (8–25cm)
Habitat:	Deep woods
Range:	Northern and western North America

This rather odd-looking plant grows in the humus of deeply shaded woods. It has no chlorophyll, so the whole plant is translucent waxy-white, with several stems that are covered in small scale-like leaves. At the top, the stem bends over and terminates in a small, bell-shaped flower. As it ages, the whole plant becomes blackened. Although it is now too rare to be harvested, Indian Pipe was once valued medicinally as a remedy for sore eyes, and as a sedative for restlessness, pains and nervous irritability. However, it is not known if the plant juices are safe and it is possibly quite toxic, so it should not be eaten.

May-apple

Scientific name:	*Podophyllum peltatum*
Family:	Barberry
Flower type:	Radially symmetrical, 2 inches (5cm) in diameter
Flowering period:	April–June
Flower color:	White
Leaf type:	Palmate, deeply lobed
Height:	12–20 inches (30–75cm)
Habitat:	Damp clearings in deciduous woodland
Range:	Eastern North America

A medium-sized plant, May-apple has a pair of large, deeply lobed palmate leaves that are borne on short stalks at the end of a single stem. The one, apple-blossom-like flower hangs downwards, and is held at the end of a short stalk that springs from the angle of the two leaf stalks. May-apple has creeping underground stems and often forms large, dense patches. Its yellow or red egg-shaped berry is edible, and can be made into pies and preserves. American Indians and early colonists used the roots as a purgative and to treat hepatitis, fevers and syphilis. An extract from the root has been found to combat cancer and malaria and a partly synthetic derivative is currently used in many cancer treatments.

Bowman's Root; Indian Physic

Scientific name:	*Porteranthus trifoliatus*
Family:	Rose
Flower type:	Radially symmetrical, $1\frac{1}{2}$ inches (3.75cm) in diameter
Flowering period:	May–July
Flower color:	White
Leaf type:	Tripartite; long elliptical, toothed leaflets
Height:	2–3 feet (60–90cm)
Habitat:	Woodland
Range:	Eastern United States

Bowman's Root is a branching plant, with alternate three-part leaves that have long, elliptical and toothed leaflets. The white to pinkish flowers are star-like, but with long, narrow, unevenly arranged petals, and are borne in a very loose terminal panicle. The alternative name of Indian Physic comes from the plant's traditional use as a laxative and emetic, with very small doses also being used for indigestion, colds and asthma. As a poultice, it was also used to treat swellings and stings. However, the plant is potentially toxic so it should not be eaten.

Shinleaf

Scientific name:	*Pyrola elliptica*
Family:	Wintergreen
Flower type:	Elongated cluster, each flower $\frac{3}{4}$ inch (1.88cm) in diameter
Flowering period:	June–August
Flower color:	White
Leaf type:	Basal, broadly elliptical
Height:	5–12 inches (12–30cm)
Habitat:	Woodland
Range:	North and northeastern North America, and parts of the west

Shinleaf is a fairly small plant, with dark green, basal, broadly elliptical leaves on short, red stalks. The bare flower stalk rises from the center of the leaves, and terminates in a loose, elongated cluster of fragrant white flowers. The flowers are rounded, rather waxy-looking, and hang downwards. *Pyrola* species contain a natural drug that is very similar to aspirin, and shinleaf gets its unusual name from a traditional practise of using the leaves as a plaster, known as a shinplaster, on bruises and wounds. American Indians used a tea made from the plant to treat epilepsy in babies, and a leaf tea for sore throats.

Above: One of the several species of *Pyrola*, many of which contain a natural drug that is similar to aspirin.

Woods Stonecrop; Wild Stonecrop

Scientific name:	*Sedum ternatum*
Family:	Stonecrop
Flower type:	Radially symmetrical, $\frac{1}{2}$ inch (1.25cm) in diameter
Flowering period:	March–May
Flower color:	White
Leaf type:	Elliptical, fleshy, whorled
Height:	Creeper, 3–8 inches (8–20cm)
Habitat:	Rocky woodlands and forests
Range:	Eastern North America

A low, and rather fleshy plant, Woods Stonecrop prefers rocky, poor soil in woodland and on banks, and also grows on dry, stony outcrops. It has creeping stems that spread horizontally along the ground, but the flower stalk is held erect and terminates in a loose, three-branched terminal cluster. The flowers are open and star-like, with four or maybe five white petals. The lower leaves are borne in whorls, usually of three or four, while the upper ones are smaller and arranged alternately along the stems. All of the leaves are entire, simple and fleshy.

Fringecups

Scientific name:	*Tellima grandiflora*
Family:	Saxifrage
Flower type:	Elongated cluster, each flower $\frac{1}{2}$ inch (1.25cm) in width
Flowering period:	April–July
Flower color:	White
Leaf type:	Roughly orbicular, scalloped, hairy
Height:	32 inches (80cm)
Habitat:	Damp woodland
Range:	Northwest North America

Although the petals of Fringecups are white or cream when they first begin to open, as the flower ages it turns a deep, rich pink. The five petals are fringed across the ends, which gives rise to the common name. The flowers are borne on long, slender stalks in elongated racemes, often several to a plant. Fringecups tends to grow in clumps, so it may be difficult to tell how many plants there are in the location. The leaves are rounded, shallowly lobed or scalloped, and mostly spring from the base of the plant on long stalks.

Early Meadow-rue

Scientific name:	*Thalictrum dioicum*
Family:	Buttercup
Flower type:	Rounded clusters, each flower $\frac{1}{4}$ inch (0.62cm) in length
Flowering period:	April–May
Flower color:	White
Leaf type:	Tripartite, with rounded, lobed leaflets
Height:	8–24 inches (20–60cm)
Habitat:	Damp woodland
Range:	Ontario and eastern North America

Although its common name may suggest that it will be found growing in open meadows, Early Meadow-rue actually prefers the shaded habitat of damp and rich woodlands. It does flower quite early on in the year, producing roughly rounded clusters of drooping, greeny-white flowers. The flowers are held on long stalks and the male and female are on totally separate plants. Both types of flower have four to five petal-like sepals, but no petals; the male flower has a cluster of long yellow stamens hanging below the sepals, while the female flower has several long purple pistils instead. The stem has many leaves in three parts, with each leaflet rounded and lobed; the leaves are borne alternately along the stem.

Rue Anemone; Windflower

Scientific name:	*Thalictrum thalictroides (Anemonella thalictroides)*
Family:	Buttercup
Flower type:	Radially symmetrical, 1 inch (2.5cm) in diameter
Flowering period:	March–May
Flower color:	White
Leaf type:	Basal, whorled, tripartite; leaflets round, lobed
Height:	4–8 inches (10–20cm)
Habitat:	Open woodland
Range:	Ontario, eastern United States

A slender and rather delicate-looking plant, Rue Anemone has either a pair or a whorl of small, basal leaves. These are in three parts, with the leaflets having rounded lobes. The stem leaves are even smaller and ovate. The flowers are open and white, sometimes tinged with pink, with 5-11 petal-like sepals, but no true petals, and with a cluster of yellow stamens and pistils in the center. American Indians made a tea from the roots to treat diarrhea and vomiting, and early physicians used the root to treat piles, but Rue Anemone is potentially poisonous.

Eastern Foamflower; False Miterwort

Scientific name:	*Tiarella cordifolia*
Family:	Saxifrage
Flower type:	Elongated cluster, each flower $\frac{1}{4}$ inch (0.62cm) in diameter
Flowering period:	April–May
Flower color:	White
Leaf type:	Palmately lobed, basal, sharp toothed, hairy, long stalked
Height:	6–12 inches (15–30cm)
Habitat:	Woodlands
Range:	Northeastern United States

Eastern Foamflower is a small plant with spiky white flowers in an elongated, open cluster. The flowers have five petals and five sepals, with ten stamens and one pistil. The leaves are palmately lobed, deeply indented at the base, sharply toothed and on long stalks from the base of the plant. In general shape, they look rather like those of the maple. Eastern Foamflower has underground stems and spreads quickly to form large colonies, so it is a useful ground cover for a shady woodland garden. American Indians used a tea made from the leaves as a mouthwash and for eye ailments, and a root tea as a diuretic and for diarrhea.

Large-flower Trillium

Scientific name:	*Trillium grandiflorum*
Family:	Lily
Flower type:	Radially symmetrical, 2–4 inches (5–10cm) in diameter
Flowering period:	April–June
Flower color:	White
Leaf type:	Diamond-shaped, long, very short stalk
Height:	8–16 inches (20–40cm)
Habitat:	Woodland, thickets
Range:	Northeast North America

Large-flowered Trillium is one of the showiest trilliums in North America, with a large white flower that turns pink as it matures. The flower has three large pointed petals and three smaller sepals, and is borne at the end of a short stalk. The stalk springs from a whorl of three diamond-shaped to ovate, dark green leaves, which have short stalks. American Indians used the root for many medicinal purposes, and the leaves can be eaten in salads or as greens – but picking them will almost certainly kill the plant.

Starflower

Scientific name:	*Trientalis borealis*
Family:	Primrose
Flower type:	Radially symmetrical, $\frac{1}{4}$–$\frac{1}{2}$ inch (0.62–1.25cm) in diameter
Flowering period:	June–July
Flower color:	White
Leaf type:	Lanceolate, whorled
Height:	4–6 inches (10–15cm)
Habitat:	Cool woods with rich soil
Range:	North, east and western United States

The stem of Starflower ends in a single whorl of five to ten, long, lanceolate, pointed and shiny green leaves, from the center of which one to three flowers are borne at the end of slender stalks. The flower has from five to nine, but usually seven, pointed white petals and is open and star-like, with quite long central yellow anthers. Starflower is not edible, but it does closely resemble Indian Cucumber (*Medeola virginiana*), except that the leaves of Starflower are net-veined, and those of Indian Cucumber are parallel-veined.

Western Trillium; Western Wakerobin

Scientific name:	*Trillium ovatum*
Family:	Lily
Flower type:	Radially symmetrical, 1–3 inches (2.5–8cm) in diameter
Flowering period:	April–June
Flower color:	White
Leaf type:	Diamond-shaped, long, very short stalk
Height:	4–16 inches (10–40cm)
Habitat:	Woodland, thickets
Range:	Northeast North America

The alternative common name of Wakerobin comes from this plant's early flowering, which is around when the robin arrives. The white flower has three large pointed petals and three smaller sepals, and is borne at the end of a short stalk. The stalk springs from the center of a whorl of three diamond-shaped to ovate, dark green leaves, which are almost sessile. There are 42 species in this genus across North America, mostly concentrated in the east but with a few in the northwest.

Sessile Bellwort; Wild Oats ►

Scientific name:	*Uvularia sessilifolia*
Family:	Lily
Flower type:	Trumpet-shaped, $1\frac{1}{4}$ inches (3.12cm) in length
Flowering period:	May–June
Flower color:	White/yellow
Leaf type:	Long, oblong, clasping
Height:	6–12 inches (15–30cm)
Habitat:	Woodland, thickets
Range:	Eastern North America

A common woodland flower, Sessile Bellwort has one or more trumpet-shaped, creamy-white or yellowish flowers, which droop down from a short, angled stalk. The leaves are sparse, long, oblong and clasping, and are quite a light green above and whitish beneath. A very similar species, Bellwort (*U. perfoliata*) is distinguished by having perfoliate leaves and orange markings within the trumpet. American Indians used the root of Sessile Bellwort to make a tea that was used to purify the blood and help broken bones to heal.

Canada Violet ▲

Scientific name:	*Viola canadensis*
Family:	Violet
Flower type:	Irregular with two symmetrical halves, $\frac{3}{4}$–1 inch (1.88–2.5cm) in diameter
Flowering period:	April–July
Flower color:	White
Leaf type:	Cordate, finely toothed
Height:	8–15 inches (20–38cm)
Habitat:	Shady deciduous woodland
Range:	Canada, eastern and central southwest United States

Since it prefers cooler temperatures, Canada Violet thrives best in northern areas and at higher altitudes elsewhere. It is a small plant, with a slender purple-green stalk and long, heart-shaped leaves. The leaves are finely toothed and have comparatively long stalks. The fragrant flowers have the typical violet shape, with two upper petals and three lower. The petals are white, but the lower are finely streaked with purple and are yellow at the base. The leaves and roots of Canada Violet were traditionally used as an emetic.

Atamasco Lily; Easter Lily

Scientific name:	*Zephyranthes atamasca*
Family:	Lily
Flower type:	Trumpet-shaped, $3\frac{1}{2}$ inches (9.25cm) in diameter
Flowering period:	March–May
Flower color:	White
Leaf type:	Basal, long, narrow
Height:	12 inches (30cm)
Habitat:	Woodland, damp clearings
Range:	Southeast United States

The alternative common name of Atamasco Lily comes from its flowering around Easter time. It is a perennial growing from an underground bulb, with several basal, long, narrow and flat blue-green leaves, and a tall leafless stalk that ends in a single upward-facing, trumpet-shaped white flower. The bulb looks rather like an onion, but has caused death in grazing cattle. There are twelve species in this genus across North America, and they are all extremely poisonous if eaten.

Tall Bellflower

Scientific name:	*Campanulastrum americanum*
Family:	Bellflower
Flower type:	Elongated spike, 1–2 feet (30–60cm) in length
Flowering period:	June–August
Flower color:	Blue
Leaf type:	Long, ovate, toothed
Height:	3–6 feet (90–180cm)
Habitat:	Rich woodland
Range:	Eastern North America

Despite its name, the flowers of Tall Bellflower are not bell-shaped, but flat-faced and radially symmetrical. They are light blue to violet in color, with a long, curved style, and borne either singly or in small clusters in the axils of the upper leaves, forming an elongated spike. The leaves are long, ovate and toothed and arranged alternately up the stem. American Indians used a tea made from the leaves to treat coughs and tuberculosis, and the crushed roots for whooping cough. There are 25 species of bellflower found across North America – although there are none in the coastal west or in the far south.

Longspur Violet ▼

Scientific name:	*Viola rostrata*
Family:	Violet
Flower type:	Irregular with two symmetrical halves, $\frac{3}{4}$ inch (1.88cm) in width
Flowering period:	March–July
Flower color:	Blue
Leaf type:	Heart-shaped, scalloped
Height:	2–6 inches (5–15cm)
Habitat:	Damp woods
Range:	Northeastern United States

This small but very attractive plant has heart-shaped leaves that are gently scalloped along the edges. The flowers have two symmetrical halves and are pale blue-violet with darker centers, and borne on the same stalk as the leaves. The lower petal has a backward-facing spur that is very long – often as much as 1 inch (2.5cm). There are several similar species found in the same general area, including Dog Violet (*V. labradorica*), which has plain, darker blue flowers and rather shorter spurs, and Prostrate Blue Violet (*V. walteri*), which is very hairy.

Dwarf Larkspur; Spring Larkspur

Scientific name:	*Delphinium tricorne*
Family:	Buttercup
Flower type:	Irregular with two symmetrical halves, $\frac{3}{4}$ inch (1.88cm) in diameter
Flowering period:	April–June
Flower color:	Purple
Leaf type:	Palmately divided, deeply lobed
Height:	6–24 inches (15–60cm)
Habitat:	Rich woodland
Range:	Eastern central United States

The most common species of its genus found east of the Plains states, Dwarf Larkspur has a tall, single stem with palmately divided leaves that have deeply lobed leaflets. The leaves are mostly borne towards the bottom of the stem, which terminates in an open raceme spike of flowers. The flowers have five petal-like sepals, with the upper one projecting backwards in a long spur. They are usually purple to blue, but are sometimes variegated blue and white.

Virginia Waterleaf

Scientific name:	*Hydrophyllum virginianum*
Family:	Waterleaf
Flower type:	Rounded cluster, each flower $\frac{1}{4}$–$\frac{1}{2}$ inch (0.62–1.25cm) in length
Flowering period:	May–August
Flower color:	Purple
Leaf type:	Pinnately divided, leaflets lanceolate, sharply toothed
Height:	1–3 feet (30–90cm)
Habitat:	Damp open woodland
Range:	Northeast North America

Virginia Waterleaf is a small perennial with a hairy stem and pinnately divided leaves, the five to seven leaflets lanceolate, sharply toothed and mottled. The markings on the leaves look rather like water stains, hence the common name. The flowers are purple-pink or sometimes white, bell-shaped, and borne in rounded clusters on long stalks that spring from the leaf axils. American Indians chewed the roots of Virginia Waterleaf for cracked lips and mouth sores, and made a root tea for diarrhea and dysentery.

Gray Beardtongue ▶

Scientific name:	*Penstemon canescens*
Family:	Figwort
Flower type:	Elongated cluster, each flower 1–$1\frac{1}{2}$inches (2.5–3.75cm) in length
Flowering period:	May–June
Flower color:	Purple
Leaf type:	Basal ovate, stalked; midstem lanceolate; upper clasping
Height:	1–3 feet (30–90cm)
Habitat:	Dry woodland
Range:	East United States

Gray Beardtongue has a tall stem covered in soft, whitish hairs, which ends in a loose, elongated cluster of roughly trumpet-shaped, purple to pink flowers. The inside of the flower is streaked with a darker purple. The basal leaves are broadly ovate, with stalks, and are arranged in a rosette. Those around the middle of the stem are more lanceolate and in opposite pairs, and the upper ones are sessile and clasping. There are at least 210 species of Beardtongue found in the United States, but they are more common in the west.

Large-flower Beardtongue ▲

Scientific name:	*Penstemon grandiflorus*
Family:	Figwort
Flower type:	Elongated cluster, each flower 2 inches (5cm) in length
Flowering period:	May–June
Flower color:	Purple
Leaf type:	Long, ovate, clasping
Height:	2–4 feet (60–120cm)
Habitat:	Woodland, thickets
Range:	Central and western United States

Living up to its common name, Large-flowered Beardtongue has very large, lavender, trumpet-shaped flowers, which are held pointing out roughly horizontal to the smooth stem. The flowers form a loose, elongated cluster at the top of the stem, above the blue-green, ovate and clasping leaves, which are arranged in opposite pairs up the plant. Large-flowered Beardtongue often grows in large colonies of very many plants, forming a quite spectacular display of rich purple when they are all in flower. Although it is naturally a wildflower of the western and central states, it is also sometimes found growing wild in areas the east having escaped from cultivation.

Lyre-leaf Sage; Cancerweed

Scientific name:	*Salvia lyrata*
Family:	Mint
Flower type:	Elongated cluster, each flower 1 inch (2.5cm) in length
Flowering period:	April–June
Flower color:	Purple
Leaf type:	Basal deeply lobed; upper smaller, shallow lobed
Height:	12–26 inches (30–65cm)
Habitat:	Sandy woodland, thickets
Range:	Southeast United States

The flowers of Lyre-leaf Sage are borne in whorls in a loose, elongated spike at the top of a straight, square-section, hairy stem. The flowers are lavender-purple in color, and long and narrow with an extended lower lip that acts as a landing platform for bees. The long basal leaves are held in a rosette, are deeply lobed and have stalks. The upper leaves are much smaller and sparser, held in opposite pairs on the stem and either have short stalks or are sessile. They have rounded teeth or shallow lobes. All the leaves are green when fresh, but often become tinged with purple later in the summer. Lyre-leaf Sage was a folk remedy for cancer, hence its alternative common name.

Larkspur Violet; Prairie Violet; Crowfoot Violet

Scientific name:	*Viola pedatifida*
Family:	Violet
Flower type:	Irregular with two symmetrical halves, $\frac{1}{2}$–$\frac{3}{4}$ inch (1.25–1.88cm) in diameter
Flowering period:	May–June
Flower color:	Purple
Leaf type:	Basal, deeply-divided; leaflets very narrow, three-lobed
Height:	3-9 inches (8-22cm)
Habitat:	Woodland clearings, plains
Range:	Central North America

The blue-violet flowers of Larkspur violet are broad and held facing outwards, at the tip of short, leafless stalks. The central lower petal has a long, prominent, backward-facing spur, and the two side petals have hairs at their base; all three are whitish at the base inside the flower. The leaves are palmate in shape, but deeply divided into very narrow leaflets, which are again divided at the ends into three lobes. The common name comes from the leaves and the color of the flowers being similar to those of the larkspur, although Larkspur Violet is a much smaller plant.

Wild Garlic

Scientific name:	*Allium canadense*
Family:	Lily
Flower type:	Umbel cluster, each flower $\frac{1}{2}$ inch (1.25cm) in diameter
Flowering period:	May–July
Flower color:	Pink
Leaf type:	Long, linear, grass-like
Height:	9–24 inches (22–60cm)
Habitat:	Woods, meadows
Range:	Eastern North America

Wild Garlic is a perennial, with long, linear, grass-like leaves, that spring from the base of the stem. The slim flower stalk ends in a rounded umbel cluster of pink to white, star-shaped flowers, which may be replaced by bulblets. Although it is called Wild Garlic, the plant smells of onion and the edible bulb tastes of onion. The leaves can be added to salads, and the bulbs used in cooking in the same way as onion or garlic. However, it is important to be very certain of the exact identification, as there are various similar onion-like wild plants that are very poisonous, like the Death Camas (*Zigadenus venenosus*).

Nodding Onion ▲

Scientific name:	*Allium cernuum*
Family:	Lily
Flower type:	Umbel cluster, each flower $\frac{1}{4}$ inch (0.62cm) in length
Flowering period:	July–August
Flower color:	Pink
Leaf type:	Basal, long, narrow, linear
Height:	12–24 inches (30–60cm)
Habitat:	Open woodland
Range:	Most of North America, except the northeast, central states and Florida

A perennial that grows afresh each year from a bulb, Nodding Onion has long, narrow, linear and basal leaves, with a bare, slender, and arching stem that ends in a drooping umbel cluster of either pink or white flowers. Although it is closely related to and very similar to the Autumn Wild Onion (*A. stellatum*) Nodding Onion can be told apart because it flowers rather earlier in the year and the flowers are held in a drooping cluster, rather than erect, and also have a less lavender tint. Cherokee Indians once used the bulbs of Nodding Onion to treat colds, colic and croup, while a poultice of the whole plant was traditionally applied to the chest for respiratory ailments.

Spreading Dogbane

Scientific name:	*Apocynum androsaemifolium*
Family:	Dogbane
Flower type:	Cyme cluster, each flower $\frac{1}{4}$ inch (0.62cm) in diameter
Flowering period:	June–July
Flower color:	Pink
Leaf type:	Ovate, long
Height:	12–20 inches (30–50cm)
Habitat:	Woodland edges, roadsides
Range:	Most of North America, except the Arctic

A rather bushy-looking plant, Spreading Dogbane has branching stems with long, ovate, sharp-tipped, blue-green leaves arranged in opposite pairs. The leaves are normally bright green, but turn bright red or yellow in autumn. The flowers are small, drooping and bell-shaped, very pale pink in color but striped inside the bell in a deeper pink. They either spring from the leaf axils, or are clustered in cymes at the top of the stems, but open all at the same time and are very sweet-smelling. Like other members of the *Apocynum* genus, Spreading Dogbane has milky sap and is very poisonous – particularly to animals. Despite this, American Indians used the root to induce sweating and vomiting, and to treat headaches, indigestion, liver disease, rheumatism and syphilis.

Cutleaf Toothwort

Scientific name:	*Cardamine concatenata (Dentaria lacinata)*
Family:	Mustard
Flower type:	Drooping cluster, each flower $\frac{3}{4}$ inch (1.88cm) in diameter
Flowering period:	April–June
Flower color:	Pink
Leaf type:	Tripalmate, sharply toothed, whorled
Height:	9–15 inches (22–38cm)
Habitat:	Moist woodland
Range:	Eastern North America

Cutleaf Toothwort is an attractive woodland plant, with tripalmate leaves that are lanceolate and sharply toothed. The leaves are usually seen arranged in whorls of three just above the midpoint of the stem, but there are also basal leaves that are only evident before the plant comes into flower. The four-petaled flowers are borne in a drooping terminal cluster and are either pink or white. The root has tooth-shaped projections – hence the common name – and has quite a peppery taste; it can be added to salads or made into a tasty relish. Cutleaf Toothwort was previously placed in a totally different genus, and had the scientific name of *Dentaria lacinata*.

Pipsissewa

Scientific name:	*Chimaphila umbellata*
Family:	Wintergreen
Flower type:	Radially symmetrical, $\frac{1}{2}$ inch (1.25cm) in diameter
Flowering period:	June–August
Flower color:	Pink
Leaf type:	Lanceolate, toothed, whorled
Height:	6–12 inches (15–30cm)
Habitat:	Dry woodland
Range:	Through the west, parts of northern and eastern North America

An evergreen perennial, Pipsissewa is found in dry woodland. It is a small plant, with shiny dark green, lanceolate, toothed leaves arranged in whorls and pink-white flowers in a small drooping cluster at the end of a bare stem. American Indians used a tea made from the leaves to treat backache, kidney and bladder problems, and as an astringent and eye drops. Early doctors also used the plant for urinary problems, and recent scientific testing has confirmed it has diuretic, antiseptic and antibacterial properties. However, the leaves can cause skin irritation. Spotted Wintergreen (*C. maculata*) is very similar, but it has spotted leaves and is not found in the west, although its range does extend further down into the south.

Carolina Spring Beauty

Scientific name:	*Claytonia caroliniana*
Family:	Purslane
Flower type:	Radially symmetrical, $\frac{1}{2}$–$\frac{3}{4}$ inch (1.25–1.88cm) in diameter
Flowering period:	March–May
Flower color:	Pink
Leaf type:	Long, ovate
Height:	6–16 inches (15–40cm)
Habitat:	Damp open woodland, lawns
Range:	Northern and southeastern North America

As its common name suggests, Carolina Spring Beauty is a spring-flowering perennial. It has long, broad, ovate, smooth, and dark green leaves, which are arranged in opposite pairs clasping the stem; there is usually one pair around the mid-stem mark. The rounded shape of the leaves of this species distinguish it from the otherwise rather similar-looking Spring Beauty (*C. virginica*) which grows in roughly the same range and habitat, but has linear leaves. The attractive flowers of Carolina Spring Beauty are quite small and have five petals that are pink or pinky-white, striped with a deeper pink and borne in a loose, terminal raceme cluster.

Spring Beauty; Narrowleaf Spring Beauty

Scientific name:	*Claytonia virginica*
Family:	Purslane
Flower type:	Radially symmetrical, $\frac{1}{2}$–$\frac{3}{4}$ inch (1.25–1.88cm) in diameter
Flowering period:	March–May
Flower color:	Pink
Leaf type:	Long, linear
Height:	6–16 inches (15–40cm)
Habitat:	Damp open woodland, lawns
Range:	Northern and east North America

A very attractive spring-flowering perennial, Spring Beauty is low-growing but forms large clumps. It has long, linear, smooth, dark green leaves, which are arranged in opposite pairs clasping the stem; there is usually one pair around mid-stem. The flowers have five petals and are pink or pinky-white, striped with a deeper pink and borne in a loose, terminal raceme cluster. The tubers of Spring Beauty were a staple food of American Indians and early colonists. They can be used raw sliced into salads, or cooked like a potato.

Common Fleabane; Philadelphia Fleabane; Daisy Fleabane

Scientific name:	*Erigeron philadelphicus*
Family:	Aster
Flower type:	Compound flower head, ½–1 inch (1.25–2.5cm) in diameter
Flowering period:	April–July
Flower color:	Pinkish white
Leaf type:	Lower long, spatulate; upper toothed, clasping
Height:	6–24 inches (15–60cm)
Habitat:	Open moist woodland, fields, overgrown places
Range:	Most of North America, except the Arctic

Common Fleabane is a slim and branching plant, with long, entire, spatulate lower leaves and smaller, clasping upper leaves that are often either toothed or lobed. The compound flower heads are made up of many slender, pinky-white ray florets, surrounding a large central yellow disk. The flower heads are borne at the end of long, branching stalks, often with several found on each plant. A tea brewed from Common Fleabane was a traditional remedy for diarrhea, kidney stones and to stop hemorrhages – it was also commonly used to treat fevers, bronchitis and coughs. However, touching the plant can sometimes lead to contact dermatitis, so it should not be collected or used medicinally without expert guidance.

Showy Tick Trefoil

Scientific name:	*Desmodium canadense*
Family:	Pea
Flower type:	Elongated cluster, each flower $\frac{1}{2}$ inch (1.25cm) in length
Flowering period:	July–August
Flower color:	Pink
Leaf type:	Pinnate, lanceolate leaflets
Height:	2–6 feet (60–180cm)
Habitat:	Damp open woodland
Range:	Northeast North America

Showy Tick Trefoil is an erect plant with a downy stem and many alternate, pinnate leaves that each have three lanceolate leaflets. The individual flowers are rather pea-like, with short stalks, and are crowded together at the end of the stem in a dense, elongated raceme cluster. They are quite large, and pink, magenta or lavender-purple in color. The seed pods are jointed, but break into single sections with hairy hooks that cling to clothing and passing animals so they can be widely spread.

Cranesbill ▶

Scientific name:	*Geranium carolinianum*
Family:	Geranium
Flower type:	Radially symmetrical, $\frac{1}{4}$–$\frac{1}{2}$ inch (0.62–1.25cm) in diameter
Flowering period:	April–June
Flower color:	Pink
Leaf type:	Palmate, deeply toothed lobes
Height:	6–20 inches (15–50cm)
Habitat:	Rocky woodland
Range:	Northeast and east North America

Cranesbill is a low-growing annual, with a branching stem and many palmate leaves that have five, deeply toothed lobes. The basal leaves have fairly long stalks, but those higher up the stem are usually much shorter. The flowers are very pale pink or lavender, with five rounded petals, and are borne in small raceme clusters at the end of the branches. The name Cranesbill comes from the fruit, which is elongated and shaped like a beak. There are 33 species in this genus found across North America.

BITTERROOT

Scientific name:	*Lewisia rediviva*
Family:	Purslane
Flower type:	Radially symmetrical, $1\frac{1}{2}$–$2\frac{1}{2}$ inches (3.75–6.25cm) in diameter
Flowering period:	May–July
Flower color:	Pink
Leaf type:	Basal rosette, long, succulent
Height:	$\frac{1}{2}$–2 inches (1.25–5cm)
Habitat:	Open coniferous woods, sagebrush
Range:	Southwest United States

Bitterroot is a small and low-growing plant, and for its size it has comparatively large and very showy pink to white flowers, with many long, lancelolate petals. There are usually several flowers growing on a single plant, each held at the end of a short stalk and growing within a basal rosette of long, linear and succulent leaves. There are 15 other species in this genus to be found across North America. Bitterroot is a species that prefers drier soil, and it is commonly found growing in open pinewoods, and also in sagebrush. It is the state flower of Montana.

WILD GERANIUM

Scientific name:	*Geranium maculatum*
Family:	Geranium
Flower type:	Radially symmetrical, 1–2 inches (2.5–5cm) in diameter
Flowering period:	April–June
Flower color:	Pink
Leaf type:	Palmate, deeply toothed lobes
Height:	1–2 feet (30–60cm)
Habitat:	Woodland, thickets
Range:	Northeast North America

Wild Geranium is a perennial that is found in woodland across the northeast. It is a fairly low-growing plant, with a branching stem and many palmate leaves that have five, deeply toothed lobes. The basal leaves have longer stalks than those higher up the stem. The flowers are pink, lavender, or occasionally white, with five rounded petals and are borne in very loose raceme clusters of a few flowers at the end of the branches. In folk medicine, the root of Wild Geranium was used to treat cancer, stop bleeding and diarrhea, and for kidney and stomach problems.

Rose-pink; Bitterbloom

Scientific name:	*Sabatia angularis*
Family:	Gentian
Flower type:	Radially symmetrical, $\frac{3}{4}$–1$\frac{1}{2}$ inches (1.88–3.75cm) in diameter
Flowering period:	June–September
Flower color:	Pink
Leaf type:	Ovate, clasping
Height:	1–3 feet (30–90cm)
Habitat:	Open woods, roadsides, meadows
Range:	Eastern United States

Rose-pink has a slender, branching stem, that is very square in section, bearing opposite pairs of small, clasping, ovate leaves. The plant also has a basal rosette of leaves. The pink flowers are star-like and slightly sweet-scented, with five petals joined at the base, and they are borne on opposite branches. There are 18 species in this genus across North America, mostly across the eastern half of the continent, some with pink and some with white flowers but all looking rather similar.

Rosy Twisted-stalk

Scientific name:	*Streptopus lanceolatus var. roseus*
Family:	Lily
Flower type:	Bell-shaped, $\frac{1}{2}$ inch (1.25cm) in length
Flowering period:	April–June
Flower color:	Pink
Leaf type:	Long, lanceolate, slightly clasping
Height:	1–3 feet (30–90cm)
Habitat:	Damp woodland, wet overgrown areas
Range:	Northwest and northeast North America

The stems of Rosy Twisted Stalk are branching and zigzagging, with long, lanceolate parallel-veined leaves that are slightly clasping. The edges of the leaves are fringed with fine, very short hairs. The flowers are tiny and bell-shaped, and hang from twisted stalks that spring from the stem just under the leaf. There are four species in this genus, all found in the cooler areas of North America. White Mandarin (*S. amplexifolius*) has greenish white flowers and the leaves are more clasping and have a white bloom beneath.

Goat's-rue

Scientific name:	*Tephrosia virginiana*
Family:	Pea
Flower type:	Rounded cluster, 3 inches (8cm) in length
Flowering period:	May–August
Flower color:	Pink
Leaf type:	Pinnate; leaflets narrowly elliptical, hoary
Height:	1–2 feet (30–60cm)
Habitat:	Sandy woodland
Range:	Ontario, northeast United States

Goat's Rue is a medium-sized perennial with pink and creamy-yellow, pea-like flowers in dense raceme clusters. The hairy stem bears compound pinnate leaves, which have 17-25 long, narrowly elliptical leaflets with a hoary surface. Goat's Rue gets its name from having once been fed to goats to increase their milk production. American Indians made a tea from the roots to strengthen children, treat tuberculosis and bladder problems and increase male potency. However, the root has also been used as a fish poison and an extract from the plant has been used as an insecticide, and it has also been shown that contact with the plant may cause dermatitis.

Wild Columbine ▶

Scientific name:	*Aquilegia canadensis*
Family:	Buttercup
Flower type:	Radially symmetrical, bell-shaped, 1–2 inches (2.5–5cm) in length
Flowering period:	May–July
Flower color:	Red
Leaf type:	Tripalmate, three-lobed leaflets
Height:	1–3 feet (30–90cm)
Habitat:	Woodland, rocky slopes
Range:	Eastern North America

A branching plant with a rather stout stem, Wild Columbine has long-stalked, deep green tripalmate leaves with three-lobed leaflets. The red flowers are drooping and bell-shaped, with long, backward and upward pointing spurs and long yellow stamens hanging down in a central column. The hollow spurs contain nectar that attracts hummingbirds and long-tongued insects. There is also a rare form of this species that has yellow and white flowers. American Indians rubbed the seeds of Wild Columbine into their hair to control head lice, and used a weak tea of the root for diarrhea and stomach problems. However, the plant is potentially poisonous, so should not be eaten.

RED COLUMBINE; CRIMSON COLUMBINE

Scientific name:	*Aquilegia formosa*
Family:	Buttercup
Flower type:	Radially symmetrical, bell-shaped, 2 inches (5cm) in diameter
Flowering period:	May–July
Flower color:	Red
Leaf type:	Compound, with tripalmate, lobed leaflets
Height:	6–36 inches (15–90cm)
Habitat:	Open woodland, near seeps
Range:	Western North America

A rather bushy perennial with a branching stem, Red Columbine has long-stalked, deep green compound leaves with tripalmate, deeply lobed leaflets. The red flowers are drooping and bell-shaped, with long, backward and upward pointing spurs and long yellow stamens hanging down in a central column. As in Wild Columbine (*A. canadensis*) the hollow spurs contain nectar that attracts hummingbirds and long-tongued insects. There are 22 species of this genus across North America, as well as many garden varieties that may escape into the wild.

RED LARKSPUR; ORANGE LARKSPUR; CHRISTMAS HORNS ▶

Scientific name:	*Delphinium nudicaule*
Family:	Buttercup
Flower type:	Radially symmetrical, 1 inch (2.5cm) in diameter
Flowering period:	May–July
Flower color:	Red
Leaf type:	Tripalmate, lobed leaflets
Height:	1–4 feet (30–120cm)
Habitat:	Rocky open woodland
Range:	Oregon to California

Red Larkspur may have a rather limited range, but is a quite tall plant with bright red blooms so it is noticeable when it is in flower. The tall stem has tripalmate leaves with lobed leaflets, and it terminates in a loose spike of red to orange flowers with quite noticeable forward-pointing sepals. The red color of the flowers attracts hummingbirds to pollinate the plant. The very similar Scarlet Larkspur (*D. cardinale*) is found in much the same range, but is generally taller with brilliant scarlet flowers.

Scarlet Fritillary

Scientific name:	*Fritillaria recurva*
Family:	Lily
Flower type:	Bell-shaped, $\frac{3}{4}$–$1\frac{1}{2}$ inches (1.88–3.75cm) in length
Flowering period:	March–July
Flower color:	Red
Leaf type:	Long, narrow, linear
Height:	1–3 feet (30–90cm)
Habitat:	Dry, hilly woods
Range:	Western United States

The only fritillary with red flowers, Scarlet Fritillary is a medium-sized perennial, with most of its long, narrow, linear leaves arranged around the middle of the stem. The drooping, bell-shaped flowers are checked with yellow inside, and are borne in a raceme cluster at the tip of the stem. The tip of the petal-like segments curves backwards, although there is a form without this feature in parts of northern California. There are 19 species in this genus in North America, all found in the west.

Wood Lily; Rocky Mountain Lily; Red Lily

Scientific name:	*Lilium philadelphicum*
Family:	Lily
Flower type:	Trumpet-shaped, 2–2½ inches (5–6.25cm) in diameter
Flowering period:	July–August
Flower color:	Red
Leaf type:	Long, linear; lower alternate; upper in whorls
Height:	12–30 inches (30–75cm)
Habitat:	Forests, particularly aspen, meadows
Range:	Western Canada, east of the Rockies, central United States

Although the Wood Lily was once very common in the wild, it has been extensively picked by those visiting its natural habitat, and has vanished from heavily grazed areas, so it has now become fairly rare. It has a tall, straight and leafy stem, with long and narrowly lanceolate leaves, which are arranged alternately towards the base of the plant and in whorls higher up. There are usually one to five trumpet-shaped flowers held standing erect at the top of the stem; these are mainly bright red although the base of the petals is tinged with yellow and spotted with deep purple on the inside. American Indians made a tea from the root of the Wood Lily to treat stomach disorders, coughs and fevers, and it was also applied externally to wounds and sores. The flowers were made into a poultice for spider bites.

Indian Pink; Pink-root

Scientific name:	*Spigelia marilandica*
Family:	Logania
Flower type:	Trumpet-shaped, 1 inch (2.5cm) in length
Flowering period:	May–June
Flower color:	Red
Leaf type:	Long, opposite, narrowly ovate, sessile
Height:	1–2 feet (30–60cm)
Habitat:	Damp woodland
Range:	Southeast United States

Indian Pink has unusual and distinctive trumpet-shaped flowers, which are a deep, bright red on the outside and creamy-yellow on the inside. They are held in a narrow, one-sided terminal cluster, and the plant flowers from the bottom of the cluster upwards. The tall stem bears long, sessile leaves that are ovate or broadly lanceolate in shape and arranged in opposite pairs. As well as growing in the wild, Indian Pink also does very well when cultivated so it is sometimes included in wildflower gardens. American Indians and early physicians used the plant to treat worms, especially in young children, but in some cases it can have quite serious and unpleasant side effects.

Purple Trillium; Stinking Benjamin; Wakerobin

Scientific name:	*Trillium erectum*
Family:	Lily
Flower type:	Radially symmetrical, $2\frac{1}{2}$ inches (6.25cm) in diameter
Flowering period:	April–June
Flower color:	Red
Leaf type:	Diamond-shaped, long, very short stalk
Height:	8–16 inches (20–40cm)
Habitat:	Woodland
Range:	North and east North America

Despite its common name, Purple Trillium has a flower that is a deep red-brown to maroon in color rather than purple. However, its alternative name of Stinking Benjamin is quite descriptive, since the rather attractive-looking flowers unfortunately smell extremely unpleasant; the stink attracts carrion flies, which pollinate the flower. The flower has three pointed petals alternating with three sepals, and is borne at the end of a rather drooping stalk. The stalk springs from the center of a whorl of three diamond-shaped to ovate leaves, which are very dark green and have quite short stalks. American Indians once used the root medicinally as an aid during childbirth, and to treat the problems arising during the menopause.

Toad Shade; Red Trillium

Scientific name:	*Trillium sessile*
Family:	Lily
Flower type:	Radially symmetrical, $1\frac{1}{2}$ inches (3.75cm) in length
Flowering period:	April–June
Flower color:	Red
Leaf type:	Diamond-shaped, long, very short stalk
Height:	4-14 inches (10-35cm)
Habitat:	Rich woodland
Range:	East North America

Toadshade is similar to Purple Trillium (*T. erectum*), with a flower that is deep red-brown to maroon and which smells extremely unpleasant. The odor of rotting meat attracts carrion flies, which pollinate the flower. The flower has three pointed petals and three sepals, but has no stalk and is held rather closed and upright, rather than open and drooping. The flower springs from a whorl of three diamond-shaped to ovate leaves, which are a very dark green, mottled with shades of lighter green.

Heartleaf Arnica

Scientific name:	*Arnica cordifolia*
Family:	Aster
Flower type:	Compound flower head, 2–4 inches (5–10cm) in diameter
Flowering period:	June–July
Flower color:	Yellow
Leaf type:	Elongated heart-shape
Height:	4–22 inches (10–55cm)
Habitat:	Open woods
Range:	Western North America

Typically, Heartleaf Arnica spreads to form rather small colonies, if the habitat is suitable. It is a medium size plant with two to four pairs of heart-shaped leaves, and one to three large, compound flower heads at the end of a long bare stalk. The yellow-orange flower heads are made up of several long, pointed ray florets, around a comparatively small and darker central disk. The bright green leaves are arranged in opposite pairs, with those at the bottom of the stem being larger and with stalks, while the upper ones are sessile. There are 32 species in this genus found across North America, but Heartleaf Arnica is much more common in the west than in the east.

Golden Star

Scientific name:	*Chrysogonum virginianum*
Family:	Aster
Flower type:	Compound flower head, 1–1½ inches (2.5–3.75cm) in diameter
Flowering period:	March–July
Flower color:	Yellow
Leaf type:	Long, ovate, bluntly toothed
Height:	3–15 inches (8–38cm)
Habitat:	Damp, shady woods
Range:	Southeast United States

Golden Star is a rather low-growing plant, reaching a maximum height of around 15 inches (38cm). It has long-stalked, ovate leaves that have bluntly toothed edges, and are borne in opposite pairs. The showy, yellow, compound flower head is held at the tip of a distinctive hairy stem. The flower head is made up of five petal-like ray florets, which are broad and toothed at the tip, set around a small, darker-colored central disk. This is the only species in this genus found in North America, and it grows in shady and damp woodland or under shady rocks in a rather restricted range.

Bluebead Lily; Corn-lily; Clinton's Lily ▲

Scientific name:	*Clintonia borealis*
Family:	Lily
Flower type:	Umbel cluster, each flower $\frac{3}{4}$–1 inch (1.88–2.5cm) in length
Flowering period:	May–July
Flower color:	Yellow
Leaf type:	Basal, oblong
Height:	6–16 inches (15–40cm)
Habitat:	Damp woodland with acid soil
Range:	Northeast North America

The unusual common name of Bluebead Lily comes from the fruits, which are bright blue bead-like berries – and are very poisonous. The plant has a basal cluster of shiny bright green, broad, oblong leaves with pointed tips, which grow from an underground rhizome. The flower stalk rises up from the center of the leaves to a height of 16 inches (40cm), and terminates in a rather drooping umbel cluster of bell-shaped, pale yellow-green flowers. The young leaves of Bluebead Lily can be added to salads or cooked as greens, but older leaves are too tough. American Indians made a poultice of fresh leaves for burns, sores and dog bites, and a tea from the plant to treat heart problems and diabetes. The root was used to help labor during childbirth.

Horse Balm; Stoneroot; Richweed

Scientific name:	*Collinsonia canadensis*
Family:	Mint
Flower type:	Elongated cluster, each flower $\frac{1}{2}$ inch (1.25cm) in length
Flowering period:	July–September
Flower color:	Yellow
Leaf type:	Long, ovate, sharply toothed
Height:	2–5 feet (60–150cm)
Habitat:	Rich woodland
Range:	Ontario and Quebec, eastern United States

A tall, and rather rather leggy plant, Horse Balm has a stout, smooth, stem with a square section, bearing opposite pairs of long, ovate, and sharply toothed leaves. The pale yellow flowers are quite tiny, but very many of them are borne in loose branching clusters that make up a large panicle. Both the leaves and the flowers give off a sharp odor of lemon when they are crushed. Traditionally, a poultice of the leaves was applied to soothe burns, bruises and sores, and a root tea was taken to treat diarrhea, dysentery and kidney and bladder problems. However, doses of the fresh leaves should be treated with caution, as they may very well cause vomiting. There are three species in this genus found in North America.

Trout Lily; Dogtooth Violet

Scientific name:	*Erythronium americanum*
Family:	Lily
Flower type:	Radially symmetrical, 1 inch (2.5cm) in diameter
Flowering period:	March–May
Flower color:	Yellow
Leaf type:	Basal sheath, long, elliptical
Height:	4–12 inches (10–30cm)
Habitat:	Woodland and meadows
Range:	Northeast North America

One of the most distinctive features of the Trout Lily is its mottled brown leaves, the patterning of which is supposed to resemble that of the Brown Trout fish – hence the flower's common name. The plant has only two leaves, which are long, elliptical to oval, and which sheath the base of the stem. The small but very showy flower is borne at the end of a bare stalk, and is yellow outside but more bronze in color inside, with slightly backward-curving sepals and petals. There may be several flowers on a plant, each with its own stalk. Trout Lily was once used medicinally in exactly the same way as White Trout Lily. There are around 18 species in this genus found across North America.

Oxeye; False Sunflower

Scientific name:	*Heliopsis helianthoides*
Family:	Aster
Flower type:	Compound flower head, 1–3 inches (2.5–8cm) across
Flowering period:	July–September
Flower color:	Yellow
Leaf type:	Elliptical, toothed
Height:	2–5 feet (60–150cm)
Habitat:	Open woodland
Range:	Eastern North America, except far north

Although it closely resembles a sunflower, Oxeye is part of the Aster family. It is quite tall, with elliptical, toothed leaves arranged in opposite pairs along a smooth stem. The solitary flower has a cone-shaped central disk and yellow ray florets that are notched at the tip. Unlike sunflowers, the rays do not fall off but stay on the flower head and become dry and papery. There are three species in this genus in North America, but Oxeye is the most common.

Whorled Loosestrife ▼

Scientific name:	*Lysimachia quadrifolia*
Family:	Primrose
Flower type:	Radially symmetrical, $\frac{1}{2}$ inch (1.25cm) in diameter
Flowering period:	May–August
Flower color:	Yellow
Leaf type:	Long, lanceolate, whorled
Height:	12–34 inches (30–85cm)
Habitat:	Open woodland, fields
Range:	Northeast North America

Whorled Loosestrife has a tall, erect stem with light green, long and lanceolate leaves arranged in whorls of three to six at regular intervals. The flowers are small and star-like, held at the tips of slender stalks that spring from the leaf axils. The five petals are yellow, but marked with red dots and often streaked right up to the tip. Early colonists used Whorled Loosestrife to soothe and calm oxen, and American Indians made a tea from it to treat kidney and bowel problems.

Prairie Coneflower; Gray-headed Coneflower

Scientific name:	*Ratibida pinnata*
Family:	Aster
Flower type:	Compound flower head, $1\frac{1}{2}$–3 inches (3.75–8cm) in diameter
Flowering period:	June–September
Flower color:	Yellow
Leaf type:	Long, pinnate; leaflets lanceolate, coarsely toothed
Height:	18–60 inches (45–150cm)
Habitat:	Dry woodland, prairies
Range:	Ontario, southeastern United States

A plant that prefers to grow in dry ground in both woodland and on prairies, Prairie Coneflower has a slender, hairy stem with very long, compound pinnate leaves that are arranged alternately. The three to seven leaflets are lanceolate and roughly toothed. The large flower head has a dome-shaped central disk, which is grayish when fresh but darkens to brown, and smells of anise when it is bruised. It is surrounded by five to ten long, narrow and very drooping yellow rays, which drop off as the flower ages.

Yellow Rattle ▶

Scientific name:	*Rhinanthus minor ssp. minor (Rhinanthus crista-galli)*
Family:	Figwort
Flower type:	Elongated cluster, each flower $\frac{1}{2}$ inch (1.25cm) in length
Flowering period:	May–August
Flower color:	Yellow
Leaf type:	Lanceolate, sessile, toothed
Height:	6–40 inches (15–100cm)
Habitat:	Thickets, open woods, fields
Range:	Northeastern and west North America

The second part of the common name of this plant comes from the seeds, which rattle within a circular capsule when they are ripe. Yellow Rattle, sometimes also called Yellow Rattlebox, has an upright, branching stem with long, lanceolate leaves. The leaves are arranged in opposite pairs and spring directly from the stem without a stalk; the outside edges of the blades are strongly toothed. The bright yellow flowers also have no stalks and are very small and rather insignificant-looking, with large, toothed bracts below each one; they are borne in a one-sided raceme.

Blue-stemmed Goldenrod; Wreath Goldenrod

Scientific name:	*Solidago caesia*
Family:	Aster
Flower type:	Rounded clusters, each flower ¼ inch (0.62cm) in length
Flowering period:	August–October
Flower color:	Yellow
Leaf type:	Elliptical, sessile, toothed
Height:	8–40 inches (20–100cm)
Habitat:	Woods, clearings
Range:	Eastern North America

Despite its name, the slender, arching stem of Blue-stemmed Goldenrod is more purple than blue, often with a whitish, waxy bloom. The stem is smooth and bears alternate, elliptical, sessile and toothed leaves with sharply pointed tips. The flowers are borne in scattered, rounded clusters from the leaf axils, with a larger terminal cluster. Individual florets are small and have only three to four rays. There are around 90 species in this genus across North America, all with yellow or yellow-cream colored flowers.

Redwood Violet; Evergreen Violet ▶

Scientific name:	*Viola sempervirens*
Family:	Violet
Flower type:	Irregular with two symmetrical halves, ½ inch (1.25cm) in diameter
Flowering period:	April–June
Flower color:	Yellow
Leaf type:	Cordate, finely toothed, thick
Height:	Creeper, 5 inches (12cm)
Habitat:	Damp woodland
Range:	Western United States

Redwood Violet is a creeper that stays close to the ground but can produce stems up to 1 foot (30cm) in length. The broad, heart-shaped leaves are thick and leathery, forming a dense mat on the ground. The leaves are finely toothed and have quite long stalks. The flowers have the typical violet shape, with two upper petals and three lower, and hang from short stalks just above the level of the leaves. The petals are yellow, but the lower three are lightly veined with maroon and the central one has a short, backward-pointing spur.

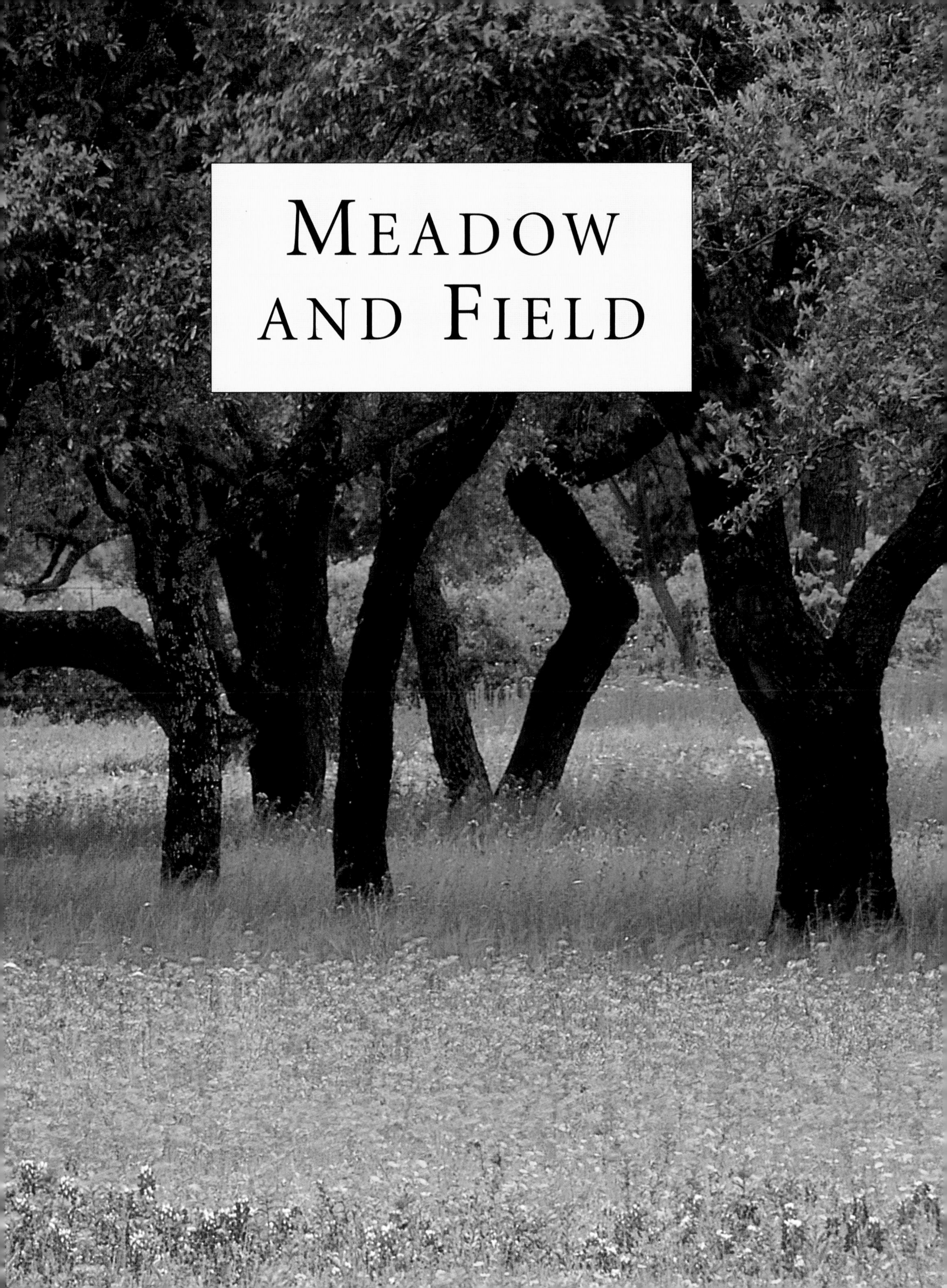

Meadow and Field

EASTERN SHOOTINGSTAR; PRAIRIE POINTERS

Scientific name:	*Dodecatheon meadia*
Family:	Primrose
Flower type:	Umbel cluster, each flower 1 inch (2.5cm) in length
Flowering period:	April–July
Flower color:	White
Leaf type:	Basal, lanceolate
Height:	9–22 inches (22–55cm)
Habitat:	Meadows, open woodland, prairies
Range:	Central Canada and southeastern and central United States

In the days of the early settlers, Eastern Shootingstar was far more numerous growing in the wild across North America than it is now. It is a medium size plant, which prefers to grow in open ground – in clearings in woodland, or in meadows and fields. It has dark green, basal, lanceolate leaves, which are sometimes tinged with red where they spring from the plant, and a long, smooth, bare stem that ends in a flat-topped umbel cluster of flowers. The petals of each flower point backwards when the flower is fully open, and they are usually white, but can sometimes be pink or lilac. There are 15 species in this genus across North America, and as Eastern Shootingstar is an attractive plant it is also often cultivated.

Wild Strawberry

Scientific name:	*Fragaria virginiana*
Family:	Rose
Flower type:	Radially symmetrical, $\frac{1}{2}$–1 inch (1.25–2.5cm) in diameter
Flowering period:	May–June
Flower color:	White
Leaf type:	Tripalmate, each leaflet obvate and toothed
Height:	Creeper, 4 inches (10cm)
Habitat:	Fields, open woodland, forest edges
Range:	Most of North America, except the Arctic

A perennial creeper, the Wild Strawberry forms runners that produce new plants. It bears small white flowers and has bright green leaves in three sections, like clover, with each leaflet obvate and toothed. However, it is better known for its sweet-tasting fruit, which looks like a much smaller version of a cultivated strawberry. The leaves can also be steeped in boiling water to make a tea that is very high in vitamin C. American Indians used this as a nerve tonic and to treat sore throats, jaundice, bladder and kidney ailments and diarrhea, and ate the berries to cure scurvy and gout.

Oxeye Daisy

Scientific name:	*Leucanthemum vulgare (Chrysanthemum leucanthemum)*
Family:	Aster
Flower type:	Compound flower head, 3 inches (8cm) in diameter
Flowering period:	May–September
Flower color:	White
Leaf type:	Lower lanceolate, lobed or deeply toothed, long petioles; upper smaller, lobed, sessile
Height:	8–32 inches (20–80cm)
Habitat:	Fields, meadows, roadsides
Range:	Most of the United States, southern Canada

A native of Europe and introduced to North America, Oxeye Daisy is naturalized across much of the continent – although it is more common in the north. It is a leafy perennial, with several stems bearing dark green, lanceolate, lobed or deeply toothed leaves with long stalks, and smaller, sessile upper leaves. The flowers are white with a bright yellow central disk, born at the tip of a long, leafless stalk. Europeans used this plant as a tonic, and American Indians made a tea from it to treat fever, and as a wash for chapped hands. It does have anti-inflammatory and spasm-relieving properties, but can cause contact dermatitis, or an allergic reaction.

Ox-eye Daisies

White Sweet Clover

Scientific name:	*Melilotus alba*
Family:	Pea
Flower type:	Raceme, 8 inches (20cm) in length
Flowering period:	April–October
Flower color:	White
Leaf type:	Compound, with three lanceolate, toothed leaflets
Height:	2–9 feet (60–270cm)
Habitat:	Fields and roadsides
Range:	Most of North America, except the Arctic

Introduced from its native Eurasia, White Sweet Clover is now found across most of North America, except in the very far north of the continent. It is a very tall plant, with widely branched stems bearing three-part, bright green leaves. Each individual leaflet is lanceolate in shape with toothed edges. The flower stalks spring from the leaf axils, and the flowers are white and pea-like and arranged in long, tapering racemes. They have a strong scent of vanilla, particularly when they are crushed, and therefore White Sweet Clover is particularly valued as a source of nectar for honey.

Blue Wild Indigo

Scientific name:	*Baptisia australis*
Family:	Pea
Flower type:	Upright raceme, each flower 1 inch (2.5cm) in length
Flowering period:	April–June
Flower color:	Blue
Leaf type:	Tripalmate, obvate leaflets
Height:	3–5 feet (90–150cm)
Habitat:	Open areas, forest margins
Range:	Northeastern North America

Having escaped from cultivation, Blue Wild Indigo is found in the wild only in the east and from New York up into Ontario. It is a perennial, with tripalmate leaves that are rather clover-like and an erect raceme of violet-blue flowers. Its sap turns purple when exposed to the air, hence its name; it resembles indigo and can be used as a dye in the same way, although it is an inferior substitute for the real thing. American Indians used a tea made from the roots as an emetic, and a poultice of root was held in the mouth to treat toothache. However, Blue Wild Indigo is currently considered to be potentially toxic, so it should not be used without expert advice.

Azure Bluet; Quaker Ladies; Innocence ▲

Scientific name:	*Houstonia caerulea (Hedyotis caerulea)*
Family:	Madder
Flower type:	Radially symmetrical, ½ inch (1.25cm) in diameter
Flower color:	Blue
Flowering period:	April–June
Leaf type:	Basal long and oblong, upper small and opposite
Height:	3–6 inches (8–15cm)
Habitat:	Grassy fields, lawns, open woods
Range:	Eastern Canada, most of eastern United States

Azure Bluet is a delicate and petite plant that prefers to grow in acid soil in small colonies. There are 30 species of bluet across North America, but none of them grows wild in the northwest. The flowers are borne at the tip of long, slender stalks, of which three or four rise from a common basal cluster of leaves. The stalks also have tiny leaves arranged in opposite pairs at intervals, and the flowers are a delicate pale blue or violet-blue, fading to white at the center and with a bright yellow central disk. Cherokee Indians used a tea made from the leaves to stop bed-wetting.

Miniature Lupine

Scientific name:	*Lupinus bicolor*
Family:	Pea
Flower type:	Raceme, each flower ¼ inch (0.62cm) in length
Flowering period:	March–May
Flower color:	Blue
Leaf type:	Palmate, with leaflets like wheel spokes
Height:	4–15 inches (10–38cm)
Habitat:	Open, grassy areas
Range:	Western United States and British Columbia

Miniature Lupine is a rather small perennial plant, with several stout, grayish, hairy, and branching stems. These bear compound palmate leaves, which have between five to seven leaflets arranged in a circle like the spokes of a wheel. The pea-like flowers are arranged in whorls at the top of the stalk, forming a short, dense raceme. The flowers are usually blue and white, but the blue may be almost violet. There are around 130 species of native lupines in North America, most of them found in the west although they are also often cultivated as garden flowers. Birds can eat the seeds without harm, but some species have been found to be poisonous to grazing cattle.

Wild Lupine

Scientific name:	*Lupinus perennis*
Family:	Pea
Flower type:	Raceme, each flower $\frac{3}{4}$ inch (1.88cm) in length
Flowering period:	April–July
Flower color:	Blue
Leaf type:	Palmate, with leaflets like wheel spokes
Height:	9–28 inches (22–70cm)
Habitat:	Dry open fields and woods
Range:	Eastern and southern United States, eastern Canada

The Wild Lupine is a much bigger plant than the Miniature Lupine, and is found in the east, not the west. It has a brownish, branched stem, bearing palmate leaves with seven to eleven leaflets arranged like the spokes of a wheel. In the southern areas of its range, the leaflets are narrower and the plant is known as Nuttall's Lupine (*L. Nuttallii*). The pea-like flowers are arranged in whorls on the stalk, forming a tall, showy raceme. The flowers are usually blue and white, but the blue may be quite violet. American Indians used a cold tea made from the leaves to treat nausea and internal hemorrhaging.

Wild Hyacinth; Camass Lily

Scientific name:	*Camassia scilloides*
Family:	Lily
Flower type:	Elongated cluster, each flower 1 inch (2.5cm) in width
Flowering period:	May–June
Flower color:	Purple
Leaf type:	Long, linear
Height:	6–22 inches (15–55cm)
Habitat:	Moist fields, open woodland, meadows
Range:	Southeastern United States, Ontario

The Wild Hyacinth is a perennial, with a globe-shaped bulb. Its leaves are long and linear, springing from the base of the plant, and the loose raceme of flowers is borne on a long, leafless stalk. Although they are normally violet-blue, the flowers can also be white or plain blue. Since the Wild Hyacinth is related to the onion its bulbs can be eaten, and in fact they were one of the staple foods for early settlers. However, it is important to be sure of identification, as the very similar Death Camas (*Zigadenus venenosus*) can be fatal if eaten. This has green, white or bronze flowers, but a similar bulb and leaves. It is normally found in the west.

Sugarbowls; Vase Flower; Lion's Beard; Leatherflower

Scientific name:	*Clematis hirsutissima (Coriflora hirsutissima)*
Family:	Buttercup
Flower type:	Urn-shaped, 1 inch (2.5cm) in length
Flowering period:	May–August
Flower color:	Purple
Leaf type:	Long, finely divided, hairy
Height:	8–24 inches (20–60cm)
Habitat:	Grassland, open fields, sagebrush
Range:	Central United States, British Columbia

Although its scientific name places it firmly in the Clematis family, Sugarbowls is not a climber like many of the other related species. It is a small, hairy, erect plant, with several stems, each of which bears just one pendent, urn-shaped flower. These are usually purple, but can range from a rather muddy purple-brown to violet. Its finely divided feathery leaves are rather reminiscent of those of the carrot, but are covered in fine hairs and are arranged in opposite pairs on the stem. As well as growing in open ground, Sugarbowls can sometimes be found in ponderosa pine forests.

Below: The shaggy fruit of *Clematis hirsutissima* gives rise to its alternative common name of Lion's Beard.

Purple Prairie Clover

Scientific name:	*Dalea purpurea (Petalostemum purpurea)*
Family:	Pea
Flower type:	Spike, $\frac{1}{2}$–3 inches (1.25–8cm) in length
Flowering period:	July–September
Flower color:	Purple
Leaf type:	Compound pinnate with narrow leaflets
Height:	1–3 feet (30–90cm)
Habitat:	Fields, meadows, openings in pine forests
Range:	Central Canada and eastern United States

Purple Prairie Clover is a tallish, slim perennial, with several grayish woolly branches, and numerous alternate compound pinnate leaves, with seven to ten narrow leaflets. The flowers are borne in dense spikes, with each flower bilaterally symmetrical. It grows in undisturbed prairie – where the ground is heavily grazed it tends to disappear. American Indians used the flowering plant to treat heart problems, and the roots for measles and pneumonia. In modern times, it has been scientifically proven that Purple Prairie Clover is strongly antibacterial.

Rough Blazing Star ▼

Scientific name:	*Liatris aspera*
Family:	Aster
Flower type:	Spike of dense flower heads, each flower $\frac{1}{4}$ inch (0.62cm) in width
Flowering period:	August–September
Flower color:	Purple
Leaf type:	Narrow, lanceolate and long, with a rough surface
Height:	15–48 inches (38–120cm)
Habitat:	Open fields, thin woodland on sandy soil
Range:	Ontario, east and southeast United States

Rough Blazing Star is a tall perennial with erect, hairy stems bearing narrow, lanceolate, alternate leaves, and shaggy-looking flower heads, which are normally rose-purple but very occasionally white. The flower heads are made up of 25-30 sessile florets, and are borne on a crowded spike. A tea made from the roots of this and other *Liatris* species was a folk remedy for kidney and bladder problems, and as a gargle for sore throats. A poultice of root was used to treat snakebites. Devil's Bit (*Chamaelirium luteum*) is also sometimes called Blazing Star, but it has a spike of white flowers and leaves in a basal rosette.

Hoary Vervain ◀

Scientific name:	*Verbena stricta*
Family:	Verbena
Flower type:	Spikes, each flower $\frac{1}{2}$ inch (1.25cm) in length
Flowering period:	June–August
Flower color:	Purple
Leaf type:	Obvate, coarsely and irregularly toothed, opposite
Height:	2–10 feet (60–300cm)
Habitat:	Dry fields
Range:	Eastern Canada, Atlantic coastal states

Found across most of the eastern North American states, Hoary Vervain has a long stem that is covered in a fine coating of whitish hairs – hence hoary as part of the common name. It can be quite a large plant, growing up to 10 feet (300cm) in height, so it is quite noticeable in its chosen habitat. The stems can either be singular or branched, and the leaves are obvate, sessile, and coarsely and irregularly toothed. They are arranged along the stem in opposite pairs. The flowers are borne in long, dense spikes, often several at the top of each plant, and they are usually purple in color – although occasionally a pink form appears.

TALL IRONWEED

Scientific name:	*Vernonia gigantea (Vernonia altissima)*
Family:	Aster
Flower type:	Loose cyme cluster, each flower $\frac{1}{4}$ inch (0.62cm) in diameter
Flowering period:	August–October
Flower color:	Purple
Leaf type:	Long and lanceolate, finely toothed
Height:	3–7 feet (90–210cm)
Habitat:	Fields, open woodland
Range:	Most of eastern North America

Tall Ironweed has an erect stem, with long, lanceolate alternate leaves that are finely toothed and downy on the underside. The deep purple-blue flower heads have 13-30 flowers and are borne in loose terminal cyme clusters. The name Ironweed comes from the fact that the stems are so hard. There are more than 20 species of Ironweed across North America, all of them in the east and southeast. American Indians used a tea made from the root as a tonic for the blood, and to relieve pain after childbirth.

DOG VIOLET

Scientific name:	*Viola labradorica*
Family:	Violet
Flower type:	Irregular with two symmetrical halves, $\frac{3}{4}$ inch (1.88cm) in width
Flowering period:	March–July
Flower color:	Purple
Leaf type:	Heart-shaped, scalloped
Height:	2–6 inches (5–15cm)
Habitat:	Damp fields and woods
Range:	Eastern Canada, west, southwest and central United States

This small but attractive plant has heart-shaped leaves that are gently scalloped at the edge. The blue-violet flowers have two symmetrical halves and are borne on the same stalk as the leaves. There are several similar species in the same general area, including Long-spurred Violet (*V. rostrata*), which has pale blue flowers, and Prostrate Blue Violet (*V. walteri*), which is very hairy. There are around 80 species of violet found across North America, and over 300 around the world. There are also many cultivated varieties, most of which are descended from European species.

BIRD'S-FOOT VIOLET ▼

Scientific name:	*Viola pedata*
Family:	Violet
Flower type:	Irregular with two symmetrical halves, $1\frac{1}{2}$ inches (3.75cm) in width
Flowering period:	March–June
Flower color:	Purple
Leaf type:	Pinnate, linear, toothed segments arranged in a fan shape
Height:	2–10 inches (5–25cm)
Habitat:	Sandy fields, dry, sunny, open woods
Range:	Ontario, Midwestern states

Bird's-foot Violet is quite easy to identify because of its very distinctive pinnate leaves that are divided into nine to fifteen segments and resemble the claws of a bird's foot. It is quite a large plant for a violet, with a smooth stem and big violet-blue flowers with conspicuous orange stamens, each held on a separate stalk. In the south, the upper two petals are often a darker violet, which makes the flower look exceptionally attractive. In some areas, Bird's-foot Violet will bloom again for a second time in the fall.

Owl's Clover *Castilleja exserta (Orthocarpus purpurascens)*

Purple Owl's-clover; Common Owl's-clover

Scientific name:	*Castilleja exserta (Orthocarpus purpurascens)*
Family:	Figwort
Flower type:	Elongated cluster, each flower $\frac{1}{2}$–2 inches (1.25–5cm) in length
Flowering period:	March–May
Flower color:	Pink
Leaf type:	Long, narrow, pinnately dissected
Height:	4–18 inches (10–45cm)
Habitat:	Fields, open woodland
Range:	Southwestern United States

Owl's-clover resembles Indian Paintbrush (*C. coccinea*), and it is now placed in the genus of *Castilleja*, having been moved from *Orthocarpus*. However, the similar-looking Yellow Owl's-clover (*Orthocarpus lutens*) has not been reclassified. Purple Owl's-clover is a small, erect plant, with long leaves pinnately dissected into a few narrow sections. The individual flowers are bilaterally symmetrical and rather more showy than those of Indian Paintbrush. They are borne in an elongated cluster and are usually pink, although they can also be found in yellow or white.

Sticky Geranium

Scientific name:	*Geranium viscosissimum*
Family:	Geranium
Flower type:	Radially symmetrical, 1 inch (2.5cm) in diameter
Flowering period:	May–July
Flower color:	Pink
Leaf type:	Palmate, deeply incised, toothed
Height:	1–3 feet (30–90cm)
Habitat:	Open meadows, woodland clearings
Range:	Western Canada, west and southwest United States

There are several very similar geraniums to be found growing in the west, and it is often very difficult to identify them exactly. Sticky Geranium has a hairy stem, which divides into several branches, and palmate, deeply incised and toothed leaves on long stalks. Most branches carry a couple of small pinky-purple flowers at the top. Where it grows this species can be very common, turning the meadows pink in spring to early summer. The genus name *Geranium* is derived from the Greek word for crane, because the fruit resembles its bill.

Dakota Verbena; Western Pink Vervain

Scientific name:	*Glandularia bipinnatifida (Verbena bipinnatifida, Verbena ambrosifolia)*
Family:	Verbena
Flower type:	Rounded cluster, each flower $\frac{1}{4}$–$\frac{1}{2}$ inch (0.62–1.25cm) in width
Flowering period:	February–September
Flower color:	Pink
Leaf type:	Bipinnate
Height:	9–18 inches (22–45cm)
Habitat:	Open fields, waste ground
Range:	Southern United States and northern Mexico

This species has several scientific names and may be listed under any of them. The genus *Glandularia* is very similar to the genus *Verbena*, and the two are closely related. Dakota Verbena has showy, rounded clusters of pink to lavender flowers and leaves that are bipinnately divided. There are 47 varieties of Verbena across North America, many of which have a much wider range than Dakota Verbena, but this grows abundantly in many areas of its range, covering the ground with a carpet of deep pink.

Henbit; Common Dead Nettle

Scientific name:	*Lamium amplexicaule*
Family:	Mint
Flower type:	Rounded cluster, each flower $\frac{1}{2}$–$\frac{3}{4}$ inch (1.25–1.88cm) in length
Flowering period:	March–November
Flower color:	Pink
Leaf type:	Ovate, scalloped, upper sessile and clasping, lower with long stalks
Height:	5–18 inches (12–45cm)
Habitat:	Fields, waste ground, roadsides
Range:	Across North America, except for the Arctic

A native of Europe, Henbit was introduced to North America and is now fully naturalized across most of North America, along with two other introduced species, Spotted Henbit (*L. maculatum*) and Red Henbit (*L. purpureum*). Henbit has pink-lavender flowers that are arranged in a whorl around a rather squarish stem, in the axils of the upper horizontal, sessile and clasping leaves. The lower leaves are larger, have quite long stalks and are arranged in opposite pairs. The young leaves can be added to salads, and the tips dried and used as an herb for cooking.

Parry's Penstemon (*Penstemon parryi*)

False Babystars

Scientific name:	*Linanthus androsaceus*
Family:	Phlox
Flower type:	Radially symmetrical, $\frac{1}{2}$–$\frac{3}{4}$ inch (1.25–1.88cm) in diameter
Flowering period:	April–June
Flower color:	Pink
Leaf type:	Long, narrow with several pointed lobes
Height:	3–12 inches (8–30cm)
Habitat:	Grassy fields, open ground
Range:	California

False Babystars is a rather small, slender plant, with a cluster of long, narrow, and deeply divided leaves arranged near the top of the stem, and sometimes a few more pairs in widely spaced rings further down. The trumpet-shaped flowers are usually bright pink, although are sometimes found in white or yellow, and are held in a loose cluster at the top of each stem. False Babystars only grows in California, west of Sierra Nevada and down to the edge of the desert in the south. There are nearly 40 species of *Linanthus* in total across California, but there are only a few occurring elsewhere in North America.

Parry's Penstemon ▲

Scientific name:	*Penstemon parryi*
Family:	Figwort
Flower type:	Elongated cluster, each flower $\frac{3}{4}$ inch (1.88cm) in length
Flowering period:	March–May
Flower color:	Pink
Leaf type:	Long, lanceolate, sessile
Height:	3–4 feet (90–120cm)
Habitat:	Grassy fields
Range:	Southern Arizona, northwest Mexico

Because it is now often included in wildflower seed mixes, the once rather limited range of Parry's Penstemon is expanding. It is a very handsome-looking plant, with several stems that have only a few long, lanceolate, smooth, sessile leaves arranged in opposite pairs. The leaves at the base of the stem are much broader than those higher up. Each stem ends in a loose, elongated cluster of funnel-shaped pink to lavender flowers. As it flowers so early in the year, Parry's Penstemon often stands out more than some other wildflowers. There are around 210 species of penstemon found across North America.

Ohio Spiderwort

Scientific name:	*Tradescantia ohiensis*
Family:	Spiderwort
Flower type:	Umbel cluster, each flower 1–2 inches (2.5-5cm) in diameter
Flowering period:	April–July
Flower color:	Pink/blue
Leaf type:	Long and linear
Height:	9–24 inches (22–60cm)
Habitat:	Dry fields, woodland edges, roadsides
Range:	Midwest United States, Atlantic coast states

Ohio Spiderwort has a smooth stem, and long and linear leaves, both of which have a whitish bloom. The three-petaled flowers are borne in a loose umbel cluster, and are usually rose-pink, but can sometimes be blue. Spiderwort is often cultivated, as it is an attractive plant. There are around 21 species across the United States, and the roots of the species were used by American Indians to make a tea for kidney and stomach problems, and as a laxative. A leaf poultice was also applied to insect bites and stings.

Indian Paintbrush; Painted-cups

Scientific name:	*Castilleja coccinea*
Family:	Figwort
Flower type:	Rounded terminal cluster, each flower 1 inch (2.5cm) in length
Flowering period:	April–July
Flower color:	Red
Leaf type:	Basal rosette of elliptical, entire leaves; upper leaves sessile and deeply lobed
Height:	8–20 inches (20–50cm)
Habitat:	Damp fields, meadows, prairies
Range:	Central Canada, southeastern United States

Most species of this genus are common across the west, but this is an eastern plant. It has an erect, hairy stem, with a basal rosette of elliptical leaves, and alternate upper leaves that are sessile and deeply lobed. The yellowish flowers are surrounded by long bracts, which are tipped in bright red and are much more noticeable than the flowers themselves. They look as if they have been dipped in paint, hence the species' common name. American Indians used a weak tea made from the flowers to alleviate rheumatism and as a secret love charm in food – and also as a poison to destroy their enemies.

Rosy Paintbrush ▶

Scientific name:	*Castilleja rhexifolia*
Family:	Figwort
Flower type:	Elongated cluster, each flower ½–1½ inches (1.25–3.75cm) in length
Flowering period:	June–September
Flower color:	Red
Leaf type:	Long, lanceolate
Height:	5–20 inches (12–50cm)
Habitat:	Fields, moist meadows
Range:	West North America

The Rosy Paintbrush is another species of Paintbrush, of which there are over 100 across North America. Like most of the others it has brightly colored bracts surrounding the flowers, which are far more conspicuous than the flowers themselves. It is an erect and leafy plant, with long, lanceolate, entire leaves arranged alternately on the stem. Many species of Castilleja are difficult to transplant because they are partially parasitic on neighboring plants, and they are also very difficult to grow from seed.

California Poppy

Scientific name:	*Eschscholzia californica*
Family:	Poppy
Flower type:	Radially symmetrical, 1–2 inches (2.5–5cm) in diameter
Flowering period:	February–September
Flower color:	Orange
Leaf type:	Bipinnate, finely dissected
Height:	9–26 inches (22–65cm)
Habitat:	Open meadows, grassy hillsides
Range:	West coast states from south Washington to south California

The state flower of California since 1903, the California Poppy is a very popular ornamental plant, but also grows abundantly in the wild in the valleys and foothills of the Pacific coast and in parts of the Rockies. It has several blue-green stems and deeply dissected, rather fern-like blue-green leaves, with a bright-colored flower held on the end of a long, bare stalk. The flower is usually plain orange, but may range from yellow-orange to a deep orange, or even have petals that grade in color from orange at the base to yellow at the tips. The flowers open only in bright sunlight, closing at night and on very cloudy days.

Overleaf: California Poppy and Fiddleneck.

Arrowleaf Balsamroot

Scientific name:	*Balsamorhiza sagittata*
Family:	Aster
Flower type:	Compound flower head, 4–5 inches (10–12cm) in diameter
Flowering period:	May–July
Flower color:	Yellow
Leaf type:	Long, arrow-shaped
Height:	9–32 inches (22–80cm)
Habitat:	Grasslands, sagebrush, open hillsides
Range:	Western North America

Arrowleaf Balsamroot has a basal rosette of very large, hairy, silver-gray leaves, which can sometimes be over 1 foot (30cm) in length, with a petiole of a similar length. Its solitary, yellow, daisy-like flower is held at the end of a long, leafless stalk. There is also a very similar species, Deltoid Balsamroot (*B. deltoidea*), which is only found in the south-western coastal states, and which can be distinguished by being less hairy and much greener in color. Arrowleaf Balsamroot has entire leaves, but some other species of balsamroot found in North America have pinnately lobed leaves.

Black Mustard

Scientific name:	*Brassica nigra*
Family:	Mustard
Flower type:	Terminal cluster, each flower ½ inch (1.25cm) in width
Flowering period:	June–October
Flower color:	Yellow
Leaf type:	Upper lanceolate, toothed; lower lanceolate, deeply lobed
Height:	2–3 feet (30–60cm)
Habitat:	Fields, waste ground
Range:	Most of North America, except the Arctic

Originally a native of Europe, Black Mustard is now naturalized and very common across most of North America, although it is rare in the southeast. It is a many branched plant, with deeply lobed, alternate lower leaves and smaller toothed upper leaves. The flowers are in small clusters at the top of each stem branch. The seeds of Black Mustard are used in pickling recipes and ground for mustard, and they are also eaten as a tonic. Brassicas have been scientifically proven to contain strong anti-cancer compounds, but eating large quantities can cause red skin blotches and occasionally ulcers.

Arrowleaf Balsamroot (*Balsamorhiza sagittata*) growing in Washington.

Yellow Bell

Scientific name:	*Fritillaria pudica*
Family:	Lily
Flower type:	Urn-shaped, $\frac{1}{2}$–1 inch (1.25–2.5cm) in length
Flowering period:	March–July
Flower color:	Yellow
Leaf type:	Linear
Height:	6–12 inches (15–30cm)
Habitat:	Grassy meadows, grasslands, sagebrush, open forests
Range:	Western Canada, west and southwest United States

Yellow Bell is a rather delicate-looking plant, with a few linear, bright green leaves arranged near the base of the stem. Each plant bears one, solitary, nodding, bell-shaped yellow flower. The flower is quite narrow in relation to its length and turns from yellow to a purplish red as it matures and begins to wither away. Fritillaries are perennials, springing from a small bulb, and there are around 19 different species found across North America. Yellow Bell is quite common within most of its range, which stretches as far west as North Dakota in the north, although only as far as northwest Colorado in the south.

Yellow Star-grass ▼

Scientific name:	*Hypoxis hirsuta*
Family:	Iris
Flower type:	Loose cluster, each flower $\frac{3}{4}$ inch (1.88cm) in diameter
Flowering period:	March-September
Flower color:	Yellow
Leaf type:	Long, linear, grass-like
Height:	3–7 inches (8–18cm)
Habitat:	Dry meadows, open woodland
Range:	Southeast United States

Unless it is in flower, this plant can easily be missed in long grass because its leaves look so similar. It has long, linear leaves and a small, star-shaped yellow flower with pointed petals at the end of a long, hairy stem. The flowers are sometimes single, or more often borne in a small, loose cluster of three. Yellow Star-grass is a perennial growing from a small bulb and is closely related to the Amaryllis, but is far less spectacular. There are nine species across North America, but none in the west.

California Goldfields

Scientific name:	*Lasthenia californica (Baeria chrysostoma)*
Family:	Aster
Flower type:	Compound flower head, $\frac{3}{4}$–1 inch (1.88–2.5cm) in diameter
Flowering period:	March–May
Flower color:	Yellow
Leaf type:	Long, linear, opposite
Height:	4–12 inches (10–30cm)
Habitat:	Open fields
Range:	Southwest United States

California Goldfields, which is also sometimes classified scientifically as *Baeria chrysostoma*, is a small annual, with red-tinged branching stems, narrow, linear opposite leaves and a bright yellow flower at the end of each branch. It prefers poor, wet soil, and despite its name is also found in parts of Oregon and Arizona. When conditions are right it will cover the ground with its golden flowers, hence its name. Spring Gold (*Crocidium multicaule*) looks very similar, but most of its leaves are arranged in a basal rosette.

Bird's-foot Trefoil

Scientific name:	*Lotus corniculatus*
Family:	Pea
Flower type:	Loose umbel cluster, each flower $\frac{1}{4}$–$\frac{1}{2}$ inch (0.62–1.25cm) in length
Flowering period:	May–September
Flower color:	Yellow
Leaf type:	Pinnate, three at tip, two at junction with stem
Height:	Creeper, 2–4 inches (5–10cm)
Habitat:	Meadows, lawns, damp ground
Range:	Most of the United States, eastern Canada

Another plant that has been introduced from Europe, Bird's-foot Trefoil is now found across much of North America, except western Canada and the Arctic. It tends to be somewhat rarer in the southern states, but otherwise is quite easy to come across in most areas. Its common name comes from the shape of the seed pods, which fan out and resemble a bird's claw. Bird's-foot Trefoil is a creeper, often with trailing stems which root on the ground. It bears pinnate leaves, and a rather loose umbel clusters of yellow, pea-like flowers. The flowers become tinged with red as they mature and wither away.

Creamcups

Scientific name:	*Platystemon californicus*
Family:	Poppy
Flower type:	Radially symmetrical, ½–1 inch (1.25–2.5cm) in diameter
Flowering period:	March–May
Flower color:	Yellow
Leaf type:	Long, narrowly lanceolate, opposite
Height:	4–12 inches (10–30cm)
Habitat:	Open grassy fields
Range:	Southwest and west United States

Cream cups is the only species within its genus, and it is only found in a very limited area of North America, in the Pacific coast states, and in parts of Nevada, Utah and Arizona. It is a rather small plant, with several stems covered in soft hairs, each of which bears a small flower. The flowers vary widely in color, from yellow to white, and often with some shading between the two. The petals drop off as the flower opens, leaving a cluster of numerous stamens and stigmas. The leaves are mainly borne towards the base of the stem, arranged in opposite pairs or whorled, and are long, narrow and lanceolate.

Common Purslane; Pusley ▼

Scientific name:	*Portulaca oleracea*
Family:	Purslane
Flower type:	Radially symmetrical, ¼ inch (0.62cm) in width
Flowering period:	May–November
Flower color:	Yellow
Leaf type:	Obvate, long with rounded tip
Height:	Creeper, 2 inches (5cm)
Habitat:	Fields, waste ground
Range:	Most of North America, except the Arctic

Although it is only a few inches high, Common Purslane may have stems that are over 1 foot (30cm) long. It is native to Europe, but has spread everywhere across North America and is fully naturalized. A sprawling plant, it has thick, fleshy, smooth, red-purple stems and fleshy, flat green leaves, which are broadly obvate with a rounded tip. The leaves are sometimes alternate, sometimes opposite. The flowers are tiny and yellow, usually solitary but sometimes in small clusters. Common Purslane is high in iron and its leaves can be used in salads or dried and used as an herb in cooking. American Indians used a poultice made from the plant for burns, and a tea for headaches and stomach-aches.

Sticky Cinquefoil ▲

Scientific name:	*Potentilla glandulosa*
Family:	Rose
Flower type:	Radially symmetrical, $\frac{1}{2}$–$\frac{3}{4}$ inch (1.25–1.88cm) in diameter
Flowering period:	May–July
Flower color:	Yellow
Leaf type:	Compound pinnate, with ovate, sharply-toothed leaflets
Height:	22 inches (55cm)
Habitat:	Open dry fields
Range:	Most of western North America, from British Columbia to California

Sticky Cinquefoil is a very pretty wildflower, with several leafy, often reddish stems, which are covered in fine, sticky hairs. Each stem is tipped with a loose cluster of yellow flowers, and the leaves are bipinnate, with ovate, toothed leaflets. It is often just known as Cinquefoil, the name coming from the French word for five, since many species in this genus have five leaflets. There are over 120 species of Cinquefoil found across the whole of North America, many of which are very similar in general appearance, although some species have either white, red or purple flowers instead of yellow.

Kidneyleaf Buttercup; Small-flowered Crowfoot

Scientific name:	*Ranunculus abortivus*
Family:	Buttercup
Flower type:	Radially symmetrical, $\frac{1}{4}$ inch (0.62cm) in diameter
Flowering period:	April–August
Flower color:	Yellow
Leaf type:	Basal leaves reniform, scalloped, upper sessile, narrow and lobed
Height:	6–24 inches (15–30cm)
Habitat:	Fields, moist open woodland, waste ground
Range:	Most of North America, except western Canada

Although Kidneyleaf Buttercup is a member of the Buttercup family, its flower has small, drooping petals and does not look much like other buttercups. The plant has branching stems, with the basal leaves kidney-shaped, scalloped and on long stalks and very different upper leaves that are sessile, narrow and lobed. There are several species that look very similar across North America, and some are considered to be toxic, causing blisters on the skin, and burns in the mouth if taken orally. American Indians used this irritating effect in a poultice to cure boils and abscesses.

CANADA GOLDENROD; MEADOW GOLDENROD

Scientific name:	*Solidago canadensis*
Family:	Aster
Flower type:	Large panicle, with tiny flower heads $\frac{1}{8}$ inch (0.31cm) in length
Flowering period:	July–September
Flower color:	Yellow
Leaf type:	Lanceolate, hairy
Height:	1–5 feet (30–150cm)
Habitat:	Meadows, open woodland
Range:	Most of North America

A tall, showy perennial, Canada Goldenrod is one of the most common goldenrods to be seen across North America, although it is generally much more widely found in the eastern half of the continent. It has a stout, hairy stem, with long, lanceolate, finely hairy leaves with three prominent veins. The leaves are arranged on the stem alternately. The tiny flower heads are born along arching branches to make up a large and handsome yellow panicle. American Indians often used Canada Goldenrod medicinally – the root was applied to soothe burns, crushed flowers were used for sore throats and they also made a tea from the flowers to treat fever and snakebites.

Missouri Goldenrod; Low Goldenrod

Scientific name:	*Solidago missouriensis*
Family:	Aster
Flower type:	Large, rounded panicle, with flower heads $\frac{1}{8}$ inch (0.31cm) in length
Flowering period:	July–August
Flower color:	Yellow
Leaf type:	Basal oblanceolate with stalks, upper lanceolate and sessile
Height:	4–34 inches (10–85cm)
Habitat:	Meadows, dry open woodland
Range:	Western North America

Despite its name, Missouri Goldenrod is found across much of western North America, and also in some southwest areas, although it is very rare in the east. It looks rather similar to Canada Goldenrod, but is smaller and has a smooth rather than hairy stem, and lanceolate, toothed and alternate leaves with three prominent veins. The tiny flower heads, which are borne on arching branches, make up a large, and rather rounded yellow panicle. Missouri Goldenrod is often the first to herald the onset of fall.

Sweet Goldenrod

Scientific name:	*Solidago odora*
Family:	Aster
Flower type:	Large, panicle, with tiny flower heads $\frac{1}{8}$ inch (0.31cm) in length
Flowering period:	July–October
Flower color:	Yellow
Leaf type:	Narrow, lanceolate, smooth
Height:	2–4 feet (60–120cm)
Habitat:	Dry meadows, dry open woodland
Range:	Nova Scotia, and across eastern and southern United States

Sweet Goldenrod is instantly identifiable by the scent of anise that its leaves give off whenever they are crushed. It has a smooth stem, with long, narrow, lanceolate, smooth and alternate leaves, which on close inspection have tiny translucent spots. The small flower heads are arranged along only one side of slightly arching branches, to make up a large, and rather open yellow panicle. A tea made from the leaves was once used for colic, stomach cramps, colds, dysentery and measles, and as a wash to cure rheumatism, headaches and neuralgia.

Chocolate Lily; Mission Bells; Checker Lily

Scientific name:	*Fritillaria affinis (Fritillaria lanceolata)*
Family:	Lily
Flower type:	Urn-shaped, $\frac{1}{2}$–1 inches (1.25–2.5cm) in length
Flowering period:	March-June
Flower color:	Brown
Leaf type:	Lanceolate, whorled
Height:	1–4 feet (30–120cm)
Habitat:	Grassy meadows, open woods
Range:	West of the Rockies

Chocolate Lily is a name also given to another member of the *Fritillaria* genus, *F. biflora*, and Spotted Mountain Bells (*F. atropurpurea*) is also commonly called Checker Lily. *F. affinis* has also been renamed, having previously been called *F. lanceolata*, so there is much confusion around these particular species They are all very similar, but *F. affinis* has mottled greenish-brown, bowl-shaped flowers on an erect stem, with long lanceolate leaves on the upper section of the stem. *F. biflora* has dark brown unmottled flowers and its leaves are on the lower part of the stem, and *F. atropurpurea* has smaller flowers and much longer, narrower leaves.

Plains and Prairie

White Wild Indigo

Scientific name:	*Baptisia alba*
Family:	Pea
Flower type:	Elongated cluster, 1 foot (30cm) in length
Flowering period:	April–June
Flower color:	White
Leaf type:	Tripalmate; leaflets spatulate
Height:	24–50 inches (60–125cm)
Habitat:	Prairies, open woods, waste ground
Range:	Eastern North America

White Wild Indigo is a rather bushy plant, with a stout, whitish-green stem and tripalmate leaves with spatulate leaflets. The flowers are pea-like, borne along the upper level of the stem in a long, erect cluster. They are either white or creamy-white. The common name comes from the blue dye that can be obtained from this species, which is similar to indigo. American Indians mixed the powdered seed of Wild White Indigo with buffalo fat to create an ointment that was applied to the skin of the stomach to treat colic, and made a tea from the leaves for use as an astringent. However, the plant should not be eaten as it is potentially toxic. White Wild Indigo was previously known as *B. leucantha*.

Carolina Larkspur; Prairie Larkspur

Scientific name:	*Delphinium carolinianum*
Family:	Buttercup
Flower type:	Elongated cluster, each flower 1 inch (2.5cm) in length
Flowering period:	May–June
Flower color:	White
Leaf type:	Compound palmate, divided leaflets
Height:	12–34 inches (30–85cm)
Habitat:	Prairies, open woodland
Range:	Central and southeast North America

A perennial of the midwest, Carolina Larkspur is a tall, slender plant with a downy stalk. It has compound palmate leaves, with the leaflets deeply divided into narrow segments. The white, or sometimes pale blue, flowers are around 1 inch (2.5cm) long, but around half of this is taken up by a backward-pointing spur on the upper sepal. The flowers are borne in a narrow, elongated raceme cluster along the top of the stem. Carolina Larkspur colonizes large areas of the prairie, and when all the plants are in flower it can look quite spectacular.

PRAIRIE MIMOSA

Scientific name:	*Desmanthus illinoensis*
Family:	Pea
Flower type:	Spherical cluster, $\frac{1}{2}$ inch (1.25cm) in diameter
Flowering period:	June–August
Flower color:	White
Leaf type:	Bipinnate, many narrow leaflets
Height:	12–50 inches (30–125cm)
Habitat:	Prairies, fields, plains
Range:	Southeast and west United States

Prairie Mimosa is a tall, erect plant with bipinnate, feathery leaves that curve gracefully off the smooth, main stem. Each leaf has 20-30 narrow, bright green leaflets. The flower clusters are small spheres, borne at the end of long stalks that spring from the leaf axils. They are made up of a mass of tiny white or very pale green flowers. The leaves of Prairie Mimosa are apparently very high in protein. American Indians used a tea made from them to soothe itching skin. There are ten species in this genus, most of which are found in the south.

RATTLESNAKE MASTER; BUTTON SNAKEROOT ◀

Scientific name:	*Eryngium yuccifolium*
Family:	Carrot
Flower type:	Spherical cluster, $\frac{3}{4}$ inch (1.88cm) in diameter
Flowering period:	July–November
Flower color:	White
Leaf type:	Linear, pointed, clasping
Height:	18–60 inches (45–150cm)
Habitat:	Prairies, open woodland
Range:	Southeast United States

With its rigid stem and spiny leaves, livestock is reluctant to eat Rattlesnake Master. Most of the leaves are arranged near the base of the erect, smooth stems, and they are long, linear, parallel-veined and clasping. The flower heads are spherical, and they are borne on stalks branching from the stem, with several on each plant. They are made up of many, very small, white to green flowers, tightly clustered and interspersed with bristly bracts. The base of each flower head is surrounded with large, pointed bracts. As they age, the flowers may take on a blue tint. American Indians used the root to make a poultice for snakebites, and to treat toothache, coughs and neuralgia. In folk medicine, a tincture of the root was used for female reproductive disorders, piles and rheumatism. This plant should not be confused with False Aloe (*Manfreda virginica*), which is also known as Rattlesnake-master. False Aloe has long, succulent leaves rather like those of a yucca and white, tubular, fragrant flowers. It produces an irritating latex.

Stemless Daisy

Scientific name:	*Townsendia exscapa*
Family:	Aster
Flower type:	Compound flower head, 1–2 inches (2.5–5cm) in diameter
Flowering period:	March–May
Flower color:	White
Leaf type:	Narrow, linear, sessile
Height:	1–3 inches (2.5–8cm)
Habitat:	Open plains; barren piñon-juniper woodland
Range:	Central North America

A tiny plant, Stemless Daisy has many narrow, linear and sessile leaves, which are held erect and are extremely densely clustered together. The flowers are borne at the end of very short stalks that spring from the mass of leaves, and hold the large flower heads just an inch (2.5cm) or so above the ground. The flower heads are made up of lots of white or pinkish ray florets, which are arranged round a yellow central disk. There are 22 species in this genus found across North America, most of them native to the central and western areas of the continent.

Soapweed Yucca ▶

Scientific name:	*Yucca glauca*
Family:	Agave
Flower type:	Elongated cluster, each flower 1½ inches (3.75cm) in diameter
Flowering period:	May–July
Flower color:	White
Leaf type:	Basal rosette, linear
Height:	2–4 feet (60–120cm)
Habitat:	Plains
Range:	Central United States

Soapweed Yucca is a large plant, with a basal rosette of long, linear sword-like, gray-green leaves that have sharply-pointed tips and hairy edges. The flowers are bowl-shaped and pendent, held in a crowded elongated cluster on a single stalk. The flowers and buds can be cooked and added to salads. American Indians made a poultice from the roots for swelling and to stop bleeding, and used the juice as a hairwash for dandruff and baldness. Modern research suggests the plant may have antifungal, antitumor and antiarthritic properties. There are 30 species in this genus found in North America, most in the southwest desert.

Identification of individual Yucca species is often difficult, as they look rather similar. Most species have the typical sword-like leaves and showy flower cluster, as illustrated above.

Blue Flax

Scientific name:	*Linum lewisii var. lewisii*
Family:	Flax
Flower type:	Radially symmetrical, 1–1½ inches (2.5–3.75cm) in diameter
Flowering period:	June–July
Flower color:	Blue
Leaf type:	Long, linear
Height:	10–26 inches (25–65cm)
Habitat:	Prairies, plains
Range:	West and central North America

Although it is a perennial, Wild Blue Flax is closely related to the European annual Common Flax (*L. usitatissimum*), from which linen fiber and linseed oil are derived, and the two plants look very similar. Common Flax has escaped from cultivation, and is now found across most of North America. Wild Blue Flax has several smooth stems with numerous long, linear gray-green leaves, and branching clusters of pale blue flowers. The flowers have five broad, rounded petals, which are often finely striped with deeper blue, and five smaller, plain-edged sepals. By contrast, the sepals of Common Flax are usually fringed. There are 35 species in this genus found in North America.

Above: Salvia officinalis growing with *Fragaria vesca.*

American Pasqueflower

Scientific name:	*Pulsatilla patens (Anemone patens)*
Family:	Buttercup
Flower type:	Radially symmetrical, $2\frac{1}{2}$ inches (6.25cm) in diameter
Flowering period:	April–May
Flower color:	Blue
Leaf type:	Basal, compound palmate; stem, sessile, linear, lobed
Height:	8–16 inches (20–40cm)
Habitat:	Prairies, plains, open grassland
Range:	Central and parts of western North America

The basal leaves of American Pasqueflower are long, hairy and compound palmate, with the leaflets deeply divided into narrow segments. Higher up the stem, just beneath the flowers, are three smaller, hairy, sessile leaves that are divided into linear lobes. The stem is softly hairy, and terminates in a solitary, bowl-shaped flower that has five to seven blue, violet or white petal-like sepals, but no petals. The seeds of American Pasqueflower are quite distinctive, as they are each tipped with a long tail that creates a feathery-looking seed head. Pasque is a corruption of the French word *Pâques*, meaning Easter, which is roughly when the plant flowers.

Blue Sage; Blue Salvia ▲

Scientific name:	*Salvia azurea*
Family:	Mint
Flower type:	Elongated cluster, each flower $\frac{1}{2}$–1 inch (1.25–2.5cm) in length
Flowering period:	July–October
Flower color:	Blue
Leaf type:	Long, linear to lanceolate, sometimes toothed, opposite
Height:	2–5 feet (60–150cm)
Habitat:	Dry prairies, open coniferous woodland
Range:	Southeast United States

Blue Sage is a tall and slender perennial, with a square stem bearing long, linear to lanceolate leaves, which are arranged in opposite pairs along its length. The lower leaves are sometimes toothed along both edges, but the upper ones are usually entire and much more linear in shape. The stem terminates in an elongated spike-like cluster of blue and rather hairy flowers. The flowers have two lips, with the lower one much bigger than the upper, and they are arranged in whorls around the stem. Blue Sage is closely related to Garden Sage (*S. officinalis*), which is often used in cooking as a flavoring herb.

Western Spiderwort

Scientific name:	*Tradescantia occidentalis*
Family:	Spiderwort
Flower type:	Radially symmetrical, 1 inch (2.5cm) in diameter
Flowering period:	June–August
Flower color:	Blue
Leaf type:	Long, linear
Height:	8–20 inches (20–50cm)
Habitat:	Plains, prairies
Range:	Central United States

Western Spiderwort has a rather smooth stem, with several very prominent joints at intervals, and which bears several long, narrow leaves arranged alternately along its length. The flowers are bright blue ranging to rose-purple in color, and have three rounded petals. They are borne at the end of a smooth stalk in a small cluster. American Indians cooked both this plant and Pine Spiderwort (*T. pinetorum*) and used them as a vegetable, and a tea made from this and other species of spiderwort was used to cure kidney and stomach problems. Plants were also often crushed and applied to insect bites and stings.

Purple Coneflower ▶

Scientific name:	*Echinacea purpurea*
Family:	Aster
Flower type:	Compound flower head, 2–4 inches (5–10cm) in diameter
Flowering period:	May–October
Flower color:	Purple
Leaf type:	Ovate, long stalked, often serrated
Height:	14–50 inches (35–150cm)
Habitat:	Prairies, open woodland
Range:	East North America

This is a wildflower that is better known around the world by its scientific name. The flowers of Purple Coneflower are used to make an herbal remedy that strengthens the immune system, and Echinacea is available as a tea, capsules or tablets in pharmacies and health food stores across the world. Purple Coneflower is a tall, daisy-like perennial, with large flower heads with drooping purple, pinkish or white rays round a cone-shaped, brown central disk. The leaves are ovate, with long stalks and prominent veins, and often with serrated edges. Purple Coneflower is easy to cultivate and makes an attractive addition to the garden.

Prairie Smoke; Old Man's Whiskers

Scientific name:	*Geum triflorum (Erythrocoma triflora)*
Family:	Rose
Flower type:	Radially symmetrical, $\frac{3}{4}$ inch (1.88cm) in length
Flowering period:	May–July
Flower color:	Purple
Leaf type:	Compound pinnate; leaflets oblong, toothed or lobed
Height:	8–16 inches (20–40cm)
Habitat:	Prairies, woodland
Range:	Central Canada, east and most of western United States

The slender stalk of Prairie Smoke rises from a basal cluster of long, compound pinnate leaves, which have oblong leaflets that are either toothed or lobed. The basal leaves are rather feathery, somewhat resembling those of a fern, and there are sometimes a few, much smaller versions, to be seen on the stem itself. The bell-shaped flowers are purple to brown-pink in color, and are usually borne in small, loose clusters of three. The common names come from the seed heads rather than the flowers, as each seed has a very long, feathery, gray-white tail, which are clustered together and make the heads look rather like old-fashioned feather dusters. Prairie Smoke often grows in patches of 100 or more plants, so the effect of the feathery seed heads can look like smoke lying over the prairie.

Illinois Tick Trefoil

Scientific name:	*Desmodium illinoense*
Family:	Pea
Flower type:	Elongated cluster, each flower ½ inch (1.25cm) in length
Flowering period:	July–August
Flower color:	Pink
Leaf type:	Segmented; three lanceolate leaflets
Height:	2–5 feet (60–150cm)
Habitat:	Prairies
Range:	Central United States

A rather tall and spindly plant, Illinois Tick Trefoil has long fruits that divide into segments and attach themselves to clothing and passing animals, so dispersing the seeds far and wide. The hairy stem has alternate leaves that are segmented into three leaflets, each of which is lanceolate in shape. The terminal leaflet has a prominent central vein underneath. The flowers are pea-like, white, pink or purple in color, and borne in an elongated raceme cluster at the top of the stem. Illinois Tick Trefoil looks similar to Showy Trefoil (*D. canadense*), but tends to be narrow and less open and bushy, while Showy Trefoil prefers open woodlands and usually has pinker flowers.

Texas Storksbill ▶

Scientific name:	*Erodium texanum*
Family:	Geranium
Flower type:	Radially symmetrical, 1 inch (2.5cm) in diameter
Flowering period:	February–June
Flower color:	Pink
Leaf type:	Ovate, three-lobed
Height:	Creeper, 6 inches (15cm)
Habitat:	Prairies and deserts
Range:	South to southwest United States

A native wildflower of North America, Texas Storkbill is a low-growing, trailing plant but it can have horizontal stems that are up to 20 inches (50cm) in length. The stems are reddish in color and roughly hairy. The leaves are generally ovate in shape, with three rather rounded lobes, the edges of which are also bluntly toothed. The pink flowers are radially symmetrical, with five rounded petals, five sepals and a cluster of ten stamens, and are borne in a loose cluster. There are nine species in this genus found in North America.

Queen-of-the-prairie

Scientific name:	*Filipendula rubra*
Family:	Rose
Flower type:	Radially symmetrical, $\frac{1}{2}$ inch (1.25cm) in diameter
Flowering period:	June–August
Flower color:	Pink
Leaf type:	Compound pinnate; leaflets deeply lobed and toothed
Height:	32–96 inches (80–250cm)
Habitat:	Prairies, meadows
Range:	Northeast North America

Queen-of-the-prairie is a tall perennial, with a stem that beats alternate arrangements of rather large and coarse-looking leaves. The leaves are compound pinnate, with deeply lobed and toothed leaflets. The individual flowers are quite small, but they are borne clustered together in large, feathery, branching terminal clusters. They are pink to red in color and sweetly scented. American Indians used a mixture made from the root of Queen-of-the-prairie as a love potion, and as a medicine to treat heart trouble. In folk medicine, the root was traditionally used as an astringent and to treat dysentery, diarrhea and bleeding.

Bush Morning Glory ▲

Scientific name:	*Ipomoea leptophylla*
Family:	Morning Glory
Flower type:	Radially symmetrical, 2–2$\frac{1}{2}$ inches (5-6.25cm) in diameter
Flowering period:	May–August
Flower color:	Pink
Leaf type:	Lanceolate, narrow
Height:	3–4 feet (90–120cm)
Habitat:	Prairies; dry, sandy soil
Range:	Central United States

Although its flowers look very similar to those of cultivated morning glories, Bush Morning Glory is not a vine but a more or less erect plant – although sometimes the lower part of the plant does lean on the ground. It has a smooth stem, with many long, narrow lanceolate leaves on quite short stalks. The attractive flowers are funnel-shaped and are deep pink to purple-red in color, often becoming darker towards the center. They are borne on short stalks that spring from the leaf axils on the upper part of the plant. Bush Morning Glory is related to the Wild Potato Vine (*I. pandurata*) and both these species are edible – the roots are boiled or baked like sweet potatoes.

Dotted Blazing Star; Dotted Gayfeather

Scientific name:	*Liatris punctata*
Family:	Aster
Flower type:	Elongated cluster, each flower $\frac{3}{4}$ inch (1.88cm) in length
Flowering period:	August–September
Flower color:	Pink
Leaf type:	Long, narrow, dotted
Height:	8–32 inches (20–80cm)
Habitat:	Plains, dry open ground, among piñon and juniper
Range:	Central North America

Dotted Blazing Star is a tall perennial with several erect stems bearing long, narrow leaves, which are bright green marked with tiny, resinous dots. The rather shaggy-looking, rose-purple flower heads are each made up of four to six disk flowers and are arranged in a dense, elongated spike. There are 34 species in this genus found across North America, mostly in the center or in the east of the continent. A tea made from the roots of this and other Liatris species was a folk remedy for kidney and bladder problems, and was used as a gargle for sore throats.

Prairie Blazing Star

Scientific name:	*Liatris pycnostachya*
Family:	Aster
Flower type:	Spike of dense flower heads, each flower $\frac{3}{4}$ inch (1.25cm) in width
Flowering period:	July–September
Flower color:	Pink
Leaf type:	Linear, with translucent dots
Height:	22–72 inches (55–180cm)
Habitat:	Damp ground on prairies
Range:	Central United States

As well as being a well-known wildflower, Prairie Blazing Star is also often cultivated as a garden plant. It is a very tall perennial with a coarse, hairy stem that has many rough, linear leaves with translucent dots. The shaggy-looking flower heads, which are normally rose-purple – although sometimes there is an odd white one – are made up of 5–12 sessile florets, and are borne on a crowded spike. Devil's Bit (*Chamaelirium luteum*) is also sometimes called Blazing Star, but it looks quite different as it has a spike of white flowers and leaves in a basal rosette.

Showy Evening-primrose

Scientific name:	*Oenothera speciosa*
Family:	Evening-primrose
Flower type:	Radially symmetrical, 1–3 inches (2.5–8cm) in diameter
Flowering period:	May–July
Flower color:	Pink
Leaf type:	Elliptical, waved or cleft edges
Height:	9–26 inches (22–65cm)
Habitat:	Prairies, plains, waste ground
Range:	Southwest and Southeast United States

This attractive plant is often cultivated in gardens, from which it escapes to the wild where – being very drought-resistant – it can soon spread across quite large areas. Showy Evening primrose is a medium-size plant, with slender, softly hairy stems bearing many elliptical leaves with wavy or cleft edges. The buds are rather drooping, but they open into pink or white flowers, borne on short stalks that spring from the leaf axils. The four broad, rounded petals are often delicately veined with a deeper shade, and have a touch of yellow at the base.

Showy Locoweed

Scientific name:	*Oxytropis splendens*
Family:	Pea
Flower type:	Elongated cluster, 2–7 inches (5–18cm) in length
Flowering period:	June–July
Flower color:	Pink
Leaf type:	Compound pinnate,softly hairy; basal, whorled
Height:	5–14 inches (12–35cm)
Habitat:	Prairies, plains
Range:	Western and central North America

Showy Locoweed has many compound pinnate, gray-green, softly hairy, and basal leaves, which are arranged in whorls. Several bare stems spring from the center of the whorled leaves, rising to 5–14 inches (12–35cm) in height. The stems are covered in silver, silky hairs and terminate in small and dense raceme clusters of 8-12, pink to lavender colored flowers. The flowers are pea-like in shape, with a pointed keel. There are around 36 species in this genus found in North America, and many of them are extremely poisonous. Several species in the genus *Astragalus* are also commonly known as locoweeds, but they can easily be distinguished visually from those in the genus *Oxytropis* by the fact that the flowers have a blunt, rather than pointed, keel.

Western Starflower; Indian Potato ▲

Scientific name:	*Trientalis latifolia*
Family:	Primrose
Flower type:	Radially symmetrical, ½ inch (1.25cm) in diameter
Flowering period:	May–July
Flower color:	Pink
Leaf type:	Ovate, whorled
Height:	4–9 inches (10–22cm)
Habitat:	Prairies, open woodland
Range:	Northwest North America

A small and rather delicate-looking plant, Western Starflower has a slender stem with a whorl of five to ten ovate, bright green leaves with sharply pointed tips. Springing from the center of the leaves are one or more thread-like stalks, terminating in a tiny, star-shaped flower. The flowers have five to nine pointed petals and are very pale pink to lavender, sometimes tipped in deeper pink. There are three species in this genus found in North America, all of which look rather similar. Starflower (*T. borealis*) has white flowers, prefers woodlands and is found in central North America, while Northern Starflower (*T. arctica*) also has white flowers and grows in wet ground, with its range extending up into Alaska.

Royal Catchfly

Scientific name:	*Silene regia*
Family:	Carnation
Flower type:	Radially symmetrical, 1 inch (2.5cm) in diameter
Flowering period:	May–July
Flower color:	Red
Leaf type:	Ovate to elliptical, sessile
Height:	2–4 feet (60–120cm)
Habitat:	Prairies, dry woodland
Range:	Midwest prairie states

A tall plant, Royal Catchfly has an erect, leafy, slender and branching stem. The bright green, ovate to elliptical, sessile leaves are arranged in opposite pairs towards the base of the stem. Royal Catchfly has bright red flowers that are borne in a loose cluster at the ends of short stalks. The flowers have five narrow, open petals that are slightly toothed at the tips, and sepals that are joined to form a short tube. There are around 30 species in this genus found in North America, widely spread across the continent.

Below: A white, trumpet-shaped flower of Bindweed (*Convulvus arvensis)* is seen growing amidst the bright red flowers of Royal Catchfly (*Silene regia*).

Curlycup Gumweed; Stickyheads

Scientific name:	*Grindelia squarrosa*
Family:	Aster
Flower type:	Compound flower head, 1 inch (2.5cm) in diameter
Flowering period:	July–October
Flower color:	Yellow
Leaf type:	Oblong, sessile, toothed, translucent spots
Height:	6–30 inches (15–75cm)
Habitat:	Prairies, waste ground
Range:	Most of North America, except the Arctic

Curlycup Gumweed has a bitter taste and livestock do not eat it, so it spreads quickly in heavily grazed areas. It is an erect plant with a branching stem bearing alternate long, oblong, sessile and toothed leaves. These are scattered with translucent spots that are glands which excrete a strong-smelling substance – possibly to repel leaf-eating insects and animals. The flower heads have dark yellow disk flowers and paler yellow ray flowers. The bracts at the base of the flower curl outwards and are pointed and sticky, hence the alternative common name of Stickyheads. American Indians made a tea from the plant to treat asthma, coughs and bronchitis, while a leaf poultice was used for wounds and skin eruptions.

Broom Snakeweed; Matchbush

Scientific name:	*Gutierrezia sarothrae*
Family:	Aster
Flower type:	Rounded cluster, each flower $\frac{1}{4}$ inch (0.62cm) in length
Flowering period:	June–September
Flower color:	Yellow
Leaf type:	Linear
Height:	8–34 inches (20–85cm)
Habitat:	Dry grassland plains, open waste ground
Range:	West central North America

A generally rounded, bushy shrub, with many slender, branching stems, Broom Snakeweed prefers dry open areas. It is a woody, aromatic, resinous plant, with long, thin linear leaves and many small yellow flower heads that are borne in lots of loose clusters, turning it into a mass of gold when it is in flower. The flowers have tiny narrow ray flowers around a very small central disk. Due to poor land management, Broom Snakeweed has rampaged across many grassland areas and it is poisonous to livestock, causing miscarriage and sometimes death. The name snakeweed comes from the plant being used in snakebite remedies, while the dried stems were tied together to make primitive brooms.

Maximilian's Sunflower

▶

Scientific name:	*Helianthus maximilianii*
Family:	Aster
Flower type:	Compound flower head, 2–3 inches (5–8cm) in diameter
Flowering period:	July–October
Flower color:	Yellow
Leaf type:	Narrowly elliptical, stiff, rough
Height:	3–10 feet (90–300cm)
Habitat:	Prairies
Range:	Central and western North America

Maximilian's Sunflower is a native American wildflower that grows across the prairies. It looks similar to other species of sunflower, with a rough, stout stem that branches near the top and bears alternate, rather widely spaced leaves. These are long, stiff and narrowly elliptical in shape, and often folded. The large yellow flower heads are made up of many pointed ray flowers around a fairly small central disk, and they are borne at the end of short stalks springing from the upper half of the plant. Maximilian's Sunflower is a valuable addition to the diet of livestock, while the seeds are an important food for wildlife.

Prairie Sunflower

Scientific name:	*Helianthus petiolaris*
Family:	Aster
Flower type:	Compound flower head, 3–5 inches (7.5–12.5cm) in diameter
Flowering period:	June-September
Flower color:	Yellow
Leaf type:	Ovate or heart-shaped, sometimes with toothed edges
Height:	2–13 feet (60–390 cm)
Habitat:	Prairies, dry open fields
Range:	Central and western North America

The Prairie Sunflower is closely related to the Common Sunflower (*H. annuus*). It is a tall plant with a coarsely hairy stem, often branched towards the top and bearing ovate or heart-shaped leaves, sometimes with toothed edges. The flower heads have bright yellow ray flowers, around a maroon central disk; the disk flowers have scales between them that are tipped with white hairs, but these can only be seen if the disk is spread apart. There are around 50 species of sunflower across North America, and many have been cultivated and hybridized to provide garden varieties.

Columbia Lily; Tiger Lily

Scientific name:	*Lilium columbianum*
Family:	Lily
Flower type:	Pendent, radially symmetrical, 2–3 inches (5–8cm)
Flowering period:	May–August
Flower color:	Yellow
Leaf type:	Long, lanceolate, whorled
Height:	20–60 inches (50–150cm)
Habitat:	Prairies, open forests
Range:	Western North America

Columbia Lily is an attractive plant with showy flowers, which unfortunately has led to it becoming quite scarce in the wild because it was often dug up to be transplanted into gardens. Destruction of its natural habitat has also caused it to decline. It is a tall plant, with a very leafy stem – the leaves are long, lanceolate and usually arranged in whorls at regular intervals. The large flowers are pendent, with several at the top of each stem at the end of short stalks. The yellow to orange petal-like segments curve strongly backward towards the base of the flower, showing the dark red, black or purple spots on the inside, with the long stamens dangling below.

Fringed Puccoon; Fringed Gromwell ▲

Scientific name:	*Lithospermum incisum*
Family:	Borage
Flower type:	Radially symmetrical, $\frac{1}{2}$–$1\frac{1}{2}$ inches (1.25–3.75cm) in diameter
Flowering period:	May–June
Flower color:	Yellow
Leaf type:	Narrowly lanceolate
Height:	3–20 inches (8–50cm)
Habitat:	Open plains, dry foothills
Range:	Most of central and eastern North America

Fringed Puccoon is a small, leafy plant, with several thick stems on each plant. The many leaves are clustered together and are comparatively long, narrowly lanceolate and very hairy. The showy flowers at the top of the stems start out with a long, narrow tube, which flares out suddenly into a trumpet-shaped, bright yellow flower, with five rounded lobes that are irregularly toothed. There are 18 species in this genus found across North America, and some have been used medicinally for thyroid problems, or as a contraceptive.

Upright Prairie Coneflower; Mexican Hat

Scientific name:	*Ratibida columnifera*
Family:	Aster
Flower type:	Compound flower head, 1–2 inches (2.5–5cm) in length
Flowering period:	July–September
Flower color:	Yellow
Leaf type:	Pinnately divided
Height:	1–4 feet (30–120cm)
Habitat:	Dry prairies, roadsides
Range:	Central North America

A branching and leafy plant, Upright Prairie Coneflower spreads across large areas and when it is in flower the ground is covered with thousands of blooms. The gray-green leaves are long and pinnately divided into several narrow segments. The flowers are borne at the end of long, bare stalks, and they have long ray florets that are either bright yellow, red-brown or combinations of the two. The central yellow-brown disk is a rounded cone-shape and the alternative common name of Mexican Hat comes from the resemblance of the flower to the shape of the wide-brimmed, high-crowned hats that are traditionally associated with Mexico.

Black-eyed Susan ▶

Scientific name:	*Rudbeckia hirta*
Family:	Aster
Flower type:	Compound flower head, 2–3 inches (5–8cm) in diameter
Flowering period:	July–October
Flower color:	Yellow
Leaf type:	Oblong to lanceolate, toothed, hairy
Height:	14–36 inches (35–90cm)
Habitat:	Prairies, fields, open woodland, waste ground
Range:	Most of North America, except desert areas and Arctic

Black-eyed Susan is both a native wildflower and a popular garden biennial. It has a coarse, erect, rough stem, with long, oblong to lanceolate, leaves that have prominent veins, bristly hairs and usually a few sparse teeth on each edge. Lower leaves have short stalks, but the upper ones are often sessile. The flower heads are daisy-like, with 8-21 bright yellow ray florets around a dark brown, dome-shaped central disk. American Indians used a root tea to treat worms and colds, and as a wash for sores and snakebites. Juice from the root was used to treat earache. Modern science has shown that the plant has immuno-stimulant properties.

Compass Plant

Scientific name:	*Silphium laciniatum*
Family:	Aster
Flower type:	Compound flower head, 3 inches (8cm) in diameter
Flowering period:	June–September
Flower color:	Yellow
Leaf type:	Large, deeply pinnately divided, roughly toothed
Height:	2–12 feet (60–400cm)
Habitat:	Prairies
Range:	Central eastern North America

Compass Plant is a very tall plant with stout, bristly stems bearing very large, rough leaves that are deeply pinnately divided, with the segments irregularly and sharply toothed along the edges. The leaves are very dark green with a prominent midrib, and are arranged alternately along the stem, either with short stalks clasping the stem or sessile. The flower heads are daisy-like, with bright yellow ray florets around a darker yellow central disk. American Indians made a tea from the roots as a general tonic, and to expel worms, and a root tea was also used traditionally for coughs, lung problems and asthma. The stems of Compass Plant exude a resinous sap that can be chewed like gum after it hardens. The common name comes from the leaves, which tend to be aligned north-south.

Rosinweed

Scientific name:	*Silphium integrifolium*
Family:	Aster
Flower type:	Compound flower head, $2\frac{1}{2}$ inches (6.25cm) in diameter
Flowering period:	June–September
Flower color:	Yellow
Leaf type:	Large, rough, slightly toothed, sessile
Height:	2–6 feet (60–180cm)
Habitat:	Prairies
Range:	Central eastern North America

A tall plant of the open prairie, Rosinweed has rather stout, hairy stems bearing comparatively large, rough-surfaced leaves that are usually slightly toothed along the edges. The leaves are dark green and are arranged in opposite pairs along the stem, springing directly from it without stalks. The flower heads are daisy-like, with fairly long, yellow ray florets arranged round a yellow central disk. There are 17 species in this genus found in North America, most of them located in eastern and central United States.

Cup-plant ▶

Scientific name:	*Silphium perfoliatum*
Family:	Aster
Flower type:	Compound flower head, 2–3 inches (5–8cm) in diameter
Flowering period:	July–September
Flower color:	Yellow
Leaf type:	Large, ovate, perfoliate, roughly toothed
Height:	3–8 feet (90–250cm)
Habitat:	Prairies
Range:	Central eastern North America

A very tall plant, Cup-plant has stout, square stems bearing large, ovate, perfoliate leaves that are sometimes sharply toothed along the edges. The upper leaves are united at the base, forming a cup. The flower heads are daisy-like, with many bright yellow ray florets around a darker yellow central disk. American Indians made a tea from the roots to treat bleeding of the lungs, back and chest pains and as an emetic. Traditionally, root tea was also used for internal bruising, liver ailments and ulcers, but the potential toxicity of the plant has not yet been established.

Rocky, Stony, Dry and Sandy Habitats

Sego Lily

Scientific name:	*Calochortus nuttallii*
Family:	Lily
Flower type:	Radially symmetrical, 1–2 inches (2.5–5cm) in diameter
Flowering period:	May–June
Flower color:	White
Leaf type:	Long, linear, narrow
Height:	6–18 inches (15–45cm)
Habitat:	Dry soil on plains and sagebrush, coniferous woodland
Range:	Western half of central United States

Although it is rather a small plant, Sego Lily is notable for being Utah's state flower. It has a stout, straight stem, usually without branches, with several long, narrow leaves along its length. The bowl-shaped flowers are usually white but are sometimes tinted pink or lavender, and have three very broad, rounded petals and three shorter, pointed sepals. They are borne in a loose umbel-like cluster, with a maximum of three flowers on each stem. The petals are marked with deep yellow at the base, with a fringe around the paler, circular central gland, and red or purple crescent marks above.

Blackfoot Daisy

Scientific name:	*Melampodium leucanthum*
Family:	Aster
Flower type:	Compound flower head, 1 inch (2.5cm) in diameter
Flowering period:	March–September
Flower color:	White
Leaf type:	Long, narrow, sessile
Height:	6–18 inches (15–45cm)
Habitat:	Rocky deserts, dry plains
Range:	South United States

Blackfoot Daisy is a low, rather bushy plant, with long, narrow, sessile hairy leaves arranged in opposite pairs. The solitary flower heads are borne at the end of branching stems and have a small yellow central disk and between 8-10 broad white ray florets with toothed tips. White Zinnia or Desert Zinnia (*Zinnia acerosa*) is found in much the same range and habitat as Blackfoot Daisy and is almost identical in appearance, except that the flower heads have fewer, broader rays and a base with overlapping scales.

HOT ROCK PENSTEMON

Scientific name:	*Penstemon deustus*
Family:	Figwort
Flower type:	Tubular, with two symmetrical halves, $\frac{1}{2}$–$\frac{3}{4}$ inch (1.25–1.88cm) in length
Flowering period:	June–July
Flower color:	White
Leaf type:	Long, ovate, sharply toothed
Height:	9–24 inches (22–60cm)
Habitat:	Open, rocky ground
Range:	West United States

Hot Rock Penstemon is unusual in that it is one of the few species of penstemon to have white flowers. It has clustered stems springing from a woody base, with long, ovate, bright green and sharply toothed leaves arranged closely together in opposite pairs. The flowers are tubular, with two symmetrical halves, and are arranged in whorls in the axils of leaf-like bracts, creating an elongated, upright cluster. The slightly unpleasant smell that is typical of many penstemons is stronger in Hot Rock Penstemon.

ROCKMAT; ROCK-SPIRAEA

Scientific name:	*Petrophyton caespitosum*
Family:	Rose
Flower type:	Long, rounded cluster, $\frac{3}{4}$–1$\frac{1}{2}$ inches (1.88–3.75cm) in diameter
Flowering period:	July–August
Flower color:	White
Leaf type:	Long, narrow
Height:	2–4 inches (5–10cm)
Habitat:	Crevices in bare rock
Range:	Southwest United States

Rockmat clings to tiny crevices in bare rock and has many gray, hairy, woody stems and numerous silky leaves that cover the surrounding area in a very thick mat of vegetation. The leaves are long and narrow but quite small, and the flowers are borne at the end of short stalks, in an elongated, round-ended cluster that looks rather like a small bottle-brush. They are white, but sometimes tinged with pink or brown, and have five sepals, five petals, 15-20 stamens and three to five pistils. There are only three species of this genus in North America, and the other two – Chelan Rockmat (*P. cinerascens*) and Olympic Mountain Rockmat (*P. hendersonii*), are found only in limited areas in Washington state.

Erect Dayflower; Slender Dayflower

Scientific name:	*Commelina erecta*
Family:	Spiderwort
Flower type:	Irregular with two symmetrical halves, 1 inch (2.5cm) in diameter
Flowering period:	May–September
Flower color:	Blue
Leaf type:	Lanceolate, narrow, sheathing
Height:	14 inches (35cm)
Habitat:	Sandy or rocky soil, open woods, overgrown ground
Range:	Central southern United States, parts of the east

Erect Dayflower can be quite variable in appearance, but is usually a smallish perennial with some trailing stems that root at the leaf nodes. The leaves are very long and narrow and sheath the stem, and the flowers are borne in small clusters at the top of the erect stems. They have two large, broad upper blue petals and one smaller whitish lower one, and each flower blooms for only one day, hence the common name. The leaves of all the plants in this species have been traditionally made into a tea to treat sore throats, urinary infections and dysentery, and for detoxifying. There are eight species of dayflower found in the United States, all of them very similar in appearance and all found in the southwest. Asiatic Dayflower (*C. Communis*) has been introduced from Asia, and is a troublesome weed in many areas.

Elegant Brodiaea; Harvest Brodiaea

Scientific name:	*Brodiaea elegans*
Family:	Lily
Flower type:	Trumpet-shaped, 1–1½ inches (2.5–3.75cm) in length
Flowering period:	April–July
Flower color:	Purple
Leaf type:	Long, narrow, basal
Height:	4–20 inches (10–50cm)
Habitat:	Dry, stony ground
Range:	West United States

The leaves of Elegant Brodiaea are long, narrow and basal, but they have usually totally disappeared by the time the flower comes out. The flower is trumpet-shaped, and ranges from purple to violet-blue in color. There are usually several on each plant, held in a loose umbel cluster at the end of the bare stalk. Another very similar species, *B. coronaria*, is also commonly known as Harvest Brodiaea. There are around 37 species in this genus in North America, all found in the west half of the continent. American Indians once ate the bulbs, calling them "grass nuts".

Chinese Houses

Scientific name:	*Collinsia heterophylla*
Family:	Figwort
Flower type:	Elongated cluster, each flower $\frac{3}{4}$ inch (1.88cm) in length
Flowering period:	April–June
Flower color:	Purple
Leaf type:	Lanceolate, scalloped
Height:	12–26 inches (30–65cm)
Habitat:	Dry, sandy, shaded soil
Range:	Southern California

When it is in flower it is immediately apparent why this wildflower is called Chinese Houses – the flowers are arranged in rings of reducing diameter up the length of the upper part of the stem, creating an inflorescence that looks just like a Chinese pagoda. The flowers are usually purple, lavender or bluish in color, but can sometimes be white, with two paler petals standing upright and two deeper-colored lying horizontal, and a fifth petal folded in the middle. Chinese Houses has only a few leaves, which are lanceolate with scalloped edges, and arranged in opposite pairs.

Sharp-lobed Hepatica

Scientific name:	*Hepatica nobilis var. acuta (Anemone acutiloba)*
Family:	Buttercup
Flower type:	Radially symmetrical, $\frac{1}{2}$–1 inch (1.25–2.5cm) in diameter
Flowering period:	February–June
Flower color:	Purple
Leaf type:	Basal, three-lobed, lobes lanceolate and pointed
Height:	4–8 inches (10–20cm)
Habitat:	Dry, rocky woodland
Range:	Northeast and eastern North America

Sharp-lobed Hepatica is a low-growing plant with basal leaves, each of which is borne at the end of a stalk and has three broadly lanceolate lobes with pointed tips. Each plant has several flower stalks, each terminating in a pretty flower with five to nine petal-like sepals. The flowers can be pale purple, lavender-blue, pink or white in color. There are only two species of hepatica in North America, both found in the same general area – the other is Round-lobed Hepatica (*H. nobilis* var. *obtusa*). They are closely related to anemones, and some experts place them in the genus *Anemone*.

Round-lobed Hepatica; Liverwort

Scientific name:	*Hepatica nobilis var. obtusa (Anemone americana)*
Family:	Buttercup
Flower type:	Radially symmetrical, $\frac{1}{2}$–1 inch (1.25–2.5cm) in diameter
Flowering period:	March–June
Flower color:	Purple
Leaf type:	Basal, three-lobed, lobes rounded
Height:	4–8 inches (10–20cm)
Habitat:	Dry, rocky woodland
Range:	Northeast and eastern North America

One of the wildflowers of very early spring, Round-lobed Hepatica is a small plant with basal leaves, each of which is borne at the end of a stalk and has three rounded lobes. There are usually several flower stalks on every plant, each ending in an attractive flower with no petals but five to nine petal-like sepals. The flowers can be pale purple, lavender-blue, pink or white in color. Early herbalists used this plant to treat liver ailments, hence its alternative common name of Liverwort. It was also used as an appetite stimulant and as a tonic, but it contains irritating compounds so is potentially risky to use.

Davidson's Penstemon

Scientific name:	*Penstemon davidsonii*
Family:	Figwort
Flower type:	Tubular, with two symmetrical halves, $\frac{3}{4}$–$1\frac{1}{2}$ inches (1.88–3.75cm) in length
Flowering period:	June–August
Flower color:	Purple
Leaf type:	Long, oval, sometimes toothed
Height:	2–6 inches (5–15cm)
Habitat:	Rock ledges
Range:	British Columbia, west United States

A low-growing, mat-forming plant, Davidson's Penstemon grows on rock ledges up to quite high elevations. It has woody stems, with many long, oval leaves arranged closely together in opposite pairs. In the northern part of its range the leaves are toothed, but in the south they are not. The flowers are tubular, with two symmetrical halves, closely clustered together on short, upright stems. They are purple to lavender-blue in color. Plants often grow in dense colonies, forming a carpet of bright color over the bare rock.

Shrubby Penstemon; Lowbush Penstemon

Scientific name:	*Penstemon fruticosus*
Family:	Figwort
Flower type:	Tubular, with two symmetrical halves, 1–2 inches (2.5–5cm) in length
Flowering period:	June–August
Flower color:	Purple
Leaf type:	Long, lanceolate or ovate, sometimes toothed
Height:	6–18 inches (15–45cm)
Habitat:	Rocky open or wooded ground
Range:	Southern British Columbia, northwest United States

A broad, bushy plant, Shrubby Penstemon grows on open and wooded rocky ground to quite high elevations. It has many long, lanceolate or ovate, bright green leaves, which may sometimes be toothed. The flowers are tubular, with two symmetrical halves, closely clustered together on short, upright stems. They are large and showy, pale purple to lavender-blue in color and plants often grow in dense colonies, forming a carpet of color over banks and rocks. There are around 210 species of penstemon in North America, most of which are concentrated across the western half of the continent.

HAIRY BEARDTONGUE

Scientific name:	*Penstemon hirsutus*
Family:	Figwort
Flower type:	Elongated cluster, each flower 1–1½ inches (2.5–3.75cm) in length
Flowering period:	May–July
Flower color:	Purple
Leaf type:	Long, narrow, oblong, sometimes toothed
Height:	10–36 inches (25–90cm)
Habitat:	Dry, rocky ground
Range:	Ontario, northeast United States

Hairy Beardtongue is a slender plant with long and narrow, oblong to lanceolate, smooth, pale green leaves arranged in opposite pairs along a softly hairy stem. The edges of the leaves are sometimes toothed, sometimes plain. The flowers are long and tubular, with two symmetrical halves, and are purple to lavender outside, but white inside. They form a loose, open cluster at the end of long stalks. The stamens are long and the fifth, sterile stamen has a small collection of hairs at the tip that protrude beyond the flower opening giving rise to the name Beardtongue.

Purple Mountain Saxifrage

Scientific name:	*Saxifraga oppositifolia*
Family:	Saxifrage
Flower type:	Radially symmetrical, $\frac{1}{2}$ inch (1.25cm) in diameter
Flowering period:	June–August
Flower color:	Purple
Leaf type:	Small, ovate, hairy-edged
Height:	1–4 inches (2.5–10cm)
Habitat:	Rocks, ledges and cliffs
Range:	Across northern North America

A low-growing plant, Purple Mountain Saxifrage forms dense mats covering the ground. Its stems are thickly clustered with small, ovate leaves that are arranged in opposite pairs, with more leaves on the lower part of the stem and less towards the tip. The leaves are sometimes tinged with purple, and have hairy edges. The flowers are bright pink or rose-purple in color and there is one borne at the tip of each stem. There are around 70 species in this genus across North America, most of which prefer cool or cold regions. Other species of saxifrage found in the same general area as Purple Mountain Saxifrage include White Mountain Saxifrage (*S. paniculata*), with white flowers and basal leaves, and Yellow Mountain Saxifrage (*S. aizoides*), with bright yellow flowers.

Mojave Aster ▲

Scientific name:	*Xylorhiza tortifolia*
Family:	Aster
Flower type:	Compound flower head, 2 inches (5cm) in diameter
Flowering period:	March–September
Flower color:	Purple
Leaf type:	Long, lanceolate, toothed
Height:	10–36 inches (25–90cm)
Habitat:	Dry, rocky desert
Range:	Southwest United States

Despite its rather inhospitable habitat, Mojave Aster can spread into quite large clumps. It is a medium-sized plant with leafy stems that spring from a woody base. The leaves are only on the lower half of the stems, and are gray-green, long, narrowly lanceolate, with spiny teeth. They are usually covered with a fine layer of grayish hair. The flower heads are comparatively large, with a central yellow disk and numerous purple to pale violet ray florets, and are borne at the tip of the stems. They appear for varying periods between March and September, depending on rainfall.

Autumn Wild Onion

Scientific name:	*Allium stellatum*
Family:	Lily
Flower type:	Rounded umbel cluster, 2½ inches (6.25cm) in diameter
Flowering period:	June–August
Flower color:	Pink
Leaf type:	Basal, narrow, linear
Height:	12–22 inches (30–55cm)
Habitat:	Rocky slopes, stony prairies
Range:	Central North America

Autumn Wild Onion has narrow, linear, grass-like, basal leaves, and an umbel cluster of flowers in a rounded dome shape at the end of a slender bare stalk. The flowers range from pink to lavender in color and have three pointed, very similar sepals and petals. They are very like those of Nodding Onion (*A. cernuum*), except that they are held erect rather than drooping. Autumn Wild Onion grows from a small bulb that has a strong scent of onion, and also tastes of onion. Early settlers ate them, either raw or parboiled, and also used them to treat colds and to keep flies and insects away.

Showy Milkweed ▲

Scientific name:	*Asclepias speciosa*
Family:	Milkweed
Flower type:	Rounded cluster, each flower $\frac{3}{4}$ inch (1.88cm) in diameter
Flowering period:	June–August
Flower color:	Pink
Leaf type:	Oblong to ovate, large, opposite
Height:	1–6 feet (30–180cm)
Habitat:	Gravel slopes, dry areas, brush
Range:	Western United States

Some milkweeds are highly poisonous, but Showy Milkweed is one of the non-toxic varieties. It is a velvety-gray plant, with a stout stem and long, large, oblong to ovate leaves arranged in opposite pairs. The sweetly scented flowers are borne in dense, rounded umbel clusters on short stalks springing from the upper leaf axils, and at the top of the stem. They are pink and star-like, with five petals and five reddish sepals, and five erect hoods that curve inwards at the center of each flower. Showy Milkweed is a perennial that often spreads to form quite large clumps, and it is one of the most widely distributed species of milkweed.

Sagebrush Mariposa Lily

Scientific name:	*Calochortus macrocarpus*
Family:	Lily
Flower type:	Radially symmetrical, 1–2$\frac{1}{2}$ inches (2.5–6.25cm) in diameter
Flowering period:	May–August
Flower color:	Pink
Leaf type:	Long, linear, narrow
Height:	9–22 inches (22–55cm)
Habitat:	Dry soil, sagebrush, coniferous forest
Range:	Eastern North America

Sagebrush Mariposa Lily has a rather stout, straight stem, with several long, narrow leaves arranged alternately along its length. The bowl-shaped flowers appear roughly triangular from above, with three broad, fan-like petals and three narrow, pointed sepals. They are borne in loose cluster – there is usually a maximum of three flowers on each stem. The petals are pink to lavender, with a whitish oblong gland at the base of each; the line where the two colors join is fringed, with a deeper pink to lilac crescent mark above. Sagebrush Mariposa Lily is fairly common in the northwest area of its range.

Farewell-to-spring

Scientific name:	*Clarkia amoena*
Family:	Evening-primrose
Flower type:	Radially symmetrical, 1–1½ inches (2.5–3.75cm) in diameter
Flowering period:	June–August
Flower color:	Pink
Leaf type:	Long, lanceolate
Height:	8–34 inches (20–85cm)
Habitat:	Dry slopes, brushy woodland clearings
Range:	West North America

Since it only comes into flower as spring turns into summer, Farewell-to-spring is aptly named. It varies widely in height, but is generally a slender, open plant with long-lanceolate leaves and fairly small bowl-shaped flowers. The four broad petals are shiny pink with a deeper pink to purple, rectangular blotch towards the base. The flowers are borne in a loose cluster, and they open during the day and remain closed at night. There are around 30 species in this genus in North America, almost all in California and its immediate neighboring states.

Tall Corydalis; Pink Corydalis

Scientific name:	*Corydalis sempervirens*
Family:	Fumitory
Flower type:	Tubular sac-like, $\frac{1}{2}$ inch (1.25cm) in length
Flowering period:	June–September
Flower color:	Pink
Leaf type:	Pinnately divided, three-lobed leaflets
Height:	6–22 inches (15–55cm)
Habitat:	Dry, rocky open areas, disturbed ground
Range:	Northeast North America, western Canada

The flowers of Tall Corydalis are instantly recognizable as they are bright pink with yellow tips. They are tubular and sac-like in shape, drooping from short stalks and arranged in a fairly tight raceme cluster at the top of erect, branching stems. The blue-green leaves are pinnately divided, with leaflets that have three very rounded lobes. When the plant is not in flower, the blue tinge to the leaf color distinguishes it from other species of corydalis. There are several species in this genus found in North America, including Golden Corydalis (*C. aurea*), which has an all-yellow flower. Historically, the roots of most species of corydalis were used to make a tea to treat menstrual problems, dysentery and diarrhea, but even quite small doses can be toxic.

Wild Bleeding Heart ▶

Scientific name:	*Dicentra eximia*
Family:	Fumitory
Flower type:	Heart-shaped, $\frac{3}{4}$ inch (1.88cm) in length
Flowering period:	May–September
Flower color:	Pink
Leaf type:	Basal, pinnately compound, divided
Height:	12–18 inches (30–45cm)
Habitat:	Rocky woodland
Range:	Eastern United States

Wild Bleeding Heart is a perennial with several long, feathery, pinnately compound, divided leaves springing from the base of the plant. The deep pink flowers are borne in a loose, branching raceme cluster at the end of a bare stalk and are shaped rather like a bleeding heart, with two outer petals forming the heart and the inner two protruding at the base to look like a drop of blood. Wild Bleeding Heart is native to North America, but there is also a very similar Asian species, Asian Bleeding Heart (*D. Spectabilis*), which is cultivated in gardens and has escaped to the wild in some areas. Asian Bleeding Heart has larger, showier flowers.

Scarlet Gaura

Scientific name:	*Gaura coccinea*
Family:	Evening-primrose
Flower type:	Elongated cluster, each flower $\frac{1}{2}$ inch (1.25cm) in diameter
Flowering period:	June–July
Flower color:	Pink
Leaf type:	Long, narrow, lanceolate
Height:	8–20 inches (20–50cm)
Habitat:	Sandy, dry soil, particularly in coniferous woodland
Range:	Central North America, some areas in west United States

Despite its name, Scarlet Gaura does not have scarlet flowers – when they first open they are white but by the following day they have turned pink and they continue to deepen in color throughout the day, although they only last for 24 hours. The plant itself has very leafy, branching hairy stems, which are gray-green in color. The leaves are long and narrow, roughly lanceolate in shape, finely hairy and very thickly crowded together. The flowers are borne in loose raceme clusters at the end of the stems, and since they are at different stages there are often several shades of pink together on one stem.

Cliff Maids; Siskiyou Lewisia

▼

Scientific name:	*Lewisia cotyledon*
Family:	Purslane
Flower type:	Radially symmetrical, 1–$1\frac{1}{4}$ inches (2.5–3.12cm) in diameter
Flowering period:	April–May
Flower color:	Pink
Leaf type:	Basal rosette, spatulate
Height:	6–12 inches (15–30cm)
Habitat:	Rock crevices
Range:	Southwest Oregon, northern California

Cliff Maids often seems to spring from the bare rock, with its roots wedged into a tiny crevice from which grows a tight basal rosette of spatulate, frilly-edged and succulent bluish-green leaves. The flowers are borne at the end of branching stalks and are brightly candy-striped in pink and white, or sometimes a plain deep pink. The succulent leaves help the plant to retain moisture, so it is very well adapted to its bare habitat. Since it is so attractive it may be tempting to replant specimens in the garden, but it will only survive for a short time even in the stoniest, driest soil. There are 15 species in this genus across North America.

Wild Bergamot

Scientific name:	*Monarda fistulosa*
Family:	Mint
Flower type:	Rounded cluster, each flower 1 inch (2.5cm) in length
Flowering period:	July–August
Flower color:	Pink
Leaf type:	Lanceolate, toothed, opposite
Height:	2–5 feet (60–150cm)
Habitat:	Dry, open ground
Range:	Most of North America, except Florida, Maritime Provinces and Newfoundland

Wild Bergamot is a very showy perennial, with a single square stem terminating in a dense, round cluster of pink to lavender flowers. The flowers are long with two lips, the upper with two lobes and the lower with three. Beneath the flower head there is a cluster of leaf-like bracts, which are pale green, often tinted with pink. The true leaves are gray-green, lanceolate and toothed and arranged in opposite pairs on the stem. American Indians made a tea from the leaves to treat colic and flatulence and early physicians also used it to expel gas and worms. The essential oil has been proved to have anesthetic, anti-inflammatory, worm-expelling and antioxidant properties.

Coyote Mint

Scientific name:	*Monardella odoratissima*
Family:	Mint
Flower type:	Rounded cluster, each flower $\frac{1}{4}$ inch (1.25cm) in diameter
Flowering period:	July–September
Flower color:	Pink
Leaf type:	Long, lanceolate
Height:	5–20 inches (12–50cm)
Habitat:	Dry, rocky soil
Range:	West and south North America

A very attractive, aromatic plant, Coyote Mint has several erect, grayish stems, which have comparatively long, lanceolate and gray-green leaves arranged in opposite pairs. The stems end in a dense, round flower head that is made up of many pink to white flowers. These are irregular in shape but with two symmetrical halves, and have five lobes, four stamens and purplish, ovate bracts. There are several very similar-looking species of Coyote Mint found in the west, varying only in details of the length of bracts and calyx, and in the flower head diameter, so it may be difficult to make a firm identification.

Purple Locoweed; Colorado Locoweed

Scientific name:	*Oxytropis lambertii*
Family:	Pea
Flower type:	Elongated cluster, $\frac{1}{2}$–1 inch (1.25–2.5cm)
Flowering period:	June–September
Flower color:	Pink
Leaf type:	Basal, pinnately compound, long
Height:	6–18 inches (16–45cm)
Habitat:	Dry, open areas
Range:	Central North America

Although it is an attractive-looking plant, Purple Locoweed is extremely toxic. It is addictive and readily eaten by livestock, to which it is often lethal. It is a medium-sized, erect plant with a stem covered in fine silvery-white hairs and many long, pinnately compound basal leaves with 9-23 stiff leaflets, which are also hairy. The pink, red-purple or bright red flowers are pea-like in shape, and are borne in dense raceme clusters at the end of long stalks. There are usually several flower stalks on each plant.

PALMER'S PENSTEMON; BALLOON FLOWER

Scientific name:	*Penstemon palmeri*
Family:	Figwort
Flower type:	Elongated cluster, each flower 1–1½ inches (2.5–3.75cm) in length
Flowering period:	May–July
Flower color:	Pink
Leaf type:	Long, lanceolate
Height:	26–60 inches (65–150cm)
Habitat:	Open rocky areas
Range:	Southeastern United States

Unlike many other of the species of penstemon, Palmer's Penstemon has very pleasantly scented flowers. It is a rather stout-stemmed plant, with only a few long, lanceolate and smooth leaves, which are arranged in opposite pairs at intervals along the stem. The upper pairs are sometimes joined together at their base, so that the stem appears to pierce them. The bright red-pink to white flowers are all puffed up like little balloons, and are arranged along only one side of the stem to form a long, narrow cluster at the top of the plant. The stamens are quite long and the sterile fifth stamen has a dense tuft of bright yellow hairs at its tip, which protrudes some way beyond the opening of the flower.

Longleaf Phlox

Scientific name:	*Phlox longifolia*
Family:	Phlox
Flower type:	Radially symmetrical, 1 inch (2.5cm) in diameter
Flowering period:	May–July
Flower color:	Pink
Leaf type:	Long, linear, narrow, opposite
Height:	6–18 inches (15–45cm)
Habitat:	Dry, rocky open ground
Range:	West and south United States

An attractive and popular wildflower, Long-leafed Phlox has many variations – a few of which are different enough to be thought of as separate species by some experts. It grows in quite dense clumps over dry, open and rocky ground, and has quite slender stems with long, narrow leaves arranged in opposite pairs. The flowers can be pink, lilac or white in color, and are formed of a slender tube that opens out at the end into five rounded lobes. The flowers are borne in loose clusters and there are often many on each plant. Longleaf Phlox is quite low-growing, so when it is in bloom the flowers form a mat of bright color carpeting the ground.

Moss Pink; Moss Phlox; Mountain Phlox ▲

Scientific name:	*Phlox subulata*
Family:	Phlox
Flower type:	Radially symmetrical, $\frac{3}{4}$ inch (1.88cm) in diameter
Flowering period:	May
Flower color:	Pink
Leaf type:	Narrowly linear, opposite
Height:	Creeper, 6 inches (15cm)
Habitat:	Dry, sandy open ground; rocky slopes
Range:	Northeast North America

Moss Pink is a creeper, forming a mat of vegetation that resembles moss – hence its common name. It grows over dry, sandy and rocky ground, and has slender stems bearing long, narrow needle-like leaves arranged in opposite pairs close together. The flowers can be pink, lavender or sometimes white, and are formed of a slender tube that opens out into five rounded lobes, each with a central notch. Moss Pink is often cultivated for rock gardens. Its alternative common name, Moss Phlox, is also the common name of *P. hoodii*, which has white to pale violet flowers and is a prairie plant.

Scarlet Larkspur; Cardinal Larkspur

Scientific name:	*Delphinium cardinale*
Family:	Buttercup
Flower type:	Radially symmetrical, $\frac{3}{4}$–1 inch (1.88–2.5cm) in diameter
Flowering period:	May–July
Flower color:	Red
Leaf type:	Orbicular, lobed; lobes deeply cut, toothed
Height:	1–9 feet (30–270cm)
Habitat:	Rocky openings
Range:	Central and southern California

Although it has a rather limited range compared to some other wildflowers, Scarlet Larkspur is very noticeable when it is in bloom because of its showy, bright red flowers. It is a tall plant with rounded, lobed leaves, with the leaflets very deeply cut and toothed. The stem terminates in a loose spike of scarlet flowers, which have five broad, forward-pointing sepals, the top one having a long, backward-pointing spur. The red color of the flowers attracts hummingbirds to pollinate the plant, and also gives rise to the plant's alternative common name of Cardinal Larkspur as it is the same shade as a cardinal's robes. The very similar Red Larkspur (*D. nudicale*) is found in much the same range, but is generally a smaller plant with red-orange flowers.

Golden-beard Penstemon

Scientific name:	*Penstemon barbatus*
Family:	Figwort
Flower type:	Elongated cluster, each flower 1–1½ inches (2.5–3.75cm) in length
Flowering period:	July–September
Flower color:	Red
Leaf type:	Long, narrow
Height:	26–36 inches (65–90cm)
Habitat:	Dry rocky slopes
Range:	South United States

Golden-beard Penstemon is a slender plant with only a few long and narrow, smooth, gray-green leaves, which are arranged in opposite pairs along the upright stem. The bright scarlet flowers are long and irregular, with two symmetrical halves, and droop from short stalks that spring from the upper leaf axils. They form a long, loose cluster at the top of the plant. The stamens are long and there is a small tuft of bright yellow hairs that protrude beyond them through the flower opening – hence the golden-beard in the common name.

Scarlet Bugler

Scientific name:	*Penstemon centranthifolius*
Family:	Figwort
Flower type:	Elongated cluster, each flower 1–1½ (2.5–3.75cm) in length
Flowering period:	May–July
Flower color:	Red
Leaf type:	Long, spatulate or lanceolate
Height:	12–45 inches (30–112cm)
Habitat:	Dry, open disturbed soil
Range:	Southwest United States

Although it looks very similar to Golden-beard Penstemon (*P. barbatus*), Scarlet Bugler is found further west and its flowers are different in shape. It is a slender plant with long, spatulate or lanceolate leaves, which are sparsely arranged in opposite pairs along the stem. The bright scarlet flowers are long and narrow and almost radially symmetrical; they droop gently from short stalks, and form a long, narrow, loose cluster at the top of the plant. Scarlet Bugler often grows in widespread dense patches, turning the ground into a sea of red.

Rock Penstemon; Cliff Penstemon

Scientific name:	*Penstemon rupicola*
Family:	Figwort
Flower type:	Tubular, with two symmetrical halves, 1–1½ inches (2.5–3.75cm) in length
Flowering period:	June–August
Flower color:	Red
Leaf type:	Long, ovate, thick, irregularly toothed
Height:	Creeper, 6 inches (15cm)
Habitat:	Rock ledges and slopes
Range:	West United States

A low-growing creeper, Rock Penstemon grows on rock ledges, rocky slopes and cliffs. It has reclining stems, with many long, ovate, thick leaves, which have small, irregular teeth and are arranged closely together in opposite pairs. As the plant spreads, it forms a thick mat over the ground. The flowers are tubular, with two symmetrical halves, clustered together on short, upright stems in a dense raceme cluster. They are bright red or rose-pink in color and as there are many flower stalks very close together the plant forms a bright carpet of color over the ground when it is in bloom.

Indian Pink

Scientific name:	*Silene californica*
Family:	Carnation
Flower type:	Radially symmetrical, 1–1½ inches (2.5–3.75cm) in diameter
Flowering period:	May–July
Flower color:	Red
Leaf type:	Ovate
Height:	8–18 inches (20–45cm)
Habitat:	Dry rocky woodland
Range:	West United States

Although it is quite widespread within its limited range – which as its scientific name suggests is mainly in California – Indian Pink is be no means that common. It is a medium-sized plant, with either trailing or erect, leafy and branching stems. The bright green leaves are ovate, quite long and arranged in opposite pairs. The flowers are a clear bright red in color, with five broad, open petals that are deeply notched at the tips. They are borne at the ends of the stems, usually those that are more erect. There are around 30 species within this genus found in North America, spread across the continent.

Cardinal Catchfly

Scientific name:	*Silene laciniata*
Family:	Carnation
Flower type:	Radially symmetrical, 1–1½ inches (2.5–3.75cm) in diameter
Flowering period:	May–July
Flower color:	Red
Leaf type:	Ovate
Height:	18–40 inches (45–100cm)
Habitat:	Dry rocky woodland
Range:	Southwest United States

Cardinal Catchfly is found in southern California and across into Texas, so its range partly overlaps that of Indian Pink (*S. californica*), which it somewhat resembles. Its flowers are bright red – the color of a cardinal's robes, hence the common name. They are borne at the ends of the stems and have five broad, open petals that are deeply notched at the tips. Cardinal Catchfly is a fairly tall plant, with erect, leafy and branching stems. The bright green leaves are ovate, comparatively long and arranged in opposite pairs. Catchfly is a common name for many members of the genus Silene – it refers to the sticky hairs on the stems that catch insects.

Fire Pink

◀▶

Scientific name:	*Silene virginica*
Family:	Carnation
Flower type:	Radially symmetrical, $1\frac{1}{2}$ inches (3.75cm) in diameter
Flowering period:	April–July
Flower color:	Red
Leaf type:	Basal, spatulate or lanceolate
Height:	8–30 inches (20–75cm)
Habitat:	Dry, sandy woodland
Range:	Southeast United States

A fairly tall plant, Fire Pink has a mixture of both erect and trailing stems, which are leafy, slender and branching. The bright green basal leaves are spatulate to lanceolate, while those on the stem are comparatively long, sessile and arranged in opposite pairs. The bright red flowers are borne in loose clusters at the ends of the stems. They have five narrow, open petals that are deeply divided at the tips, and sepals that are joined to form a tube. Fire Pink resembles Indian Pink (*S. californica*) and Cardinal Catchfly (*S. laciniata*) but is found in the east, not the west.

Texas Betony; Scarlet Hedge Nettle

Scientific name:	*Stachys coccinea*
Family:	Mint
Flower type:	Elongated spike, each flower $\frac{3}{4}$–1 inch (1.88–2.5cm) in length
Flowering period:	March–September
Flower color:	Red
Leaf type:	Deltoid, toothed
Height:	36–40 inches (90–100cm)
Habitat:	Rock crevices with rich soil
Range:	South United States

Despite its alternative common name, Texas Betony is not a stinging plant although it is covered in a fine coating of hair that looks like that of true nettles. It is an erect, leafy plant, with a stout, square stem bearing nearly triangular, toothed leaves that are arranged in opposite pairs. The bright red to scarlet flowers are tubular, with the upper lip turning upwards and the lower downwards. They are borne in whorls at intervals along the stem, creating an elongated spike. There are around 30 species of this genus across North America, but others in the same range have pink flowers rather than red.

Scarlet Globe-mallow; Red False Mallow ▼ ▶

Scientific name:	*Sphaeralcea coccinea*
Family:	Mallow
Flower type:	Radially symmetrical, 1–1½ inches (2.5–3.75cm) in diameter
Flowering period:	May–August
Flower color:	Orange
Leaf type:	Palmately dissected, toothed
Height:	18–22 inches (45–55cm)
Habitat:	Arid, open ground
Range:	Central United States

Scarlet Globe-mallow is fairly easy to recognize as a species because of its bright orange flowers with their five broad petals, which are unusual in its range. However, it may be more difficult to identify it precisely, as there are other, very similar species of globe-mallow within the same general area. Scarlet Globe-mallow is a leafy, branching, softly hairy plant, with palmately dissected, irregularly toothed leaves. The flowers are orange to orange-red, and are borne in narrow clusters that spring from the upper leaf axils. Scaly Globe-mallow (*S. leptophylla*) shares the same range in the south and has gray hairs that are more like scales.

Great Plains Paintbrush; Downy Painted-cup

Scientific name:	*Castilleja sessiliflora*
Family:	Figwort
Flower type:	Sickle-shaped, 1–2½ inches (2.5–6,25cm) in length
Flowering period:	March–September
Flower color:	Yellow
Leaf type:	Lower narrow, upper lobed
Height:	6–12 inches (15–30cm)
Habitat:	Dry, rocky ground; open coniferous forests
Range:	Great Plains to Texas and Arizona

Great Plains Paintbrush has multiple, clustered, hairy stems, with long, narrow lower leaves and upper leaves that usually have three to five rather narrow lobes. The leaves are also softly hairy and each plant has many, all clustered together and curving outwards from the stems. The yellow-pink flowers are not very distinctive amongst the leaves – they are long and sickle-shaped, with a very protruding curved corolla and yellow to pink bracts. Designed to thrive in poor soil, Great Plains Paintbrush is a very small and compact plant in really dry areas, but becomes larger and looser where conditions are more conducive to growth.

Canyon Dudleya

Scientific name:	*Dudleya cymosa*
Family:	Stonecrop
Flower type:	Rounded cluster, each flower $\frac{1}{2}$ inch (1.25cm) in length
Flowering period:	April–July
Flower color:	Yellow
Leaf type:	Basal rosette, lanceolate, succulent
Height:	5–9 inches (12–22cm)
Habitat:	Rocky ground
Range:	Southwest United States

A low, compact plant, Canyon Dudleya has a tight basal rosette of lanceolate, pointed and thick, fleshy leaves, which are gray-green in color, often with a reddish tinge. The small, erect yellow flowers are borne on reddish stalks in a dense, branching flat-topped cluster. The main flower stalk grows from a leaf axil rather than from the center of the rosette, and sometimes has very small leaves toward the bottom half. There are several species of Dudleya in California and they look similar and also often hybridize, so it may be difficult to make a firm identification.

WESTERN WALLFLOWER ▲

Scientific name:	*Erysimum capitatum*
Family:	Mustard
Flower type:	Radially symmetrical, $\frac{3}{4}$ inch (1.88cm) in diameter
Flowering period:	March–July
Flower color:	Yellow
Leaf type:	Basal rosette; stem leaves; narrow, lanceolate, toothed
Height:	8–34 inches (20–85cm)
Habitat:	Dry, stony ground
Range:	West North America

Western Wallflower has erect stems, sometimes branching towards the top, with some alternate stem leaves towards the base, as well as a rosette of leaves at the bottom. All the leaves are narrowly lanceolate, with small teeth along each edge. The flowers have four petals and can range in color from yellow, through orange and burnt orange to almost maroon. They are borne in a dense and showy raceme cluster at the end of each of the stems. There are around 25 species of wallflower in North America, including Plains Wallflower (*E. asperum*) which is extremely similar to Western Wallflower, but is generally found slightly further to east. Where their ranges overlap the two species often interbreed, which can make a firm identification rather difficult.

HOARY PUCCOON; INDIAN-PAINT

Scientific name:	*Lithospermum canescens*
Family:	Borage
Flower type:	Rounded cluster, each flower $\frac{1}{2}$ inch (1.25cm) in diameter
Flowering period:	April–June
Flower color:	Yellow
Leaf type:	Linear, sessile
Height:	4–18 inches (10–45cm)
Habitat:	Dry, rocky and sandy ground
Range:	Central Canada to Southeast United States

A small plant, the leaves and stems of Hoary Puccoon are covered with fine, soft, grayish hairs, making it look hoary – hence the first part of the common name. Puccoon comes from an American Indian word for a plant that provides dye. The leaves are narrowly lanceolate and sessile, and arranged alternately along the stems, which terminate in a rounded cluster of yellow-orange flowers. The flowers are tubular, with five rounded, open lobes. American Indians used a tea made from the leaves of Hoary Puccoon to wash down patients in fever to prevent convulsions. Hairy Puccoon (*L. caroliniense*) is very similar in appearance to Hoary Puccoon, but has coarser hairs.

NORTHERN BLAZINGSTAR

Scientific name:	*Mentzelia laevicaulis (Nuttallia laevicaulis)*
Family:	Stickleaf
Flower type:	Radially symmetrical, 2–5 inches (5–12cm) in diameter
Flowering period:	July–September
Flower color:	Yellow
Leaf type:	Long, narrow, lanceolate, irregularly toothed
Height:	12–32 inches (30–80cm)
Habitat:	Dry, gravelly or sandy soil
Range:	Western North America

Despite its preference for arid habitat areas, Northern Blazingstar has very showy and attractive yellow flowers. It is a medium-height plant, with a stout white stem that branches towards the top, each branch bearing a star-like flower with lanceolate, pointed petals. The leaves are long, narrow and lanceolate, with large and irregular teeth and barbed hairs that stick to clothing. Eveningstar (*M. decapetala*) looks very similar but has creamy-white flowers. Despite the similarity in common names, Northern Blazingstar is not related to the *Liatris* genus of blazing stars, which belong to the Aster family.

Common Cinquefoil; Old-field Cinquefoil

Scientific name:	*Potentilla simplex*
Family:	Rose
Flower type:	Radially symmetrical, $\frac{1}{2}$–$\frac{3}{4}$ inch (1.25–1.88cm) in diameter
Flowering period:	March–June
Flower color:	Yellow
Leaf type:	Palmately compound, five long leaflets
Height:	2–6 inches (5–15cm)
Habitat:	Dry, poor soil
Range:	Most of east North America

Common Cinquefoil is a low, spreading plant with supple downy stems and palmately-compound leaves. The leaves have five long, pointed leaflets that are toothed at the tip. The solitary flowers are borne at the end of long stalks that rise from the leaf axils, with the first flower springing from the axil of the second leaf. The flowers are yellow, with five sepals and five rounded petals. Common Cinquefoil is very similar to Indian Strawberry (*Duchesnea indica*), which has three-lobed leaves, and to Canadian Dwarf Cinquefoil (*P. canadensis*), which has smaller five-lobed leaflets and its first flower rising from the axil of the first leaf.

Roadside and Waste Ground

Yarrow; Sneezeweed; Milfoil

Scientific name:	*Achillea millefolium*
Family:	Aster
Flower type:	Flat-topped corymb cluster, each flower 2–5 inches (5–12.5cm) in diameter
Flowering period:	May–October
Flower color:	White
Leaf type:	Long, thin, lance-shaped, and finely pinnately divided
Height:	12–39 inches (300–100cm)
Habitat:	Open areas, fields, waste places
Range:	Across North America

Yarrow is a perennial plant, with aromatic, blue-green, feathery leaves, and tiny white flowers in large, rounded, flat-topped, terminal clusters – although there is also a more unusual rose-pink flowered form, which is sometimes transplanted into gardens. It not only occurs in North America but also in Eurasia, and its Latin name honors the legendary Greek, Achilles, who is supposed to have used a poultice made from the flowers to stop wounds bleeding on the battlefield. Early Americans often used Yarrow for the same purpose, although it can sometimes cause dermatitis.

Pearly Everlasting

Scientific name:	*Anaphalis margaritacea*
Family:	Aster
Flower type:	Flat-topped cluster, each flower $\frac{1}{4}$ inch (0.62cm) in diameter
Flowering period:	July–September
Flower color:	White
Leaf type:	Long and very narrow lanceolate
Height:	1–3 feet (30–90cm)
Habitat:	Dry fields, roadsides, waste ground
Range:	Most of North America

Pearly Everlasting is a perennial plant with a thick, white, woolly stem. It bears long, thin alternate leaves that are smooth and dark green above and densely hairy underneath. The stem is topped with a flat-topped cluster of spherical pearly-white flowers – the male and female flowers grow on separate plants, and the male flower can be quickly and easily distinguished by a yellow tuft to be seen in its center. The flowers remain intact after they are dried, so they are often used in flower arrangements. American Indians used a tea made from this plant to cure colds, coughs and throat infections, and it can also be made into a poultice for burns, sores and bruising.

Indian Hemp

Scientific name:	*Apocynum cannabinum*
Family:	Dogbane
Flower type:	Cyme cluster, each flower $\frac{1}{4}$ inch (0.62cm) in diameter
Flowering period:	June–August
Flower color:	Greenish-white
Leaf type:	Lanceolate to obvate, with a sharply pointed tip
Height:	1–2 feet (30–60cm)
Habitat:	Roadsides, edges of thickets
Range:	Most of North America

Indian Hemp is an erect plant with several branches on the upper stem and numerous whitish flowers borne in terminal clusters. The leaves are pale green above, and usually whitish on the underside. The stem turns red when the plant is mature, and is filled with a milky-white sap. Although this plant is poisonous, American Indians used the berries to make a weak tea for heart problems, and the stem fiber to make cords and cloth. The scientific name *apocynum* means "noxious to dogs" – hence the family name of Dogbane – and animals tend to avoid most of the plants in this genus.

Shepherd's Purse

Scientific name:	*Capsella bursa-pastoris*
Family:	Mustard
Flower type:	Elongated cluster, each flower $\frac{1}{4}$ inch (0.62cm) in diameter
Flowering period:	All year
Flower color:	White
Leaf type:	Lanceolate and lobed
Height:	6–24 inches (15–60cm)
Habitat:	Gardens, waste ground, field edges
Range:	Across North America

Although it originates from Europe, Shepherd's Purse is now found in most areas of the world. It is a small plant with a basal rosette of deeply lobed leaves, although the main stem also has a few smaller, narrower, arrow-shaped, clasping leaves. The small, elongated cluster of flowers is borne at the tip of a long stalk, and the distinctive, elongated heart-shaped seed pods are the same general shape as a medieval shepherd's purse – hence the plant's name. The leaves of Shepherd's Purse can be used in salads, although they may be rather peppery, and the dried seeds as seasoning in soups and stews. A tea made from the seeds and leaves is used medicinally to stop bleeding.

Poison Hemlock

Scientific name:	*Conium maculatum*
Family:	Carrot
Flower type:	Flat-topped umbel cluster, 2 inches (5cm) in diameter
Flowering period:	May–August
Flower color:	White
Leaf type:	Triangular in outline, bipinnate
Height:	3–9 feet (60–300cm)
Habitat:	Waste places
Range:	Much of eastern United States

Introduced from Eurasia, Poison Hemlock is a tall, erect plant with many branches, feathery, dark green, parsley-like leaves and many flat-topped, umbel clusters of flowers. The stems are hollow, grooved and spotted with purple. All parts of the plant are extremely poisonous – eating it causes death by paralyzing the respiratory nerves, and contact can cause dermatitis. It is reputed to be an extract from this plant that was used to kill Socrates, the Greek philosopher. Poison Hemlock is a biennial, so flowers are only produced in its second year. It is a member of the Parsley family, and the leaves produced in its first year have been mistaken for Parsley, with fatal results.

Queen Anne's Lace; Wild Carrot

Scientific name:	*Daucus carota*
Family:	Carrot
Flower type:	Compound umbel cluster, 4–5 inches (10–12cm) in width
Flowering period:	May–October
Flower color:	White
Leaf type:	Long and many pinnate
Height:	12–18 inches (30–45cm)
Habitat:	Waste ground, dry fields, roadsides
Range:	Most of North America

Although Queen Anne's Lace was originally a native of Europe, it was introduced to North America many years ago. It is now also widespread across most of this continent – except for the colder Arctic areas – and in some areas is so plentiful it is considered to be an invasive weed. It is a fairly tall plant, with a stem covered in bristly hairs and feathery green leaves. The attractive white flower clusters often have one single red-purple flower at the center of each cluster. This plant is the ancestor of the carrot, so its leaves smell carrot-like when crushed and its tap root can be cooked and eaten – although it is important to be very sure of the exact identification, as it may be confused with Poison Hemlock.

Flowering Spurge

Scientific name:	*Euphorbia corollata*
Family:	Spurge
Flower type:	Umbel cluster, width 2–10 inches (5–25cm)
Flowering period:	June-September
Flower color:	White
Leaf type:	Lower linear to oval and alternate, upper leaves whorled
Height:	9–36 inches (22–90cm)
Habitat:	Dry open areas, roadsides
Range:	Eastern and central United States, southeastern Canada

A deep-rooted perennial, Flowering Spurge has smooth stems ending in a loose umbel cluster of small, white flowers. Its lower leaves are linear and alternate, but the upper ones are smaller and whorled. It is common on roadsides in eastern states, but does not grow wild further west. American Indians made a poultice from the roots to apply to snakebites, and a tea from the leaves to treat diabetes. A tea made from the roots was also used for rheumatism and as a laxative – the common name Spurge comes from the Latin *expurgare*, meaning to purge. The stems exude a milky sap when cut, which may cause blistering of the skin.

Snow-on-the-mountain ▼

Scientific name:	*Euphorbia marginata*
Family:	Spurge
Flower type:	Loose clusters, each flower $\frac{1}{4}$ inch (0.62cm) in diameter
Flowering period:	June–August
Flower color:	White
Leaf type:	Lower leaves oval and alternate, upper leaves whorled
Height:	1–3 feet (30–90cm)
Habitat:	Waste areas
Range:	Midwest North America

Snow-on-the-mountain is another member of the Spurge family. Its smooth stems end in a loose cluster of small, white flowers, which spring from the center of white-margined bracts. Its lower leaves are linear and alternate, but the upper ones are much smaller and whorled and have white edges. Snow-on-the-mountain is native to the prairie states of the Midwest, but it also grows in other areas of eastern North America, having escaped to the wild from cultivation. The stems exude a milky sap when they are cut or bruised, which may be irritating to the skin.

English Plantain

Scientific name:	*Plantago lanceolata*
Family:	Plantain
Flower type:	Cylindrical head, each flower $\frac{1}{4}$ inch (0.62cm) in length
Flowering period:	April–November
Flower color:	White
Leaf type:	Narrow, lanceolate
Height:	6–22 inches (15–55cm)
Habitat:	Roadsides, waste ground, garden lawns
Range:	Most of North America, except the Arctic regions

As its name suggests, the English Plantain originates from Europe, but it is now spread widely across much of North America and is fully naturalized. It has long, narrow, lance-shaped leaves with three ribs and a short, cylindrical flower head held above the leaves at the end of a bare, grooved stalk. Traditionally, a tea made from the leaves was used to cure coughs and bronchial infections, and its effectiveness has been proven scientifically – it contains a mild antibiotic and has an anti-inflammatory action. The leaves can also be applied to the skin to alleviate insect stings, blisters and ulcers, but in rare cases they may cause dermatitis.

Bouncing Bet; Soapwort

Scientific name:	*Saponaria officinalis*
Family:	Carnation
Flower type:	Rounded cluster, each flower 1 inch (2.5cm) in diameter
Flowering period:	July–September
Flower colour:	White, sometimes tinged pink
Leaf type:	Long, oval
Height:	12–30in (30–75cm)
Habitat:	Roadsides, disturbed areas
Range:	Across North America, except the far north

Bouncing Bet was introduced from its native Europe, and it is now found across most of North America. It spreads quickly via underground stems and soon forms quite large colonies. It is a tall perennial, with a smooth, thick stem that often has one or two branches, and long, oval leaves that are arranged in opposite pairs and have 3-5 conspicuous ribs. The flowers are in dense, rounded terminal clusters and are white, or sometimes very pale pink, and have notched petals. When the foliage is crushed and mixed with water a lather can be generated, hence the common name of Soapwort, while Bouncing Bet comes from an old-fashioned term for a washerwoman. American Indians used a poultice of the leaves to treat boils and Poison Ivy rash, and in Europe a root tea was traditionally used for lung disease, asthma, gall disease and jaundice, but large doses are poisonous.

White Campion; Evening Lychnis; White Cockle

Scientific name:	*Silene latifolia (Lychnis alba)*
Family:	Carnation
Flower type:	Radially symmetrical, 1 inch (2.5cm) in diameter
Flowering period:	June–September
Flower color:	White
Leaf type:	Long, lanceolate
Height:	1–3 feet (30–90cm)
Habitat:	Roadsides, waste ground, fields
Range:	Most of North America, except desert areas

White Campion was introduced from Europe, but is now naturalized across much of North America. It has a many-branched stem, with long, light green, opposite leaves, which are covered in downy hair, and very sweetly scented flowers. The flowers open at night, and are pollinated by moths; male and female flowers are on separate plants. It is very easy to confuse this plant with Night-flowering Catchfly (*S. noctiflora*), which also has hairy leaves and white flowers – the main differences are that Night-flowering Catchfly has sticky hairs and the female flower has only three styles, while the female flowers of White Campion have five styles. Occasionally White Campion has pale pink flowers.

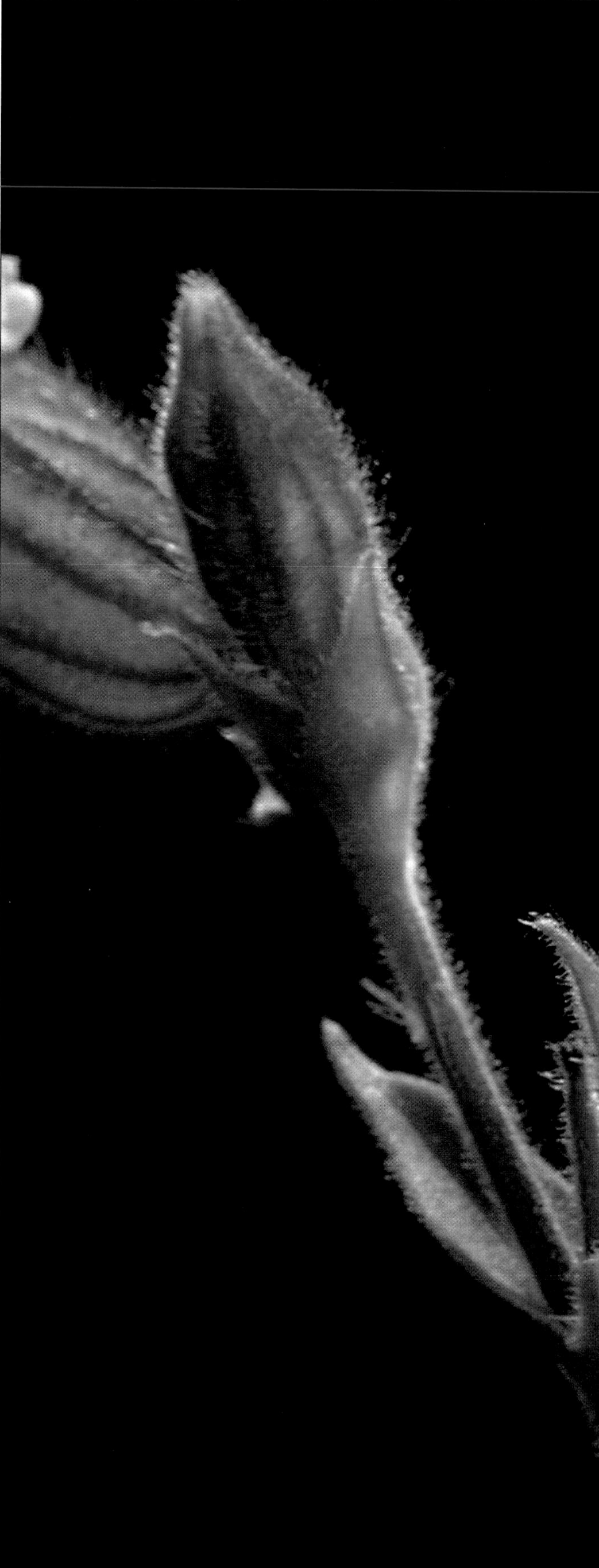

Bladder Campion; Maiden's Tears

Scientific name:	*Silene vulgaris (Silene cucubalus)*
Family:	Carnation
Flower type:	Radially symmetrical, 1 inch (2.5cm) in diameter
Flowering period:	April–August
Flower color:	White
Leaf type:	Long, lanceolate, often clasping
Height:	9-30 inches (22–75cm)
Habitat:	Fields, roadsides
Range:	Much of North America, except the Arctic

Another introduction from Europe, Bladder Campion is distinctive because of its inflated, balloon-like calyx, which not only has clear lengthways veins like other varieties of *Silene*, but also a distinct network of smaller veins. Its stem is not as branched as that of White Campion, and the leaves are opposite, smooth and often clasping. The flower petals are very deeply notched. Like White Campion, Bladder Campion flowers at night and is pollinated by moths. It can also be confused with Night-flowering Catchfly (*S. noctiflora*), but this species is hairy, sticky, and has broader leaves.

Chicory

Scientific name:	*Cichorium intybus*
Family:	Aster
Flower type:	Radially symmetrical, 2 inches (5cm) in diameter
Flowering period:	April–October
Flower color:	Blue
Leaf type:	Long, lanceolate, toothed or lobed
Height:	1–6 feet (30–180cm)
Habitat:	Roadsides, waste ground, field borders
Range:	Across the United States

Chicory is a perennial herb, which was introduced to North America from Eurasia and is now abundant across the continent. It is a tall plant with rather sparse, long, partly clasping leaves and large, attractive flowers borne directly from the upper parts of the main branches. The flowers are usually a clear violet-blue – although occasionally a white- or pink-flowered form appears – and the tips of the petals are toothed. They do not last long in the sunshine, usually wilting by midday. The long tap root of Chicory is commonly roasted and used as a substitute for coffee, and its leaves can be used in salads.

Virginia Spiderwort

Scientific name:	*Tradescantia virginiana*
Family:	Spiderwort
Flower type:	Umbel cluster, each flower 1–2 inches (2.5–5cm) in width
Flowering period:	April–July
Flower color:	Purple
Leaf type:	Long, linear
Height:	1–3 feet (30–90cm)
Habitat:	Roadsides, thickets, meadows
Range:	Ontario and southeast United States

Virginia Spiderwort has a single smooth stem with long, narrow alternate leaves, which sheath the stem. The violet-blue flowers – very occasionally white – are borne on a hairy stalk in umbel-like clusters, above a pair of long, leaf-like bracts. American Indians used a tea made from this and other species of Spiderwort to cure kidney and stomach problems, and plants were also crushed and applied to insect bites and stings. There are about 21 species of Spiderwort in North America, all found across the southeast and in central Canada. They are also sometimes found elsewhere, but have probably escaped from cultivation.

Corncockle ►

Scientific name:	*Agrostemma githago*
Family:	Carnation
Flower type:	Radially symmetrical, 1 inch (2.5cm) in diameter
Flowering period:	June–September
Leaf type:	Long, narrow lanceolate
Height:	1–3 feet (30–90cm)
Habitat:	Roadside, disturbed soil
Range:	Across North America

A native of Europe, the Corncockle is a rather slim plant with stiffly erect leaves arranged in opposite pairs and flowers on the end of long stalks. Its stem is covered in fine white hairs, and has several upward-pointing branches. In England the Corncockle was once a common weed in grain fields and its poisonous seeds had to be manually picked out of harvested wheat – the word "corn" is also used to cover wheat grain in Europe. Bread made with contaminated wheat is quite capable of poisoning a human, and even today the plant remains a problem in grain-producing areas. The Corncockle has now spread across much of Canada and the United States, and is fully naturalized.

Common Milkweed

Scientific name:	*Asclepias syriaca*
Family:	Milkweed
Flower type:	Umbel cluster, 2 inches (5cm) in width
Flowering period:	June–August
Flower color:	Pink
Leaf type:	Large oblong or oval
Height:	2–6 feet (60–200cm)
Habitat:	Roadsides, fields, waste ground
Range:	Most of southern Canada and northeastern United States

The Common Milkweed is the most widely spread Milkweed in North America. It is a tall perennial, with opposite long, light green leaves, which are downy gray beneath, and rather drooping globe-shaped clusters of flowers. The leaves exude a milky-white sap when bruised, hence its common name. Its foliage is the only food of Monarch butterfly larvae, and the toxic sap makes the butterfly poisonous to predators. Despite this, the plant had a wide range of medicinal uses for early Americans, including wart removal, and as a laxative and contraceptive. Its silky seed tassels were also used to stuff pillows and mattresses.

Deptford Pink

Scientific name:	*Dianthus armeria*
Family:	Carnation
Flower type:	Radially symmetrical, $\frac{1}{2}$ inch (1.25cm) in width
Flowering period:	May–September
Flower color:	Pink
Leaf type:	Long, thin, and grass-like
Height:	6–24 inches (15–60cm)
Habitat:	Roadsides, dry fields
Range:	Most of North America, except the Arctic and the prairie states

Another introduction from Europe, the Deptford Pink is named for Deptford in England, where it was once found in great numbers. It has a tall, erect stem, generally smooth and slender but quite swollen at each leaf node, with long, thin, opposite leaves. The flowers are bright pink, often with white spots, and resemble very simple carnations – the plant comes from the same family – and are borne singly on the tips of the stems. There are several varieties of Pink growing wild in North America, many of which have escaped from gardens.

Stork's Bill

Scientific name:	*Erodium cicutarium*
Family:	Geranium
Flower type:	Radially symmetrical, ½ inch (1.25cm) in diameter, borne in umbels
Flowering period:	April–October
Flower color:	Pink
Leaf type:	Basal rosette, each leaf ovate and bi-pinnate
Height:	6–12 inches (15–30cm)
Habitat:	Waste ground, roadsides, field borders
Range:	Most of North America

Stork's Bill is part of the Geranium family, but it does not resemble most of the other species in this family found in North America. It originates from the Mediterranean area of Europe, but is now commonly found across much of the United States and Canada. It is a rather small plant, with reddish, branched stems, small, fern-like basal leaves and simple pink-purple flowers in loose umbel clusters. The name Stork's Bill comes from the seed pod, which is a beaked capsule resembling a stork's bill. The leaves can be added to bath water to relieve rheumatism, and the plant is also a source of vitamin K.

Annual Garden Phlox ▲

Scientific name:	*Phlox drummondii*
Family:	Phlox
Flower type:	Cyme cluster, each flower 1 inch (2.5cm) in diameter
Flowering period:	May–July
Flower color:	Pink
Leaf type:	Lanceolate to ovate
Height:	9–18 inches (22–45cm)
Habitat:	Waste ground, roadsides, fields
Range:	Southeast United States, from Maryland to Florida and west to Oklahoma

Although Annual Garden Phlox is a southern plant, it is sometimes found further north and west, having escaped from cultivation. It is a plant with many branches and lots of bright green leaves – the lower leaves are opposite and the upper leaves are alternate, unlike most other species of Phlox. The flowers are normally a deep rose-pink, but can vary in shade through pale pink to white. There are around 60 species of Phlox that are native to North America, but within its region this is one of the most common.

Red Clover

Scientific name:	*Trifolium pratense*
Family:	Pea
Flower type:	Spherical cluster, $\frac{1}{2}$–1 inch (1.25–2.5cm) in width
Flowering period:	May–September
Flower color:	Pink
Leaf type:	Tripalmate
Height:	6–20 inches (15–50cm)
Habitat:	Lawns, roadsides, fields
Range:	Across North America, except the Arctic

Red Clover originates from Europe, but was planted across North America as pasture for farm animals, and as a crop to make hay. It is also used in traditional crop rotation to improve the nitrogen content of the soil. It is a short but leggy perennial, with tripalmate leaves, each oval leaflet of which often has a chevron of lighter green or white across the center. The flowers are dense, rounded heads, made up of 30-90 small, pea-like individual flowers, and are borne on erect, hairy stems. Folk medicine used Red Clover flower tea as a mild sedative and for asthma and bronchitis, and as a wash to treat sores, burns and ulcers. Extracts of Red Clover are now sold in tablet form as it is reputed to ward off cancer.

Scarlet Pimpernel; Poor Man's Weatherglass

Scientific name:	*Anagallis arvensis*
Family:	Primrose
Flower type:	Radially symmetrical, $\frac{1}{4}$ inch (0.62cm) in diameter
Flowering period:	June–August
Flower color:	Red
Leaf type:	Ovate, long
Height:	4–12 inches (10–30cm)
Habitat:	Roadsides, waste ground, garden lawns
Range:	Eastern Canada, western United States and along the eastern coastal states to Texas

An annual, the Scarlet Pimpernel creeps across the ground, and its flowers are borne on long, slim stalks from the axil of each bright green leaf. Although the flowers are more usually red or red-orange there are also blue and white varieties, which are both rare. The Scarlet Pimpernel originates from Europe, but is now found across much of North America. Its European name of Poor Man's Weatherglass was given because the flowers open only when the sun is shining, closing when it is wet or overcast. Although the plant may look very attractive, it is also poisonous and can cause dermatitis.

Indian Blanket; Firewheel; Gaillardia

Scientific name:	*Gaillardia pulchella*
Family:	Aster
Flower type:	Radially symmetrical, 1–3 inches (2.5-8cm) across
Flowering period:	June–August
Flower color:	Red
Leaf type:	Lower lobed, upper lanceolate
Height:	1–2 feet (30–60cm)
Habitat:	Roadsides, sandy fields, grassland
Range:	Across southwest, south and eastern United States, eastern Canada

Indian Blanket is common across much of the southeast of North America, particularly along roadsides, but it has also escaped from cultivation into the wild and so can sometimes be found in other areas. It is a very popular garden plant because it is attractive, tolerates dry conditions and is very easy to grow. The stem is branched and covered in soft, downy hairs, and each stem ends in a showy flower that is usually red tipped with yellow, although there are also pink and all-yellow variants. The lower alternate leaves are shallowly lobed, but the upper ones are smaller and lanceolate. Indian Blanket has several alternative names, including Firewheel and Showy Gaillardia.

Butterfly Weed; Orange Milkweed; Pleurisy Root

Scientific name:	*Asclepias tuberosa*
Family:	Milkweed
Flower type:	Umbel cluster, 2 inches (5cm) in width
Flowering period:	June–August
Flower color:	Orange
Leaf type:	Lance-shaped, long and narrow
Height:	12–18 inches (30–45cm)
Habitat:	Roadsides and fields
Range:	Most of the United States and southern Canada

The leafy and hairy stem of the Butterfly Milkweed bears alternate leaves – the only Milkweed to do so. The leaves also have a clear sap, rather than a milky-colored one, but the plant is often more noticeable for its spectacular clusters of bright orange flowers, which attract passing butterflies. This accounts for one common name, while Pleurisy Root comes from its once having been used to treat pleurisy and other lung problems. Although it is such an attractive plant, it is not often cultivated in gardens – despite being voted as the fourth most showy wildflower in America in a poll of naturalists and scientists.

Overleaf: Butterfly Weed (*Asclepias tuberosa*)

Greeneyes; Chocolate Flower

Scientific name:	*Berlandiera lyrata*
Family:	Aster
Flower type:	Radially symmetrical, $1\frac{1}{2}$ inches (3.75cm) in diameter
Flowering period:	May–October
Flower color:	Yellow
Leaf type:	Long, with scalloped edges, sometimes pinnately divided
Height:	1–4 feet (30–120cm)
Habitat:	Roadsides, grassy areas on stony soil
Range:	Southwestern United States

Greeneyes is a rather leafy plant, with long, velvety, alternate leaves, which are deeply scalloped or pinnately divided, borne on many short branches. The flowers appear at the tips of long bare stalks and are bright yellow with a maroon-red center. Its genus name honors a French-Swiss physician, Jean-Louis Berlandier, who collected plants across its growing area in the nineteenth century. There are five species of Berlandiera in the United States, but Greeneyes is the most common in most areas. The flowers may smell of chocolate, so it is also sometimes called Chocolate Flower.

Above: Species of Coreopsis can hybridize, which leads the flowers to have the characteristics of both species.

Lanceleaf Coreopsis; Tickseed

Scientific name:	*Coreopsis lanceolata*
Family:	Aster
Flower type:	Radially symmetrical, 2–3 inches (5–8cm) in diameter
Flowering period:	May–July
Flower color:	Yellow
Leaf type:	Lance-shaped, lower ones more elliptical, upper rather oblong
Height:	1–2 feet (30–60cm)
Habitat:	Water ground, roadsides, disturbed and poor soil
Range:	Midwest North America, also in the northeast from cultivation

Lanceleaf Coreopsis is a native American wildflower, originating in the Midwest, but now also common across the northeast – probably after having escaped from cultivation in gardens. It is quite a tall plant, branching at the base and with bright yellow daisy-like flowers at the end of long stalks. The leaves are broadly lance-shaped, but the lower ones are more elliptical, while the upper ones are wider and more oblong. There are about 40 species of Coreopsis in North America, mostly with yellow flowers, but the petals of the Lanceleaf Coreopsis have rather unusual scalloped tips and the central disk is yellow, not brown.

Garden Coreopsis

Scientific name:	*Coreopsis tinctoria*
Family:	Aster
Flower type:	Radially symmetrical, 2 inches (5cm) in diameter
Flowering period:	August–September
Flower color:	Yellow
Leaf type:	Lobed lower, entire upper
Height:	2–4 feet (60–120cm)
Habitat:	Waste places, roadsides, gardens
Range:	West and southern North America, also parts of the east

Garden Coreopsis is native to North America, but is much more widespread after having escaped from cultivation. It gets its name because it is often grown as a showy garden flower. It is a quite tall, smooth-stemmed annual, with numerous branches on which are borne many bright yellow flowers, which have a red-maroon central disk with the same color at the base of the rays. The lower leaves are usually stalked and divided once or twice into lobes, but upper leaves tend to be entire. American Indians used the roots to make a tea to treat diarrhea and as an emetic.

Golden Yarrow

Scientific name:	*Eriophyllum lanatum*
Family:	Aster
Flower type:	Compound flower head, 2½ inches (7.25cm) in diameter
Flowering period:	May–August
Flower color:	Yellow
Leaf type:	Long, irregularly lobed
Height:	5–24 inches (12–60cm)
Habitat:	Dry, open areas
Range:	West coast states, from British Columbia to California, east to west Wyoming

Golden Yarrow is a medium size plant with several, branching stems and long leaves, which are thickly covered in a layer of fine white hairs, giving it a grayish, furry look. Each stem ends in a leafless stalk, which bears a yellow compound flower head with yellow ray florets and an orange central disk. Golden Yarrow prefers very dry areas, and its hairs conserve water by reflecting the heat and keeping air movement away from the surface of the plant. It is often a very common plant where it grows, and when in flower can cover the ground in a rich yellow carpet of flowers. There are five species of Yarrow in total that are found all across North America.

Lanceleaf Goldenrod; Grassleaf Goldenrod ▼

Scientific name:	*Euthamia graminifolia (Solidago graminifolia)*
Family:	Aster
Flower type:	Flat-topped cluster, each tubular flower ¼ inch (0.62cm)
Flowering period:	June–September
Flower color:	Yellow
Leaf type:	Narrow lance-shaped
Height:	2–4 feet (60–120cm)
Habitat:	Damp roadsides and fields, wet open woodland
Range:	Northeast North America

There are over 90 species of Goldenrod growing across North America, and it can be difficult to tell many of them apart. Lanceleaf Goldenrod is fairly distinctive, with a more slender stem than other species, covered in fine white hairs and with narrow, lance-shaped alternate leaves with parallel veins. The stem branches at upper levels, and each branch ends in a flat-topped cluster of small, yellow, tubular flowers. The flowers are quite fragrant, unlike many of the other varieties. Goldenrods were previously classified in the genus *Solidago*, but are now in the genus *Euthamia*. Goldenrod leaves can be dried and made into a tea that is used as a tonic.

Common Sunflower

Scientific Name:	*Helianthus annuus*
Family:	Aster
Flower type:	Compound flower head, 3–5 inches (7.5–12.5 cm) in diameter
Flowering period:	June–September
Flower color:	Yellow
Leaf type:	Ovate or heart-shaped, sometimes with toothed edges
Height:	2–13 feet (60–390cm)
Habitat:	Dry open fields, roadsides, plains, foothills
Range:	Most of North America

The Common Sunflower is a tall, leafy plant with a coarse, hairy stem, which is often branched at higher levels and bears bright yellow ray flowers, around a maroon central disk. The flower face follows the sun as it moves across the sky. This plant has been cultivated in North America from early times; the seeds are edible and used for cooking oil and livestock fodder, and Native Americans obtained a dull blue dye from the seeds and a yellow dye from the flower heads, which they used in traditional basketwork and weaving. They also ground sunflower seeds to make bread flour and used the oil for cooking and to dress hair. During the 19th century, many believed that growing the Common Sunflower near a house would protect the occupants from malaria. This particular species of sunflower is the state flower of Kansas.

Jerusalem Artichoke

Scientific name:	*Helianthus tuberosus*
Family:	Aster
Flower type:	Compound flower head, 3 inches (8cm) in diameter
Flowering period:	August–October
Flower color:	Yellow
Leaf type:	Lanceolate or ovate
Height:	6–10 feet (180–300cm)
Habitat:	Roadsides, field edges
Range:	Eastern and northwestern United States

The Jerusalem Artichoke is a perennial with a stout, grooved, hairy, branching stem, bearing opposite lower leaves, and alternate upper leaves. The leaves are rather rough and thick, and are finely toothed. The plant tends to grow in colonies, rather than as a single specimen. It was cultivated by American Indians as its tubers can be eaten raw or cooked like potatoes and are very nutritious and low in starch. A tea made with the leaf and stalk was also once used to treat rheumatism. Today the Jerusalem Artichoke is sometimes grown as a crop, so its tubers may be found in food markets. Despite its common name, this plant has nothing to do with Jerusalem and is actually a member of the Aster family like the Sunflower.

Common St.-John's-Wort

Scientific name:	*Hypericum perforatum*
Family:	St.-John's-Wort
Flower type:	Cluster, each flower $\frac{3}{4}$ inch (1.88–2.5cm) in width
Flowering period:	June–September
Flower color:	Yellow
Leaf type:	Small, long, elliptical
Height:	12–30 inches (30–75cm)
Habitat:	Fields, roadsides, waste places
Range:	Most of central North America, except the Prairie states

Common St.-John's-Wort was introduced from Europe and is now found in abundance across much of North America, to the point where it is considered a weed in some states. It has a branching, bushy stem, with small, long and elliptical leaves and with each branch ending in a small cluster of bright yellow flowers, which have tiny black dots on the edges of the petals. St.-John's-Wort has become one of the best-known and popular herbal remedies for mild depression. A tincture of the flowers was once used to treat skin ulcers, cuts and bruises, and a tea to treat dysentry, diarrhea and worms. However, eating the plant can cause photodermatitis in both cattle and humans.

Common Evening-primrose

Scientific name:	*Oenothera biennis*
Family:	Evening-primrose
Flower type:	Umbel cluster, each flower 1–2 inches (2.5–5cm) in diameter
Flowering period:	June–September
Flower color:	Yellow
Leaf type:	Lanceolate and toothed
Height:	2–5 feet (60–150cm)
Habitat:	Fields, roadsides
Range:	Most of North America, except the Arctic regions

The Evening primrose is a tall night-blooming biennial – its flowers normally close by midday. It has a leafy stalk, often hairy and sometimes tinged with purple, with large, yellow flowers in a loose umbel cluster at the top. Evening primrose oil is a natural source of gamma-linoleic acid and can help in imbalances and abnormalities of essential fatty acids, as well as being useful to treat a wide range of illnesses, including migraine, arthritis, dyslexia and eczema. American Indians used a tea made from the roots for bowel pains, and rubbed the root on muscles to give them strength.

Rough-stemmed Goldenrod

Scientific name:	*Solidago rugosa*
Family:	Aster
Flower type:	Panicle cluster, each flower 1/8 inch (0.31cm) in length
Flowering period:	July–November
Flower color:	Yellow
Leaf type:	Long, sharply toothed
Height:	1–6 feet (30–180cm)
Habitat:	Roadsides, woodland edges, neglected fields
Range:	Central and eastern North America

Like other Goldenrods, the Rough-stemmed Goldenrod has a long stem, with small, yellow flowers clustered along arching branches, which form a roughly triangular-shaped showy panicle. Its distinguishing feature is its rough, very hairy stem, and its leaves, which are long, sharply toothed, hairy, rough and wrinkled. The lower leaves can be as much as 12 inches (30cm) long; the leaves are alternate and are often deeply veined. In all, there are around 90 species of Goldenrod across the whole of North America.

Common Dandelion

Scientific name:	*Taraxacum officinale*
Family:	Aster
Flower type:	Compound flower head, 1–2 inches (2.5–5cm) in diameter
Flowering period:	March–September
Flower color:	Yellow
Leaf type:	Basal rosette, deeply toothed and lobed
Height:	3–8 inches (8–20cm)
Habitat:	Waste ground, roadsides, fields, garden lawns
Range:	Across North America

The Common Dandelion is originally from Eurasia, but is now found across most of the world – particularly in suburban lawns. The leaves, which form a basal rosette, are deeply and irregularly toothed and lobed; the young leaves can be eaten as greens. The flower stem rises from the center and exudes a milky sap when broken; it bears a flower head made up of many rays. The seeds each have a parachute of bristles that form a spherical downy head before they are dispersed. A tea made from the roots of the Common Dandelion is used to treat liver, gallbladder, kidney and bladder problems; it has been scientifically proven that there are anti-inflammatory compounds in both the root and the leaves.

Yellow Goatsbeard

Scientific name:	*Tragopogon dubius*
Family:	Aster
Flower type:	Compound flower head, $1\frac{1}{2}$–2 inches (3.75–5cm) in diameter
Flowering period:	July–August
Flower color:	Yellow
Leaf type:	Basal, clasping, broad but narrowing to a sharp tip
Height:	1–3 feet (30–90cm)
Habitat:	Fields, roadsides, waste places
Range:	Most of North America, except the Arctic

Originally from Europe, Yellow Goatsbeard has established itself across most of North America. It resembles a dandelion, but has long, grass-like leaves. It is a biennial, with a coarse stem, long, pointed, clasping leaves, and one flower head, which opens early in the day but is usually closed by midday. The stem is thickened just below the flower, which is usually yellow but can sometimes be reddish or purple. The seeds each have feather-like bristles, and as they ripen form a large, downy sphere, very like that of a dandelion but much larger. The leaves can be eaten in salads or cooked as greens, and the tap root cooked like a potato or roasted and ground to make a coffee substitute.

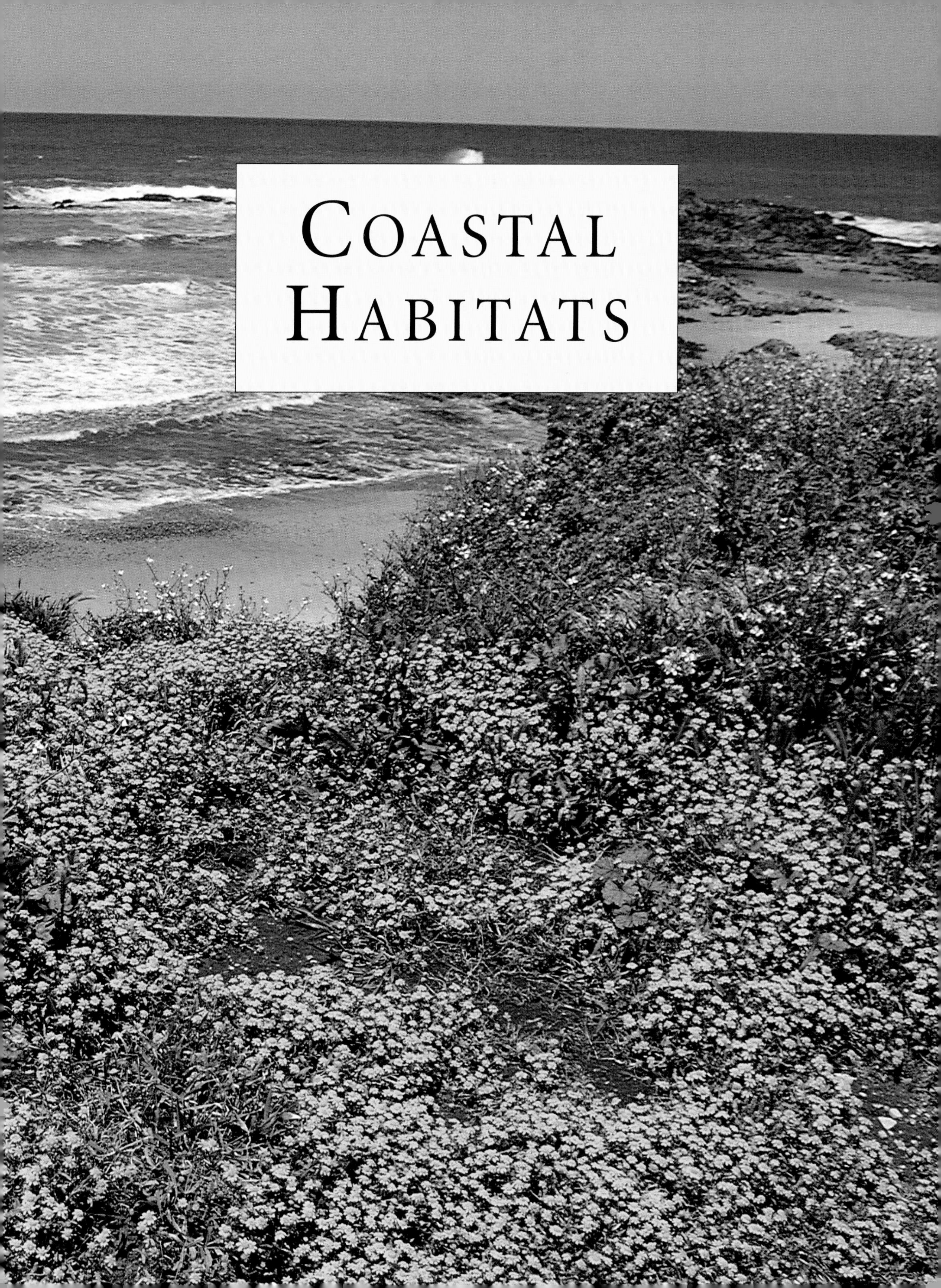

COASTAL HABITATS

BEACH STRAWBERRY

Scientific name:	*Fragaria chiloensis*
Family:	Rose
Flower type:	Radially symmetrical, $\frac{1}{2}$–1 inch (1.25–5cm) in diameter
Flowering period:	April–August
Flower color:	White
Leaf type:	Tripalmate, each leaflet obvate, sharply toothed
Height:	Creeper, 6 inches (15cm)
Habitat:	Coastal bluffs, dunes
Range:	Pacific coast

A perennial creeper, Beach Strawberry forms runners that root at intervals to produce new plants; the young plants often stay connected to the main one for some time. The bright green leaves are in three sections, like clover leaves, with each leaflet obvate and sharply toothed. The small white flowers are borne on short, hairy stalks, and have five pointed sepals and five broad petals. The fruit looks like a much smaller version of a cultivated strawberry and is rich in anticancer elements. It is edible and can be used in most strawberry recipes.

SEA-MILKWORT

Scientific name:	*Glaux maritima*
Family:	Primrose
Flower type:	Radially symmetrical, $\frac{1}{4}$ inch (0.62cm) in diameter
Flowering period:	July
Flower color:	White
Leaf type:	Oblong to oval, fleshy
Height:	3–12 inches (8–30cm)
Habitat:	Salt marshes, seashores
Range:	Pacific coast, much of Canada, northeast United States

A small plant that prefers salt water marshes, Sea-milkwort has a thick, fleshy stem bearing oblong to oval, succulent, gray-green leaves arranged in opposite pairs. The small flowers are sessile, and spring from the leaf axils; they have no petals but five petal-like sepals. They are cup-shaped and usually white, pinky-cream or pale lavender. American Indians once boiled the roots and ate them to induce sleep. Sea-milkwort is a spreading plant, and often forms quite large patches, but it is not common and should not be removed from the wild.

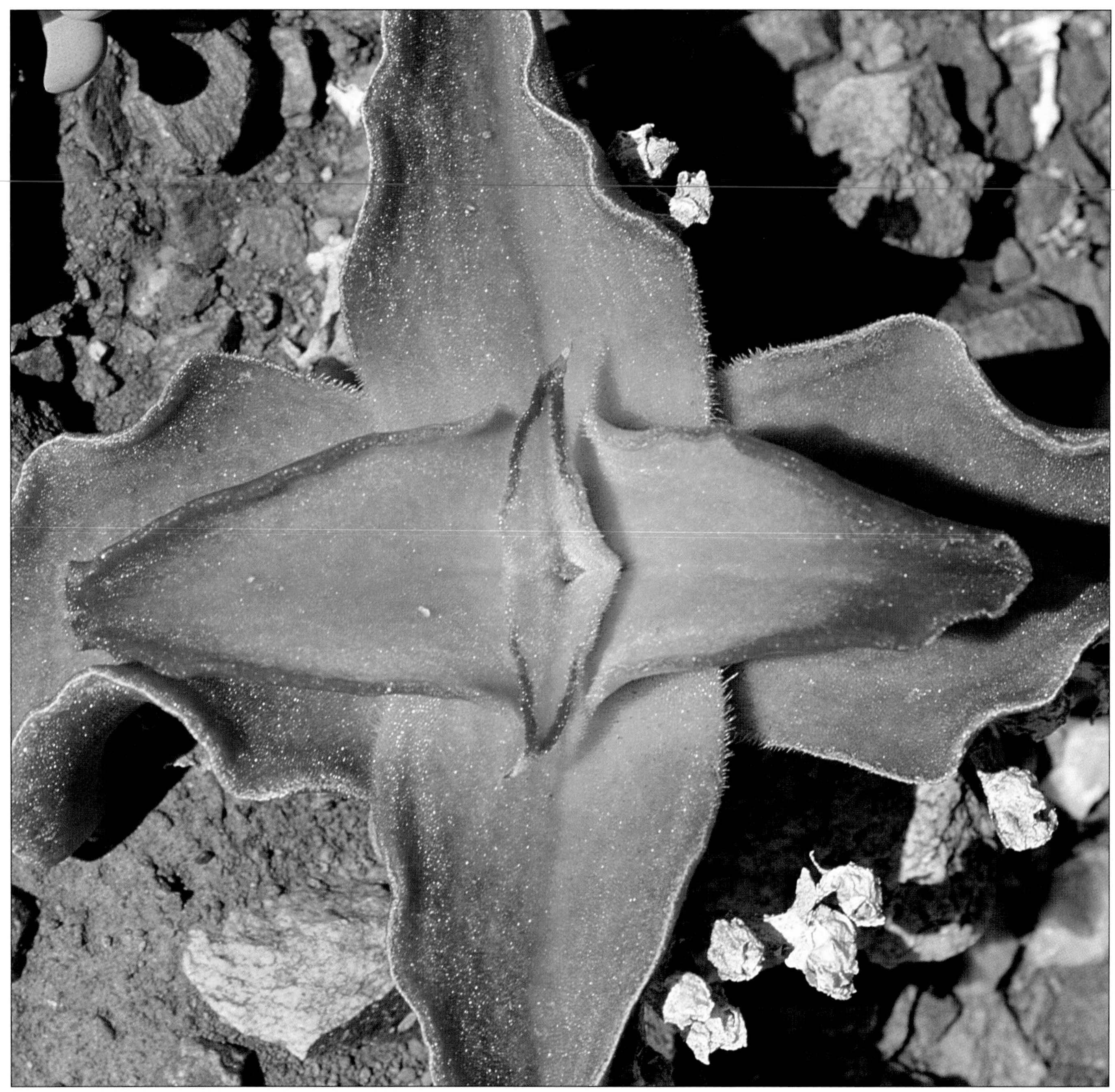

Crystalline Ice Plant

Scientific name:	*Mesembryanthemum crystallinum*
Family:	Ice Plant
Flower type:	Radially symmetrical, 1 inch (2.5cm) in diameter
Flowering period:	April–October
Flower color:	White
Leaf type:	Spatulate to ovate, wavy-edged
Height:	Creeper, 4 inches (10cm)
Habitat:	Open slopes near the coast, deserts
Range:	Southwest Pacific coast

Crystalline Ice Plant is a creeper with trailing, reddish-green, succulent stems, which are covered with a fine layer of tiny, clear beads that contain water. The beads look like crystals, hence the plant's common name, and if touched they burst and give the stems a wet feel. The leaves are long, spatulate to ovate, and wavy-edged. The flowers are white or reddish-white, with many, very narrow, thread-like petals. Crystalline Ice Plant was introduced from South Africa, but has become naturalized within its small range. It is also found in southern Europe.

Blue-eyed Grass

Scientific name:	*Sisyrinchium angustifolium*
Family:	Iris
Flower type:	Radially symmetrical, $\frac{1}{2}$ inch (1.25cm) in diameter
Flowering period:	May–July
Flower color:	Blue
Leaf type:	Basal, linear, grass-like
Height:	6–20 inches (15–50cm)
Habitat:	Fields, meadows
Range:	Most of North America, except Prairie States

It is very difficult to make an identification of Blue-eyed Grass with any certainty, as even the experts disagree on whether some of the variants are separate species or not. As its common name suggests, Blue-eyed Grass has long, linear, rather grass-like leaves in a cluster at the base of the plant. The flowers are borne at the end of a long, flat stem, usually with only one in bloom at any one time. The six petal-like segments open out widely at the ends, and are blue to blue-violet in color. They are notched twice at the tip, with a longer, central point.

New York Aster

Scientific name:	*Symphyotrichum novi-belgii (Aster novi-belgii)*
Family:	Aster
Flower type:	Compound flower head, 1–2 inches (2.5–5cm) in diameter
Flowering period:	August–October
Flower color:	Purple
Leaf type:	Lanceolate, clasping
Height:	10–60 inches (25–150cm)
Habitat:	Shorelines, wet meadows
Range:	Atlantic coast

A large plant, with a slender, smooth, branching stem, New York Aster has many long, lanceolate leaves that partly clasp the stem and are arranged alternately. The compound flower heads are borne mainly towards the ends of the branches, and they have many ray florets around the yellowish or reddish central disk florets. The rays are usually purple-blue, but they can be white or rose-pink. The narrow bracts are greenish-white. New York Aster is abundant near the coast, but is commonly found only up to 100 miles inland.

California Thrift ▶

Scientific name:	*Armeria maritima*
Family:	Leadwort
Flower type:	Rounded cluster, $\frac{1}{2}$–1 inch (1.25–2.5cm) in diameter
Flowering period:	March–August
Flower color:	Pink
Leaf type:	Basal cluster, linear
Height:	4–18 inches (10–45cm)
Habitat:	Beaches, coastal areas
Range:	Pacific coast, Arctic

A rather low-growing plant, California Thrift prefers to be in coastal areas and is not found very far inland. It has a dense tussock of narrow, linear grayish-green leaves, all of which are at its base. The bare flower stalk springs from the leaves and terminates in a small, rounded, ball-shaped cluster of pink to lilac flowers, which are mixed with papery bracts. There are only two species in this genus in North America, but there are many others in dry areas of the Mediterranean and in Asia.

Threadleaf Sundew

Scientific name:	*Drosera filiformis*
Family:	Sundew
Flower type:	Radially symmetrical, $\frac{1}{2}$ inch (1.25cm) in diameter
Flowering period:	June–August
Flower color:	Pink
Leaf type:	Long and covered in sticky hairs
Height:	4–12 inches (10–30cm)
Habitat:	Wet coastal sand
Range:	Northeast and southeast Atlantic coast

Threadleaf Sundew is a perennial carnivorous plant, with basal leaves that are long, thin and thread-like, with reddish hairs that exude drops of sticky sap to catch small insects. The lavender to pink flowers are small and arranged along one side of a leafless stalk in an elongated raceme cluster. The plant is able to survive in very poor sandy soil as it gets its nutrients from the insects caught on its sticky leaves. The Threadleaf Sundew plants found in the separate southern section of the range are larger than those in the north, and are sometimes classed as a different species, *D. tracyi*.

Seaside Daisy

Scientific name:	*Erigeron glaucus*
Family:	Aster
Flower type:	Compound flower head, $2\frac{1}{2}$ inches (6.25cm) in diameter
Flowering period:	April–July
Flower color:	Pink
Leaf type:	Basal rosette, spatulate, sometimes toothed
Height:	6–18 inches (15–45cm)
Habitat:	Coastal bluffs, dunes
Range:	Southwest Pacific coast

A slightly succulent plant, Seaside Daisy has a basal rosette of long, spatulate leaves that are often toothed toward the tip and narrow to a flat stalk at the base. The compound flower heads are made up of very many short, slender, pale pink to white ray florets, surrounding a central yellow disk. The flower heads are borne at the end of short, bristly, sticky-haired stalks, with several on each plant. There are over 140 species in this genus found across North America, but some of them are unattractive weeds.

Crimson-eyed Rosemallow; Swamp Rosemallow

Scientific name:	*Hibiscus moscheutos (Hibiscus palustris)*
Family:	Mallow
Flower type:	Radially symmetrical, 4–8 inches (10–20cm) in diameter
Flowering period:	June–September
Flower color:	Pink
Leaf type:	Ovate to lanceolate, toothed or lobed
Height:	30–84 inches (75–210cm)
Habitat:	Tidal marshes, swamps
Range:	East and southeast Pacific coast, central United States

Crimson-eyed Rosemallow is a tall, coarse plant with long, ovate to lanceolate, pointed leaves that are toothed or lobed and softly hairy underneath. The large, showy bowl-shaped flowers have five broad lobes and many stamens, and are strongly musk-scented. The flowers are usually white or pink, but can be deep purple-red in the center; they are borne on short stalks springing from the leaf axils. As well as salt water marshes, Crimson-eyed Rosemallow thrives in very wet, inland areas. The leaves and roots were once used to treat dysentery, and lung and urinary ailments.

Seashore Mallow

Scientific name:	*Kosteletzkya virginica*
Family:	Mallow
Flower type:	Radially symmetrical, $1\frac{1}{2}$–2 inches (3.75–5cm) in diameter
Flowering period:	June–October
Flower color:	Pink
Leaf type:	Ovate, hairy, basal lobes
Height:	12–34 inches (30–85cm)
Habitat:	Salt water to fresh water marshes
Range:	Southeast coastal states

A medium-size plant, Seashore Mallow prefers to grow in brackish water marshes, although it can sometimes be found further inland in freshwater areas. It has a branching, hairy stem that bears ovate, gray-green leaves, which have a rough, hairy surface and shallow lobes at the base only. The leaves are arranged alternately along the stem and are palmately veined. The rose-pink flowers are either borne on the end of stalks that spring from the leaf axils, or at the tip of the stems. They have five broad petals and many stamens that form a column in the center of the flower.

Railroad Vine; Goat's-hoof Vine ▲

Scientific name:	*Ipomoea pes-caprae*
Family:	Morning Glory
Flower type:	Radially symmetrical, 2 inches (5cm) in length
Flowering period:	All year
Flower color:	Pink
Leaf type:	Long, broadly ovate, folded at center
Height:	Vine, stems to 20 feet (600cm) long
Habitat:	Beaches, coastal dunes
Range:	Southeast Atlantic coast

A West Indian plant, Railroad Vine was introduced to North America and has become naturalized – it is also found in other warm areas of the world. It is a vine, with a long stem that creeps along the ground, almost to the water's edge, and roots at the nodes. The stem bears long, broadly ovate to rounded, bright green leaves, folded at the center and deeply notched at the tip. The alternative common name of Goat's-hoof Vine comes from the leaf shape, which resembles a goat's hoofprint. The flower stalks stand erect off the stem, bearing a pink to purple-red, trumpet-shaped flower.

Beach Pea ▲

Scientific name:	*Lathyrus japonicus*
Family:	Pea
Flower type:	Rounded cluster, each flower $\frac{3}{4}$ inch (1.88cm) in length
Flowering period:	June–September
Flower color:	Pink
Leaf type:	Compound pinnate; leaflets oval
Height:	Vine, stems to 24 inches (60cm)
Habitat:	Beaches, gravel ground
Range:	Pacific coast, northwest Atlantic coast, Great Lakes

Beach Pea has a flower rather like a sweetpea, and is found on both beaches and the gravel shores of the Great Lakes. The same species is also found in China and Japan. It is a vine, with trailing, angled, fleshy stems that can extend up to 24 inches (60cm). The leaves are compound pinnate, with oval leaflets each tipped with a bristle. The upper leaflets are modified into tendrils that bind the plant to surrounding objects or plants. The pink to lavender flowers are borne in rounded clusters at the end of long stalks, with six to ten flowers on each stalk.

Marsh Rose-gentian; Sea Pink

Scientific name:	*Sabatia dodecandra*
Family:	Gentian
Flower type:	Radially symmetrical, $1\frac{1}{2}$–$2\frac{1}{2}$ inches (3.75–6.25cm) in diameter
Flowering period:	June–September
Flower color:	Pink
Leaf type:	Lanceolate, clasping
Height:	12–24 inches (30–60cm)
Habitat:	Salt marshes and meadows
Range:	Southeast Atlantic coast

Marsh Rose-gentian has a rounded, slender, branching stem, with opposite pairs of small, slightly clasping, lanceolate leaves and a basal rosette of slightly larger leaves. The pink flowers are rather flat, with 8 to 13 petals joined at the base, and are borne on opposite branches. There are 18 species in this genus found across North America, mostly across the eastern half of the continent. Some have pink and some have white flowers, but they all look rather similar and it can be quite hard to identify a particular species with certainty.

Saltmarsh Fleabane

Scientific name:	*Pluchea odorata (Pluchea purpurascens)*
Family:	Aster
Flower type:	Rounded cluster, each flower $\frac{1}{4}$ inch (0.62cm) in diameter
Flowering period:	June–October
Flower color:	Pink
Leaf type:	Lanceolate, sometimes toothed or scalloped
Height:	15–48 inches (38–120cm)
Habitat:	Saltwater marshes
Range:	Atlantic coast, Southwest Pacific coast

When it is in bloom, Saltmarsh Fleabane can be quite conspicuous with its bright pink flowers amidst the rather dull browns and greens of marsh grasses. It is an erect plant with a smooth stem, which bears lanceolate, bright green leaves that are sometimes toothed or scalloped. The leaves either have short stalks, or are sometimes sessile, and are arranged alternately along the stem. The unusual flower heads have no ray florets, only disk florets, and are held in small, flat-topped clusters. They are pink to lavender in color, and smell very strongly of camphor. There are around six herbaceous species in this genus, which are found across North America.

Above: Sesuvium species

Western Sea Purslane

Scientific name:	*Sesuvium verrucosum*
Family:	Ice Plant
Flower type:	Radially symmetrical, $\frac{1}{4}$ – $\frac{1}{2}$ inch (0.62–1.25cm) in diameter
Flowering period:	April–October
Flower color:	Pink
Leaf type:	Long, obvate, fleshy
Height:	12–36 inches (30–90cm)
Habitat:	Open, salty soil
Range:	Southern United States

Western Sea Purslane is the only species of its genus that grows in the west side of the southern United States, hence the first part of its common name. It is a small, succulent plant, with thick, branching gray-green stems, which are sometimes reclining and sometimes held more erect. The leaves are long, obvate and fleshy, and are borne in opposite pairs on the stem. The flowers are open and star-like, with five petal-like sepals, which are pink on the inside and green outside and joined at the base; the petals are absent. In the center of the flower there is a cluster of many stamens.

Red Clintonia; Andrew's Clintonia ▲

Scientific name:	*Clintonia andrewsiana*
Family:	Lily
Flower type:	Rounded cluster, 1–2 inches (2.5–5cm) in diameter
Flowering period:	May–July
Flower color:	Red
Leaf type:	Basal rosette, long, elliptical
Height:	10–20 inches (25–50cm)
Habitat:	Coastal, shady woods
Range:	Pacific coast states

An attractive plant with bright red flowers, Red Clintonia grows near the coast, but only in shady forested areas – particularly Redwood forests. It is a medium-size plant with a basal rosette of long, broadly elliptical leaves, from which springs the flower stalk. The stalk often has no leaves, but it terminates in a small rounded cluster of long, bell-shaped red flowers; sometimes there is another, small cluster below the main one. There are four species in this genus found in North America, two in the east and two in the west.

Beach Primrose

Scientific name:	*Camissonia cheiranthifolia*
Family:	Evening-primrose
Flower type:	Radially symmetrical, $\frac{1}{2}$–$1\frac{1}{2}$ inches (1.25–3.75cm) in diameter
Flowering period:	May–August
Flower color:	Yellow
Leaf type:	Ovate, hairy
Height:	Creeper, 6 inches (15cm)
Habitat:	Beaches
Range:	Pacific coast

A member of the Evening-primrose family, Beach Primrose is a low-growing creeper that grows on sandy beaches. It has a central rosette of ovate leaves, which are covered with a fine coating of gray hairs. From the rosette spring very long, leafy stems, which often extend up to 48 inches (120cm) away from the main plant. The stem leaves are similar to the basal leaves, but are usually much smaller in size, and are arranged alternately down the length of the stem. The flowers are bright yellow, with 4 rounded petals, and are borne toward the end of the stems.

Powdery Dudleya ▲

Scientific name:	*Dudleya farinosa*
Family:	Stonecrop
Flower type:	Rounded cluster, each flower $\frac{1}{4}$ inch (0.62cm) in length
Flowering period:	April–September
Flower color:	Yellow
Leaf type:	Basal rosette, ovate, succulent
Height:	5–15 inches (12–38cm)
Habitat:	Coastal bluffs
Range:	Pacific coast

A low, compact plant, Powdery Dudleya has a tight basal rosette of ovate, thick, fleshy leaves, which are pale green in color, often covered with a whitish powder – hence the common name. The small yellow flowers are borne on whitish, erect stalks in a dense, rounded cluster. The flower stalks grow from a leaf axil rather than from the centre of the rosette, and have very small leaves arranged alternately along their length. There are several species of coastal Dudleya, but this is the only one found in the northern section of its range.

Carolina Lily

Scientific name:	*Lilium michauxii*
Family:	Lily
Flower type:	Bell-shaped, 2–3 inches (5–8cm) in length
Flowering period:	May–August
Flower color:	Yellow
Leaf type:	Long, oblanceolate, whorled
Height:	1–4 feet (30–120cm)
Habitat:	Coastal plains, upland woods and thickets
Range:	Southeast United States

The Carolina Lily is found from Virginia to Texas and down into Florida, usually on the coastal plain but also up into the lower foothills of mountains in the area. It has a tall stem, with long, oblanceolate leaves usually arraned in whorls. The showy, nodding, bell-shaped red-yellow flowers are marked with red-brown spots, and have strongly backward-curving, petal-like segments that reach round to almost touch the base of the flower. There are up to six flowers on each stem, either on long stalks springing from the leaf axils or in a cluster at the top.

Seaside Goldenrod

Scientific name:	*Solidago sempervirens*
Family:	Aster
Flower type:	Elongated cluster, each flower $\frac{1}{4}$–$\frac{1}{2}$ inch (0.62–1.25cm) in length
Flowering period:	June–November
Flower color:	Yellow
Leaf type:	Lanceolate or oblong, fleshy; upper clasping
Height:	12–96 inches (30–250cm)
Habitat:	Sandy soil, salt water marshes
Range:	Atlantic coast

Seaside Goldenrod is a tall, succulent plant, with fleshy, smooth green stems bearing long, lanceolate or oblong leaves arranged alternately. The basal leaves can be as long as 12 inches (30cm) and are held on long stalks, but the upper ones decrease in size higher up the stem and are sessile. All the leaves are quite thick and fleshy, and unlike many other species in this genus, the edges are smooth, not toothed. The small, showy flower heads are bright yellow, with 7-10 ray florets around a central disk. They are borne in a loose panicle cluster along only one side of branches arching off the stem.

Sea Oats ▶

Scientific name:	*Uniola paniculata*
Family:	Grass
Flower type:	Elongated cluster, 6–18 inches (15–45cm) in length
Flowering period:	July
Flower color:	Brown
Leaf type:	Linear, grass-like
Height:	30–84 inches (75–210cm)
Habitat:	Coastal sands
Range:	Southeast Atlantic coast

Sea Oats prefers to grow on coastal sands and is sometimes used to control erosion on beaches. It is a very tall, eye-catching plant, with long, grass-like leaves and a tall, smooth stem that ends in a spectacular curving plume. The flowers forming the plume have no sepals or petals, but are made up of stamens and pistil enclosed in bracts, and grouped in brownish spikelets. Sea Oats should not be disturbed in the wild, as it is illegal to damage it.

MOUNTAIN AND HILLSIDE

Western Springbeauty

Scientific name:	*Claytonia lanceolata*
Family:	Purslane
Flower type:	Radially symmetrical, $\frac{1}{4}$–$\frac{3}{4}$ inch (0.62–1.88cm) in diameter
Flowering period:	April–June
Flower color:	White
Leaf type:	Narrowly lanceolate, succulent
Height:	3–9 inches (8–22cm)
Habitat:	Foothills to high altitudes, commonly near snow banks
Range:	Western North America

A flower of the early spring, Western Springbeauty is a low-growing plant that prefers moist, high altitude ground, particularly near snow level. Its slender, reddish stem has a pair of narrowly lanceolate, succulent, dark green leaves around the halfway point, and ends in a loose raceme cluster of bowl-shaped flowers. The flowers have five petals and two sepals and are white to pink, with paler colors usually streaked with fine, darker pink lines. Western Springbeauty grows from a small, round underground stem that looks like a bulb. This is edible, either raw or cooked like a potato, but since the plant is rather rare it should not be eaten except in an emergency.

White Mountain-avens ▲

Scientific name:	*Dryas octopetala*
Family:	Rose
Flower type:	Radially symmetrical, 1 inch (2.5cm) in diameter
Flowering period:	July–August
Flower color:	White
Leaf type:	Small, lanceolate, scalloped, with edges rolled under
Height:	Creeper, 6 inches (15cm)
Habitat:	Open, rocky ground to above timberline
Range:	North and northwest North America

Although it is a very low-growing plant, White Mountain-avens can spread across quite large areas of ground via its stems, which put out roots where they touch the earth. The leaves are quite small, lanceolate and with scalloped and rolled edges and are arranged alternately. They are dark green in color and the undersides are quite often very hairy. The solitary flower is white, or sometimes a pale creamy-yellow, and is borne at the end of a short, erect stalk. The eight to ten petals are broad and held open in a shallow bowl. There are 18 species in this genus found across North America, all of which prefer the cold or much cooler regions of the continent.

Showy Fleabane; Showy Daisy

Scientific name:	*Erigeron speciosus*
Family:	Aster
Flower type:	Compound flower head, 2 inches (5cm) in diameter
Flowering period:	May–September
Flower color:	White
Leaf type:	Narrowly lanceolate, clasping
Height:	12–32 inches (30–80cm)
Habitat:	Open woodland at medium elevations
Range:	Northwest and western central United States

The large flower heads make Showy Fleabane one of the most attractive of its species. It has a smooth stem, with many long, narrow, lanceolate to ovate leaves on the lower two thirds. The leaves are smooth, but have three noticeable veins and the base curves round to clasp the stem. Towards the top, the stem branches into as many as 12 bare stalks, each of which ends in a large flower head with 75-100 very narrow ray florets around a yellow central disk. The ray florets are usually white in color, but may sometimes be pink or lavender.

Partridgefoot ►

Scientific name:	*Luetkea pectinata*
Family:	Rose
Flower type:	Elongated cluster, 1–2 inches (2.5–5cm) in length
Flowering period:	May–August
Flower color:	White
Leaf type:	Basal, fan-shaped, finely divided
Height:	3–6 inches (8–15cm)
Habitat:	High elevations
Range:	Northwest North America

A tiny plant, Partridgefoot has a dense cluster of deep green basal leaves, which form a thick mat over the ground. They are roughly fan-shaped, but deeply dissected into narrow segments and look rather like a bird's splayed feet – hence the plant's common name. The several flower stalks grow from the mat of leaves, and are reddish in color and mainly bare - although they may have a few small leaves towards the base. The white flowers are borne at the end of each stalk in a dense, elongated cluster, and are open and star-like with five sepals, five petals, five pistils and 20 stamens. There is only one species in this genus found in North America.

Fivespot

▲

Scientific name:	*Nemophila maculata*
Family:	Waterleaf
Flower type:	Radially symmetrical, 1–2 inches (2.5–5cm) in diameter
Flowering period:	April–June
Flower color:	White
Leaf type:	Pinnately lobed
Height:	3–12 inches (8–30cm)
Habitat:	Open hillsides
Range:	West United States

An attractive, low-growing and branching plant, Fivespot has many long, slender stalks with pinnately lobed leaves, which are arranged in opposite pairs on short stalks. The leaves usually have between three and nine lobes, and are smooth and bright green in color. The charming flowers are bowl-shaped, with five wide lobes that are mainly white, but which each have a large, deep purple spot at the tip – hence the common name of Fivespot. Each flower is held at the end of its own long, slender stalk. There are 11 species in this genus found in North America, two in the eastern half of the continent and nine in the west. Fivespot is closely related to Baby Blue Eyes (*N. menziesii*), which has pale blue flowers darkening evenly to deep purple at the tip of the lobes.

Western Pasqueflower; Mountain Pasqueflower

Scientific name:	*Pulsatilla occidentalis (Anemone occidentalis)*
Family:	Buttercup
Flower type:	Radially symmetrical, 1–2 inches (2.5–5cm) in diameter
Flowering period:	May–September
Flower color:	White
Leaf type:	Basal, finely divided; stem, whorled, narrowly segmented
Height:	8–22 inches (20–55cm)
Habitat:	Mountain meadows
Range:	Western North America

The several stems of Western Pasqueflower are surrounded by basal leaves that are deeply divided into very narrow segments. Higher up the stems, whorled round just beneath the flowers, are three smaller, hairy, sessile leaves that are also deeply divided into many narrow segments. The stem is softly hairy, and terminates in a solitary, bowl-shaped flower that has five to seven white or cream petal-like sepals, which are hairy on the back. There are no petals, but a great many stamens, creating the look that is distinctive of pasque flowers. The seeds are each tipped with a long plume that creates a feathery, shaggy, rounded seed head.

Coulter's Matilija Poppy

Scientific name:	*Romneya coulteri*
Family:	Poppy
Flower type:	Radially symmetrical, 6–8 inches (15–20cm) in diameter
Flowering period:	May–August
Flower color:	White
Leaf type:	Deeply pinnately lobed, lobes sometimes toothed
Height:	32–100 inches (80–260cm)
Habitat:	Mountain brushland
Range:	Southern California

A tall leafy plant, Coulter's Matilija Poppy has stout, branching stems with many long, gray-green, deeply pinnately lobed leaves, with the lobes sometimes toothed. The leaves are arranged alternately along the stems, which divide into several stalks near the end, each bearing one white or cream flower. The flowers have three sepals, which drop as the flower opens, and six broad petals around a thick rounded cluster of many feathery stamens and 7-12 stigmas. Coulter's Matilija Poppy grows in large patches, so its showy flowers can create a spectacular effect.

Beargrass; Indian Basket Grass

Scientific name:	*Xerophyllum tenax*
Family:	Lily
Flower type:	Elongated rounded cluster, 4–22 inches (10–55cm) in length
Flowering period:	June–August
Flower color:	White
Leaf type:	Basal, long, linear
Height:	50-60 inches (125-150cm)
Habitat:	Open woods above timberline
Range:	Western North America

Beargrass, as its common name might suggest, has rather grass-like leaves, which are very long and narrow and grow in a tightly packed, massive clump. The stout flower stalks spring from the center of the clump of leaves, bearing many tiny, white flowers in a dense, cylindrical and domed, raceme cluster, which looks a little like a bottle-brush. The individual flowers have six segments in a flat, open star-like shape. The alternative common name of Indian Basket Grass comes from American Indians having traditionally used the leaves to weave into baskets.

Overleaf: An open mountain meadow filled with Beargrass in flower.

Colorado Blue Columbine

Scientific name:	*Aquilegia caerulea (Aquilegia coerulea)*
Family:	Buttercup
Flower type:	Radially symmetrical, 2–3 inches (5–8cm) in diameter
Flowering period:	July–August
Flower color:	Blue
Leaf type:	Compound palmate, leaflets cleft and lobed
Height:	28–34 inches (70–85cm)
Habitat:	Mountains, high altitude aspen woods
Range:	Rocky Mountains from south Montana to New Mexico

Colorado Blue Columbine is a very attractive plant and is Colorado's state flower. It is a bushy perennial with several stems bearing many compound palmate leaves, with the rather rounded leaflets further cleft and lobed. The flowers are large and showy, with five pointed, petal-like sepals on the outside and five curving petals inside, each of which has a long, backward-pointing spur. The sepals are normally sky blue and the petals pale blue to white, with the spur a deeper blue, but since this species has been extensively cultivated and has hybridized with other wildflowers there are many variations on this.

Harebell; Bluebell

Scientific name:	*Campanula rotundifolia*
Family:	Bellflower
Flower type:	Bell-shaped, $\frac{1}{2}$–1 inch (1.25–2.5cm) in length
Flowering period:	July–September
Flower color:	Blue
Leaf type:	Basal orbicular; stem linear, alternate
Height:	6–30 inches (15–75cm)
Habitat:	Open rocky areas at moderate to high elevations
Range:	West and eastern United States, eastern Canada

This pretty wildflower is not confined to North America – it is also found across Europe and Asia. It has a smooth, slender stem with sparse, linear leaves arranged alternately along the stem; the rounded, slightly heart-shaped basal leaves appear quite early in the plant's development and die back before it flowers. The blue to violet-blue flowers are bell-shaped, with five pointed lobes that curve outwards, and they are borne at the end of short stalks at the top of the plant. The blue of the flowers has a deeper intensity in those plants that grow in shade. There are 29 species in this genus found in North America, most of them with blue flowers – although there are some with white.

Explorer's Gentian

Scientific name:	*Gentiana calycosa*
Family:	Gentian
Flower type:	Funnel-shaped, 1–1$\frac{1}{2}$ inches (2.5–3.75cm) in length
Flowering period:	July–September
Flower color:	Blue
Leaf type:	Ovate, opposite, lower sheathing
Height:	3–12 inches (8–30cm)
Habitat:	Meadows at high elevations, along streams
Range:	Western Rocky Mountains

A leafy plant, often with several growing together in a clump, Explorer's Gentian can create an attractive show when it is in flower. The flowers are funnel-shaped and erect, borne at the top of the stems, and are usually bright blue in color – although they may have some greenish streaks. The leaves are ovate and arranged in opposite pairs, with the lower leaves sheathing the stem. Gentians are popular in rock gardens, but they should not be dug up from the wild as many species are quite rare, and it can be difficult to tell them apart. Their roots were once used medicinally as a tonic.

Tall Mountain Shootingstar

Scientific name:	*Dodecatheon jeffreyi*
Family:	Primrose
Flower type:	Radially symmetrical, $\frac{3}{4}$–1 inch (1.88–2.5cm) in length
Flowering period:	June–August
Flower color:	Purple
Leaf type:	Basal rosette, oblanceolate
Height:	15–24 inches (38–60cm)
Habitat:	Wet mountainsides
Range:	Northwest United States

Tall Mountain Shootingstar is very well named, as its flower stalk grows up to 24 inches (60cm) – much higher than that of many of the other shootingstar species. It has a basal rosette of deep green and oblanceolate leaves, which are covered in tiny, glandular hairs. The bare flower stalk springs from the center of the rosette of leaves, and the red-pink to purple flowers are borne in a small to medium cluster, suspended and nodding from the top of the stalk. The four or five petals are swept sharply back and upwards, with the stamens and stigma pointing down, creating the very typical shootingstar flower shape. A perennial, Tall Mountain Shootingstar can form quite large colonies when it is growing in the right conditions.

Baby-blue-eyes ▲

Scientific name:	*Nemophila menziesii*
Family:	Waterleaf
Flower type:	Radially symmetrical, $\frac{1}{2}$–$1\frac{1}{2}$ inches (1.25–3.75cm) in diameter
Flowering period:	April–June
Flower color:	Purple
Leaf type:	Pinnately divided, each segment deeply lobed
Height:	3–12 inches (8–30cm)
Habitat:	Open hillsides
Range:	West United States

Baby-blue-eyes is a low-growing, branching plant, with long, slender stalks bearing many pinnately divided leaves, with each segment deeply lobed. The leaves are arranged in opposite pairs at the end of short stalks. The pretty flowers are bowl-shaped, with five wide lobes that are deep purple at the tip, often fading almost to white at the base and speckled with black. Each flower is held at the end of its own long, slender stalk. Baby-blue-eyes is often cultivated and is regularly included in commercial wildflower seed mixes, so it may also be found outside its area where it has escaped into the wild. Baby blue-eyes is also a common name given to *N. phacelioides*, which has longer, more oval segmented leaves and prefers sandy, open woodland.

Silky Phacelia; Purple Fringe; Alpine Phacelia

Scientific name:	*Phacelia sericea*
Family:	Waterleaf
Flower type:	Elongated cluster, each flower $\frac{1}{4}$ inch (0.62cm) in length
Flowering period:	June–August
Flower color:	Purple
Leaf type:	Pinnately lobed
Height:	14–18 inches (35–45cm)
Habitat:	Rocky ground at high elevations
Range:	West North America

A common wildflower at high altitudes, Silky Phacelia has several erect stems that are densely covered in fine silver-gray hairs. The gray-green leaves are roughly lanceolate in overall shape, but are deeply pinnately lobed and also covered in silver-gray hairs. The leaves are mostly borne towards the base of the stems. The purple flowers are very small, but are thickly clustered in coils around the stalk, producing a tight, cylindrical flower spike, which is given a rather spiky appearance by the numerous stamens that extend outwards. There are around 140 species in this genus found in North America, most of them in the west.

Sky Pilot

Scientific name:	*Polemonium viscosum*
Family:	Phlox
Flower type:	Radially symmetrical, ½–1 inch (1.25–2.5cm) in diameter
Flowering period:	June–August
Flower color:	Purple
Leaf type:	Compound pinnate; leaflets lobed at base, sessile
Height:	2–20 inches (5–50cm)
Habitat:	Open, rocky places at high altitude
Range:	Rocky Mountains

Sky Pilot gets its common name because it thrives at high altitudes above the timberline, and does less well lower in the mountains. It has clumps of stout stems that are covered in sticky, glandular hairs, with long, narrow, sessile, compound pinnate leaves. The leaflets are divided at the base into several lobes, and each leaf is also covered in glandular hairs. All the hairs exude a rather unpleasant, skunk-like smell. The attractive, funnel-shaped flowers are borne at the end of the stem, with several in a very loose corymb cluster. They are most usually purple-blue, but sometimes white or yellow.

Red Ribbons ▲

Scientific name:	*Clarkia concinna*
Family:	Evening-primrose
Flower type:	Rounded cluster, each flower 1–2 inches (2.5–5cm) in diameter
Flowering period:	May–June
Flower color:	Pink
Leaf type:	Broadly elliptical
Height:	8–12 inches (20–30cm)
Habitat:	Shady mountain slopes
Range:	Southwest coastal ranges

Red Ribbons is a low-growing plant with branching stems bearing many broad, elliptical leaves. The rather complex-looking, bright pink flowers have four narrow petals that flare widely towards the tip, where they are deeply divided into three spreading lobes. In Red Ribbons the three lobes are all roughly the same width, but in the taller but otherwise very similar Beautiful Clarkia (*C. pulchella*) the central lobe is noticeably longer and wider than the other two. Beautiful Clarkia grows in more open ground and its range spreads further north.

Rocky Mountain Bee Plant

Scientific name:	*Cleome serrulata*
Family:	Caper
Flower type:	Rounded cluster, each flower $\frac{1}{2}$ inch (1.25cm) in length
Flowering period:	July–September
Flower color:	Pink
Leaf type:	Tripalmate; leaflets long, lanceolate
Height:	9–60 inches (22–150cm)
Habitat:	Mountain foothills, rangelands
Range:	West and south United States

Rocky Mountain Bee Plant is a bushy plant that has several branching stems, each of which bears many alternate tripalmate leaves with long, lanceolate, and dark green leaflets. The lower leaves have short stalks, but the upper leaves are nearly sessile. The stems terminate in loose raceme clusters of flowers that are usually pink to lavender in color – although occasionally they can be white. The flowers have four long, narrow petals and six even longer stamens, so the overall effect of the cluster is of a softly spiky, slightly elongated globe. The sweet nectar attracts many bees, hence the plant's common name. The long seed pods are borne on the end of short stalks, and they are already evident lower down the raceme when the top is still in flower. The seeds are very nourishing, but not very pleasant to eat.

Rock Fringe; Rose Epilobium

Scientific name:	*Epilobium obcordatum*
Family:	Evening-primrose
Flower type:	Radially symmetrical, $\frac{3}{4}$–$1\frac{1}{2}$ inches (1.88–3.75cm) in diameter
Flowering period:	July–October
Flower color:	Pink
Leaf type:	Ovate
Height:	Creeper, 6 inches (15cm)
Habitat:	Mountain meadows at high altitude, rocky slopes
Range:	West United States

Rock Fringe is low-growing, like many alpine plants, mainly to protect it from cold mountain winds in its exposed habitat. Its short, creeping stem has very many blue-green ovate leaves, which are arranged in opposite pairs. The flowers are held at the tip of short stalks that spring from the upper leaf axils. They are quite large in comparison with the rest of the plant, and the four, deep pink petals are heart-shaped. There are around 40 species in this genus found across North America, but most of them grow much taller.

Pink Monkeyflower; Lewis's Monkeyflower

Scientific name:	*Mimulus lewisii*
Family:	Figwort
Flower type:	Irregular with two symmetrical halves, 1–2 inches (2.5–5cm) in length
Flowering period:	June–August
Flower color:	Pink
Leaf type:	Elliptical, toothed, sessile
Height:	14–48 inches (35–120cm)
Habitat:	Damp open ground at high altitude
Range:	Central western North America

Its large, showy flowers and vivid coloring make Pink Monkeyflower one of the most attractive and noticeable of mountain wildflowers. It is quite a tall plant, with many long, ovate, often toothed leaves arranged in opposite pairs along a branching stem. The leaves are sessile and covered in a fine layer of sticky hairs, as is the stem. The flowers are irregular and in two symmetrical halves, with three lobes curving downwards and two curving upwards. They are deep pink to red, with a patch of yellow hairs and darker red fine streaks on the central lower lobe. The bright color of the flowers attracts hummingbirds in the summer season to pollinate the plant.

Moss Campion; Moss Pink

Scientific name:	*Silene acaulis*
Family:	Carnation
Flower type:	Radially symmetrical, $\frac{1}{2}$ inch (1.25cm) in diameter
Flowering period:	July–August
Flower color:	Pink
Leaf type:	Long, narrow, mostly basal
Height:	1–3 inches (5–8cm)
Habitat:	Damp rocky crevices above timberline
Range:	Northern North America

As well as North America, Moss Campion is found across the Northern Hemisphere in cool alpine areas. It is a low-growing, mat-forming plant, with many short stems bearing masses of long, very narrow leaves arranged in opposite pairs, mostly towards the base of the stems. The flowers are held on short stalks just above the dense mat of leaves, and are deep pink, or sometimes lilac, in color. The tubular calyx opens out at the end into five broad lobes that are often notched at the tip. There are around 30 species in this genus found in North America, widely spread across the continent.

Giant Red Paintbrush ▶

Scientific name:	*Castilleja miniata*
Family:	Figwort
Flower type:	Elongated cluster, each flower $\frac{1}{2}$–$1\frac{1}{2}$ inches (1.25–3.75cm) in length
Flowering period:	May–August
Flower color:	Red
Leaf type:	Narrowly lanceolate
Height:	12-38 inches (30-95cm)
Habitat:	Mountain meadows, forest clearings
Range:	Most of northern and western North America

Giant Red Paintbrush gets its common name from its resemblance when it is in flower to a rather ragged paintbrush that has been dipped in bright red paint. It is a tall plant with a single stem bearing many narrowly lanceolate alternate leaves; the upper ones may be smooth or covered in slightly sticky hairs. The stem ends in an elongated rounded cluster of bright crimson, tubular flowers with four pointed lobes, with brightly colored bracts beneath. The bracts are usually red, but may very occasionally be yellow or orange. There are around 109 species in this genus found in North America.

Yellow Columbine

Scientific name:	*Aquilegia flavescens*
Family:	Buttercup
Flower type:	Radially symmetrical, $1\frac{1}{2}$–3 inches (3.75–8cm) in diameter
Flowering period:	June–August
Flower color:	Yellow
Leaf type:	Compound palmate, deeply cleft and lobed
Height:	16–48 inches (40–120cm)
Habitat:	Damp shade
Range:	Western North America

Yellow Columbine is a branching, bushy perennial with compound palmate leaves and very attractive, showy, bright yellow flowers on fairly long stalks. The flower petals have a very long spur that extends backwards, with the tip turned to form a hook, which makes them very distinctive. Although columbines come in a variety of colors including white, red and blue – and the hybridized and cultivated versions offer an even wider range of colors – many of the yellow-flowered varieties are quite rare in the wild.

Glacier Lily; Yellow Fawn-lily ▶

Scientific name:	*Erythronium grandiflorum*
Family:	Lily
Flower type:	Radially symmetrical, 1–2 inches (2.5–5cm) in length
Flowering period:	March–June
Flower color:	Yellow
Leaf type:	Basal, broadly lanceolate
Height:	8–12 inches (20–30cm)
Habitat:	Open mountain forests
Range:	West United States

Glacier Lily has two, broad, lanceolate, basal leaves, which sheath the base of the short bare flower stalk that springs from between them. The stalk often branches towards the top, with a flower suspended from the tip of each branch; there are one to five flowers on each stem. The flowers are yellow, ranging from very pale to deep gold, and each have six petal-like segments that curve strongly backwards to touch the base, with six long stamens dangling down from the center. Modern science has shown that Glacier Lily contains antimutagenic compounds, and other species in the genus have been used medicinally.

Cutleaf Coneflower

Scientific name:	*Rudbeckia laciniata (Rudbeckia ampla)*
Family:	Aster
Flower type:	Compound flower head, 3–6 inches (8–15cm) in diameter
Flowering period:	June–October
Flower color:	Yellow
Leaf type:	Deeply pinnately divided, toothed
Height:	26–120 inches (65–300cm)
Habitat:	Mountain meadows, damp slopes
Range:	Western and across southern North America

Cutleaf Coneflower is a tall and erect plant, with a leafy, branching stem. The leaves are long, and deeply pinnately divided into five to seven lobes, which are further toothed along the edges. The lower leaves are borne on long stalks, while the upper ones are sessile. Each of the stem branches terminates in a solitary large flower head, which has six to ten drooping yellow ray florets arranged aaround a greeny-brown, domed or conical central disk. American Indians made a tea with the roots of this plant, mixed with some others, which was used to relieve indigestion, and the flowers were included in a poultice for burns. However, Cutleaf Coneflower has been found in recent times to be quite toxic to livestock.

Spotted Saxifrage

Scientific name:	*Saxifraga bronchialis (Ciliaria austromontana)*
Family:	Saxifrage
Flower type:	Loose rounded cluster, each flower $\frac{3}{4}$ inch (1.88cm) in diameter
Flowering period:	June–August
Flower color:	Yellow
Leaf type:	Basal, long, narrow, hairy
Height:	4–8 inches (10–20cm)
Habitat:	Rocky slopes at high altitudes
Range:	Northwest North America, Rocky Mountains

A mat-forming plant, Spotted Saxifrage spreads to create small clumps of green on rocky ground at higher altitudes. The leaves are mostly basal, and are small, long and narrow, with stiff hairs along the edges. The several stems also usually have a few, even smaller, alternate leaves arranged at widely spaced intervals along their length. The stems terminate in an open, branching and loose cluster of small yellow or creamy-white flowers, which are spotted inside with purple or dark red. The flowers have five pointed petals, and ten long, and rather spiky stamens. There are around 70 species in this genus found in North America, mainly in cool and cold regions.

Rocky Mountain Goldenrod

Scientific name:	*Solidago multiradiata*
Family:	Aster
Flower type:	Elongated cluster, each flower $\frac{1}{4}$ inch (0.62cm) in length
Flowering period:	June–September
Flower color:	Yellow
Leaf type:	Long, lanceolate, hairy stalks
Height:	4–30 inches (10–75cm)
Habitat:	Alpine areas
Range:	Rocky Mountains, northern North America

Rocky Mountain Goldenrod has several stout, erect stems all clumped together, with many long, lanceolate, alternate leaves, which have bristly hairs along the edges of their stalks. The rather small flower heads are compound, with five to ten tiny yellow rays around a small central disk. They are densely arranged to form a long, narrow cluster. There are around 90 species in this genus, found across North America in a very wide variety of habitats. Narrow Goldenrod (*S. spathulata*) is very similar to Rocky Mountain Goldenrod and is found up to quite high elevations, but has smooth leaf stalks.

American Globeflower;

Scientific name:	*Trollius albiflorus (Trollius laxus ssp. albiflorus)*
Family:	Buttercup
Flower type:	Radially symmetrical, 1–1½ inches (2.5–3.75cm) in diameter
Flowering period:	June–August
Flower color:	White/yellow
Leaf type:	Palmately lobed, irregularly toothed
Height:	6–18 inches (15–45cm)
Habitat:	Wet ground at high altitude
Range:	Rocky Mountains

American Globeflower has one or more leafy stems, the green-yellow leaves deeply palmately divided into five to seven lobes, which are irregularly toothed. Each stem ends in a shallow bowl-shaped white or greenish-cream flower, with five to nine, broad petal-like sepals and many small yellow petals. The petals are shorter than the stamens, so may not be apparent. There are also several cultivated species, which often have more curving sepals to create deeper bowl-shaped flowers. There is also a yellow-flowered version, Yellow Globeflower (*T. laxus* ssp. *laxus*) which is found in the east and is quite rare.

Left: Yellow Globeflower, which is the same as White Globeflower but with yellow flowers.

Northern Mule's Ears

Scientific name:	*Wyethia amplexicaulis*
Family:	Aster
Flower type:	Compound flower head, 3–5 inches (8–12cm) in diameter
Flowering period:	May–August
Flower color:	Yellow
Leaf type:	Long, lanceolate; lower partly sheathing
Height:	12–32 inches (30–80cm)
Habitat:	Hillsides and meadows at moderate elevations
Range:	Central western North America

The stout stems of Northern Mule's Ears spring from a clump of long, broadly lanceolate, deep green leaves on short stalks. The stems have much smaller leaves, the bases of which wrap round to partly sheath the stem. The compound flower heads are made up of 13-21, deep yellow elliptical ray florets, round a flattish, slightly deeper yellow central disk. The disk florets have scales at the base, and long, lanceolate bracts. There may be several flower heads on each plant, of varying sizes. There are 14 species in this genus found in North America, all in the western half of the continent.

WATER PLANTS

Water Plantain ▲

Scientific name:	*Alisma plantago-aquatica*
Family:	Water Plantain
Flower type:	Rounded cluster, each flower $\frac{1}{4}$–$\frac{1}{2}$ inch (0.62–1.25cm) in diameter
Flowering period:	July–August
Flower color:	White
Leaf type:	Ovate, long stalked
Height:	36–50 inches (90–125cm)
Habitat:	Shallow water, marshes
Range:	Most of North America

A rather spindly, branching plant, Water Plantain has long ovate leaves that spring from the base on long stalks – although those underwater may be much narrower. The tiny flowers are white, or sometimes pale pink, and are borne in whorls of four or more at the ends of the branches in open, umbel-like clusters. They have three sepals, three rounded petals and several stamens and pistils in a ring. American Indians made a poultice from the root of Water Plantain to apply to bruises, swellings and wounds, and in Chinese medicine the plant is used as a diuretic. Scientific experiments have shown that it may lower blood pressure and reduce glucose levels in the blood.

Buckbean; Bogbean ▶

Scientific name:	*Menyanthes trifoliata*
Family:	Buckbean
Flower type:	Rounded cluster, each flower $\frac{1}{2}$ inch (1.25cm) in diameter
Flowering period:	May–August
Flower color:	White
Leaf type:	Compound; three broadly oval leaflets
Height:	4–12 inches (10–30cm) above water level
Habitat:	Shallow lakes, bogs
Range:	Northeast and western North America

Buckbean is quite distinctive in its habitat, with long stalks bearing compound leaves divided into three, broadly ovate to lanceolate leaflets. The flowers are open and star-like, either pure white or tinged with purple, with five to six pointed lobes that are heavily fringed or bearded. They are borne at the end of a long, stout stalk in an open raceme cluster. Traditionally, a tea made from the dried leaf or the roots was used as a digestive tonic and for fevers, rheumatism and liver ailments. It is astringent, and can be used to stop bleeding. The leaves are currently used in Germany to treat dyspepsia and loss of appetite, but the fresh plant causes vomiting.

Above: A close-up view of *Menyanthes trifoliata*

Fragrant Water-lily

Scientific name:	*Nymphaea odorata*
Family:	Water-lily
Flower type:	Radially symmetrical, 4–5 inches (10–12cm) in diameter
Flowering period:	June–September
Flower color:	White
Leaf type:	Floating, orbicular
Height:	3–5 inches (8–12cm) above water level
Habitat:	Ponds, very slow-flowing streams
Range:	Most of North America

Fragrant Water-lily has sweet-smelling white flowers, with many pointed petals and numerous bright yellow stamens. The flowers are held just above the surface of water, on stalks that can be as long as 48 inches (120cm), and they only open in the afternoon. The shiny, green, rounded leaves float on the surface of water, and are shiny dark green on the top, and purple-red beneath. American Indians made a tea from the spongy roots to treat coughs, tuberculosis and mouth sores, and a root poultice for swellings. Traditionally a root tea was drunk for chronic diarrhea, but large doses may be toxic.

Arrow Arum

Scientific name:	*Peltandra virginica*
Family:	Arum
Flower type:	Elongated cluster, 3–8 inches (8–20cm) in length
Flowering period:	April–June
Flower color:	White
Leaf type:	Large, arrow-shaped, fleshy, prominent veins
Height:	12–20 inches (30–50cm) above water level
Habitat:	Shallow ponds, swamps, slow-moving streams and waterways
Range:	Eastern North America

The large, arrow-shaped leaves of Arrow Arum are a very common sight in shallow waterways across the eastern half of North America. The leaves are quite fleshy, with rather prominent veining, and are borne on long stalks so they stand erect above the level of the water. In contrast, the flowers are rather inconspicuous – they consist of tiny white to greeny-yellow flowers in a narrow spadix, which is almost concealed by the green to white colored, leaf-like spathe that is wrapped around it. When it is growing in the right conditions, Arrow Arum can quite quickly spread to form very large colonies.

True Watercress

Scientific name:	*Rorippa nasturtium-aquaticum*
Family:	Mustard
Flower type:	Rounded cluster, each flower $\frac{1}{8}$ inch (0.31cm) in diameter
Flowering period:	April–October
Flower color:	White
Leaf type:	Compound, leaflets oval
Height:	6–10 inches (15–25cm) above water level
Habitat:	Streams, cool slow-running water
Range:	Most of temperate North America

True Watercress is a European plant, which was introduced to North America and has become naturalized. It has long stems floating on the surface of the water, bearing compound leaves with 3–9 oval leaflets – the end one larger than those further down. The leaves may be partly or completely submerged. The small, white flowers have four rounded petals, and are borne in a rounded cluster. True Watercress is prized for its leaves, which are high in vitamins A and C, have a spicy flavor and can be added to salads or made into soup. Medicinally, it is used as a blood purifier and for lethargy, rheumatism, bronchitis, scurvy and goiter. However, it must be collected from clean water, as it absorbs toxins and heavy metals.

Grass-leaf Arrowhead

Scientific name:	*Sagittaria graminea*
Family:	Water Plantain
Flower type:	Elongated cluster, each flower $\frac{1}{2}$ inch (1.25cm) in diameter
Flowering period:	March–November
Flower color:	White
Leaf type:	Linear, grass-like
Height:	12–24 inches (30–60cm) above water level
Habitat:	Shallow water
Range:	Central and eastern United States

The long, linear, grass-like leaves of Grass-leaf Arrowhead spring from a submerged rhizome and stand erect above the water level. The spindly flower stalks are long and rise well above the water; they have small, white flowers, which are whorled on short branches. The flowers have three sepals and three broad white petals and the male and female flowers are borne on the same plant; the upper flowers usually have stamens, while the lower ones have pistils. There are more than 30 species in this genus found in North America.

Arrowhead

Scientific name:	*Sagittaria latifolia*
Family:	Water Plantain
Flower type:	Elongated cluster, each flower $\frac{1}{2}$–$1\frac{1}{2}$ inches (1.25–3.75cm) in diameter
Flowering period:	June–September
Flower color:	White
Leaf type:	Basal, arrow-shaped
Height:	12–36 inches (30–90cm) above water level
Habitat:	Shallow water
Range:	Most of United States

Arrowhead has basal, arrow-shaped leaves, with prominent veining, standing erect above the water level and surrounding the tall flower stalks. The small, white flowers are whorled at the ends of short branches, and have three sepals and three broad white petals; some flowers have stamens, while others have many pistils arranged in a sphere. American Indians made the submerged rhizome into a tea to treat indigestion, and into a poultice for wounds and sores. Early settlers cooked and ate the roots like a potato, and called it Duck Potato.

LIZARD'S-TAIL

Scientific name:	*Saururus cernuus*
Family:	Lizard's-tail
Flower type:	Elongated cluster, 5–12 inches (12–30cm) in length
Flowering period:	May–September
Flower color:	White
Leaf type:	Long, cordate
Height:	24–60 inches (60–150cm)
Habitat:	Shallow water
Range:	Southeastern United States

The unusual common name of Lizard's-tail comes from the long, wavy, drooping flower cluster on this attractive perennial. It is a medium-size plant, with elongated, heart-shaped leaves on long stalks, which spring from branching stems growing from a stout rhizome. The tiny white flowers are very sweetly scented, and are arranged in a long, slender, tapering spike that waves and droops at the tip. American Indians made a poultice of the roots to apply to wounds and inflammations, while a tea made from the whole plant was used as a wash for general illness and rheumatism. Scientific research has shown that the plant has compounds with sedative properties. Lizard's-tail spreads easily and can form quite large colonies.

Water Hyacinth

Scientific name:	*Eichhornia crassipes*
Family:	Pickerelweed
Flower type:	Elongated cluster, each flower 2 inches (5cm) in length
Flowering period:	May–September
Flower color:	Blue
Leaf type:	Roundly ovate or reniform
Height:	6–16 inches (15–40cm) above water level
Habitat:	Lakes, streams, swamps
Range:	Southeast United States

Water Hyacinth is a tropical plant that was introduced to North America from South America and is now naturalized in warmer areas in the south. Any found further north are likely to be discarded aquarium plants. It has bright green, roundly ovate or kidney-shaped leaves, the stalks of which often have inflated bulbs acting as floats. The attractive blue to lavender flowers are funnel-shaped and borne in a showy spike. They have six lobes – the upper one is larger than the others and has a bright yellow spot in the center. Water Hyacinth is found around the world, and is often considered to be a weed if it clogs waterways, but it is also useful to remove excessive nutrients and toxins from polluted water.

Pickerelweed

Scientific name: *Pontederia cordata*
Family: Pickerelweed
Flower type: Elongated cluster, each flowerr $\frac{1}{2}$ inch (1.25cm) in length
Flowering period: July–November
Flower color: Purple
Leaf type: Basal, cordate
Height: 12–24 inches (30–60cm) above water level
Habitat: Freshwater marshes, shallow edges of ponds and lakes
Range: Eastern North America

Pickerelweed is a stout plant with a submerged rhizome, and creeping stems that allow it to spread quickly. It has basal, heart-shaped, smooth green leaves on long stems that extend up above the water level. The flower spikes are on long stalks, and are made up of many purple to blue, funnel-shaped flowers, thickly clustered in an elongated, rounded cone. The flower has two lips, with the lower lip in three parts and the upper divided into three lobes; the central lobe has two yellow spots. The young leaves of Pickerelweed can be added to salads, or cooked as a pot herb.

Swamp Loosestrife; Water Willow

Scientific name:	*Decodon verticillatus*
Family:	Loosestrife
Flower type:	Cluster, each flower $\frac{1}{2}$ inch (1.25cm) in length
Flowering period:	July–August
Flower color:	Pink
Leaf type:	Long, lanceolate, whorled
Height:	24–96 inches (60–250cm)
Habitat:	Shallow water, swamps, bogs
Range:	Eastern North America

Swamp Loosestrife has many arching, intertwining, and woody stems, and can form large colonies at the edges of areas of water. The leaves are long, narrowly lanceolate and willow-like – hence the alternative common name of Water Willow. They are sometimes whorled around the stem in groups of three or four, sometimes arranged in opposite pairs. The pink flowers are bell-shaped, with five short stamens and five, very long, protruding stamens, giving them a rather spiky appearance. They are borne in tufts in the axils of the upper leaves.

Sweetflag ▼

Scientific name:	*Acorus calamus*
Family:	Sweetflag
Flower type:	Spike, each flower $\frac{1}{8}$ inch (0.31cm) in length
Flowering period:	May–August
Flower color:	Yellow
Leaf type:	Long, linear, parallel-veined
Height:	12–50 inches (30–125cm)
Habitat:	Streams, swamps, marshes, along rivers
Range:	Most of North America

Sweetflag grows in water, or very wet soil. It has long, narrow, linear leaves that are parallel-veined and spring from a thick rhizome. The unusual flower spike is made up of many densely clustered yellow flowers arranged to form a diamond pattern. The spike sticks out at an angle around halfway up a stalk that otherwise looks like another leaf. The young rhizomes can be eaten raw or added to salads, and are also sometimes candied – although they have a pungent flavor. American Indians ate the root for stomach problems and as a stimulant on long journeys. There are two species in North America, one native and the other introduced from Eurasia, but they are almost impossible to tell apart, to the extent that some authorities class them as the same species.

Water Arum; Wild Calla

Scientific name:	*Calla palustris*
Family:	Arum
Flower type:	Spike, 1 inch (2.5cm) in length
Flowering period:	June–August
Flower color:	Yellow
Leaf type:	Cordate, long
Height:	6–12 inches (15–30cm)
Habitat:	Cool wetlands, pond edges
Range:	Northern and northeast North America

A perennial plant, Water Arum grows in water or in the very wet, boggy areas around it. It has many comparatively large, glossy, dark green, heart-shaped leaves that are borne on long stalks. The flower consists of a spadix of tiny yellow flowers, surrounded by a broad white spathe. It is on a long stalk, which extends roughly horizontally outwards so the flower is held just above water level. American Indians made a tea from the dried roots to treat flu, shortness of breath and bleeding, and a root poultice for swellings and snakebites. However the raw plant can irritate the skin and internal mucous membranes. Water Arum is also found in the northern regions of Europe and Asia.

Fringed Loosestrife ▼

Scientific name:	*Lysimachia ciliata*
Family:	Primrose
Flower type:	Radially symmetrical, $\frac{3}{4}$ inch (1.88cm) in diameter
Flowering period:	June–August
Flower color:	Yellow
Leaf type:	Long, ovate, opposite
Height:	4–48 inches (10–120cm)
Habitat:	Shallow ponds, edges of streams
Range:	Most of the United States and southern Canada

The erect stem of Fringed Loosestrife is sometimes branched, and sometimes single. It bears long, lanceolate to ovate leaves in opposite pairs, with the leafstalks having a fringe of hairs – hence the plant's common name. The yellow flowers have five broad petals that have tiny teeth at the tip, with a sharp central point. They are solitary and borne at the end of short stalks that spring from the leaf axils; they usually point outwards, although they can also be seen hanging down. There are 16 species in this genus found across North America, some native and some naturalized from Europe.

YELLOW LOTUS; AMERICAN LOTUS

Scientific name:	*Nelumbo lutea*
Family:	Lotus
Flower type:	Radially symmetrical, 6–10 inches (15–25cm) in diameter
Flowering period:	July–September
Flower color:	Yellow
Leaf type:	Floating, round, flat; erect, bowl-shaped
Height:	6–36 inches (15–90cm) above water level
Habitat:	Ponds, slow-flowing streams
Range:	Ontario, eastern United States

Even when it is not in flower, Yellow Lotus can be recognized by its round floating leaves, which are attached to the leafstalk in the center with the veins radiating outwards. The leaves held above the water do not open out flat, but stay in a bowl shape. The flowers are bright yellow and fragrant, with many pointed petals and petal-like sepals. In the center of the stamens is a large, rather strange-looking, upside-down cone-shape with many small holes, each of which holds a pistil. This develops into the seed receptacle, which is held clear of the water. The young leaves and stalks of Yellow Lotus can be used as a pot herb, while the seeds can be eaten raw, roasted or boiled. Mature seeds can be eaten like nuts, or ground into flour and used in baking recipes. The tubers can be cooked and eaten in the same way as sweet potatoes.

Yellow Pond-lily; Indian Pond Lily; Spatterdock

Scientific name:	*Nuphar lutea*
Family:	Water-lily
Flower type:	Radially symmetrical, 2–4 inches (5–10cm) in diameter
Flowering period:	May–September
Flower color:	Yellow
Leaf type:	Floating, cordate
Height:	1–6 inches (2.5–15cm) above water level
Habitat:	Ponds, slow-flowing streams
Range:	Western North America

Yellow Pond-lily has heart-shaped leaves with rounded ends, which are borne on very long stalks from stems under the mud, so they float on the surface of water. The flowers are bright yellow and bowl-shaped, with up to nine petal-like sepals and small, narrow inconspicuous petals that may not be noticed among the stamens. American Indians made a tea from the roots to treat blood diseases, heart trouble and chills with fever, and a poultice for swellings, boils and wounds. The rhizome was also a folk remedy for impotence, but large doses are potentially toxic.

Yellow Water-lily; Mexican Water-lily

Scientific name:	*Nymphaea mexicana*
Family:	Water-lily
Flower type:	Radially symmetrical, 4–5 inches (10–12cm) in diameter
Flowering period:	May–September
Flower color:	Yellow
Leaf type:	Floating, orbicular
Height:	3–5 inches (8–12cm) above water level
Habitat:	Ponds, very slow-flowing streams
Range:	Southeast and parts of west North America

The rounded leaves of Yellow Water-lily float on the surface of water, except when many plants are crowded together, in which case they may be held above it. They are dark green with some brown blotches on the top, and a more red-brown beneath, with some darker spots. The flowers are bright yellow, with many pointed petals and numerous stamens. The flowers are held above the surface of water on long stalks, and they open in the afternoon. The tubers of Yellow Water-lily can be cooked and eaten in the same way as sweet potatoes.

Golden Club Arum

Scientific name:	*Orontium aquaticum*
Family:	Arum
Flower type:	Spike, 1–2 inches (2.5–5cm) in length
Flowering period:	April–June
Flower color:	Yellow
Leaf type:	Long, elliptical to oblong, floating or more erect
Height:	12–24 inches (30–60cm) above water level
Habitat:	Shallow, still water
Range:	Southeast United States

A rather attractive perennial, Golden Club Arum has long, elliptical to oblong, dark-green leaves on long stalks that normally float on the surface of the water – or sometimes lie just above it. The flower is a long spadix with a compact cluster of golden yellow flowers, borne at the top of a thick white stalk; the spathe is not developed, so it appears as a tubular leaf at the base of the flower stalk. There is only one species in this genus found in North America, but it is quite common in the swamps of the south.

Floating Bladderwort ▲

Scientific name:	*Utricularia inflata*
Family:	Bladderwort
Flower type:	Rounded cluster, each flower $\frac{3}{4}$ inch (1.88cm) in diameter
Flowering period:	May–October
Flower color:	Yellow
Leaf type:	Submerged threadlike; basal whorled, inflated
Height:	1–8 inches (2.5–20cm) above water level
Habitat:	Ponds and ditches
Range:	Southeastern United States

Swollen Bladderwort is a carnivorous plant, with underwater bladders that catch unwary crustaceans to supplement its nutrients. It has a basal whorl of three to eight leaves, with the part nearest the stem inflated to create a float and the tips divided into many threadlike segments. Underwater the leaves are also divided into threadlike segments bearing the bladders, which have a flap-like opening surrounded by trigger hairs. The yellow flowers are held at the end of a short flower stalk in a raceme, with 6 to 17 flowers in each cluster.

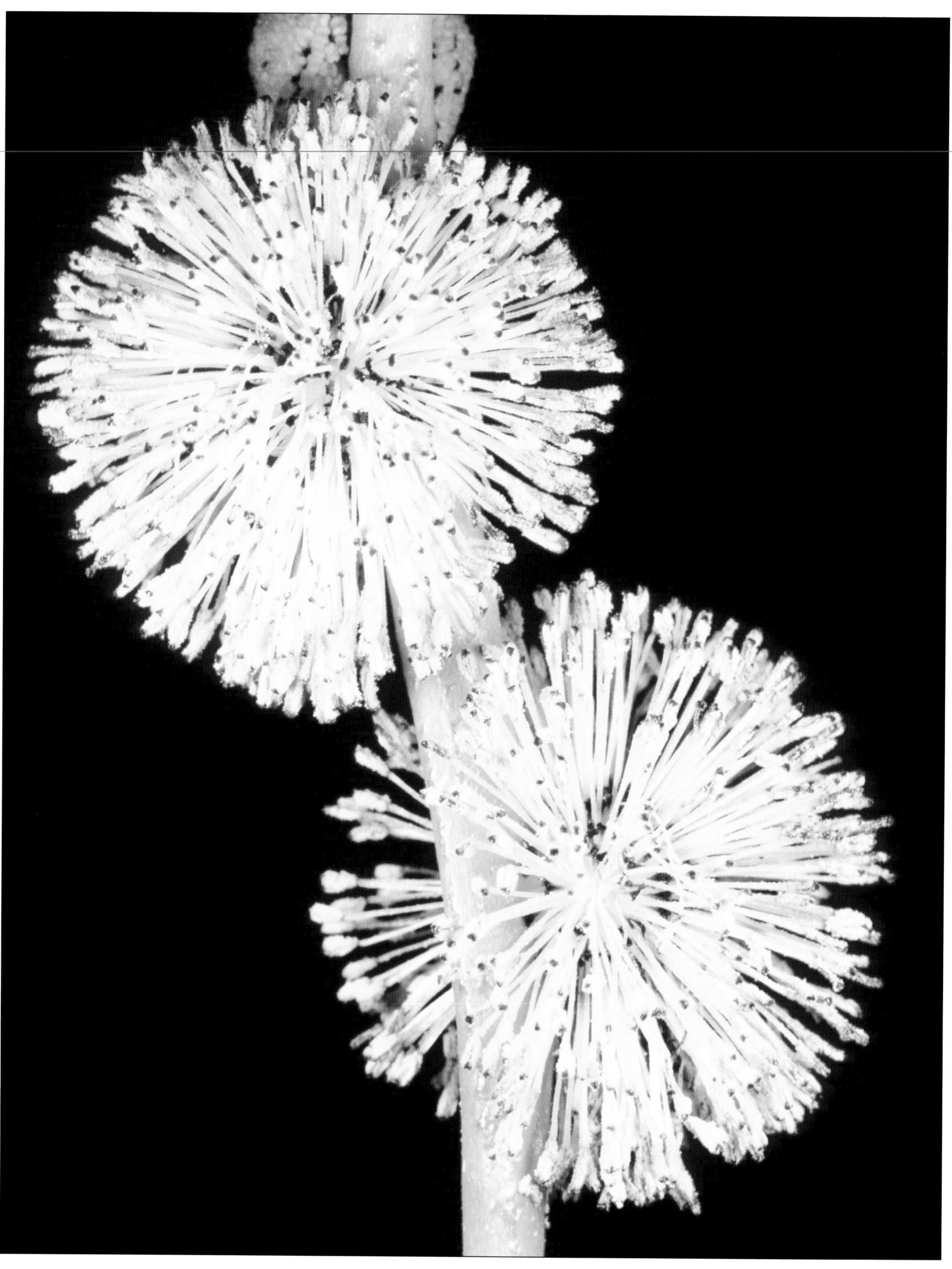

American Bur-reed

Scientific name:	*Sparganium americanum*
Family:	Bur-reed
Flower type:	Spherical cluster, 1 inch (2.5cm) in diameter
Flowering period:	May–August
Flower color:	Green
Leaf type:	Linear, grass-like
Height:	12–38 inches (30–95cm)
Habitat:	Shallow water, muddy water edges
Range:	Eastern North America

Bur-reed is an erect plant, with long, linear, grass-like leaves that spring from an underground rhizome. The leaves are often up to 36 inches (90cm) long, but are often partly submerged. The small, spherical flower heads are made up of tiny green flowers, which have scales instead of petals and sepals, and are borne at intervals along zig-zag stalks. Bur-reed is a plant that prefers to be half in and half out of the water, and it forms dense colonies along the edges of streams, lakes and ponds. Great Bur-weed (*S. eurycarpum*) is very similar in appearance, but often reaches a height of up to 84 inches (210cm).

Broadleaf Cattail; Common Cattail ▶

Scientific name:	*Typha latifolia*
Family:	Cattail
Flower type:	Elongated cluster, 6 inches (15cm) in length
Flowering period:	May–July
Flower color:	Brown
Leaf type:	Long, linear; sheathing
Height:	36–100 inches (90–260cm)
Habitat:	Shallow water, freshwater marshes
Range:	Most of North America, except Arctic

There is only one genus in this family, with ten species that are found all round the world. Broadleaf Cattail is a tall plant, with long, stiff, linear leaves that sheath the stem. The slender flower spike is made up of tiny yellowish male flowers at the top, with brown female flowers beneath. The flowers have bristles instead of sepals and petals; the female flowers have one pistil and the male three stamens. American Indians made a poultice from the roots to apply to wounds, sores and burns, and the fuzz from the female flowerhead was used to prevent chafing in babies. Broadleaf Cattail spreads quickly via creeping roots, and creates a good habitat for wildlife, but it may be poisonous to grazing animals.

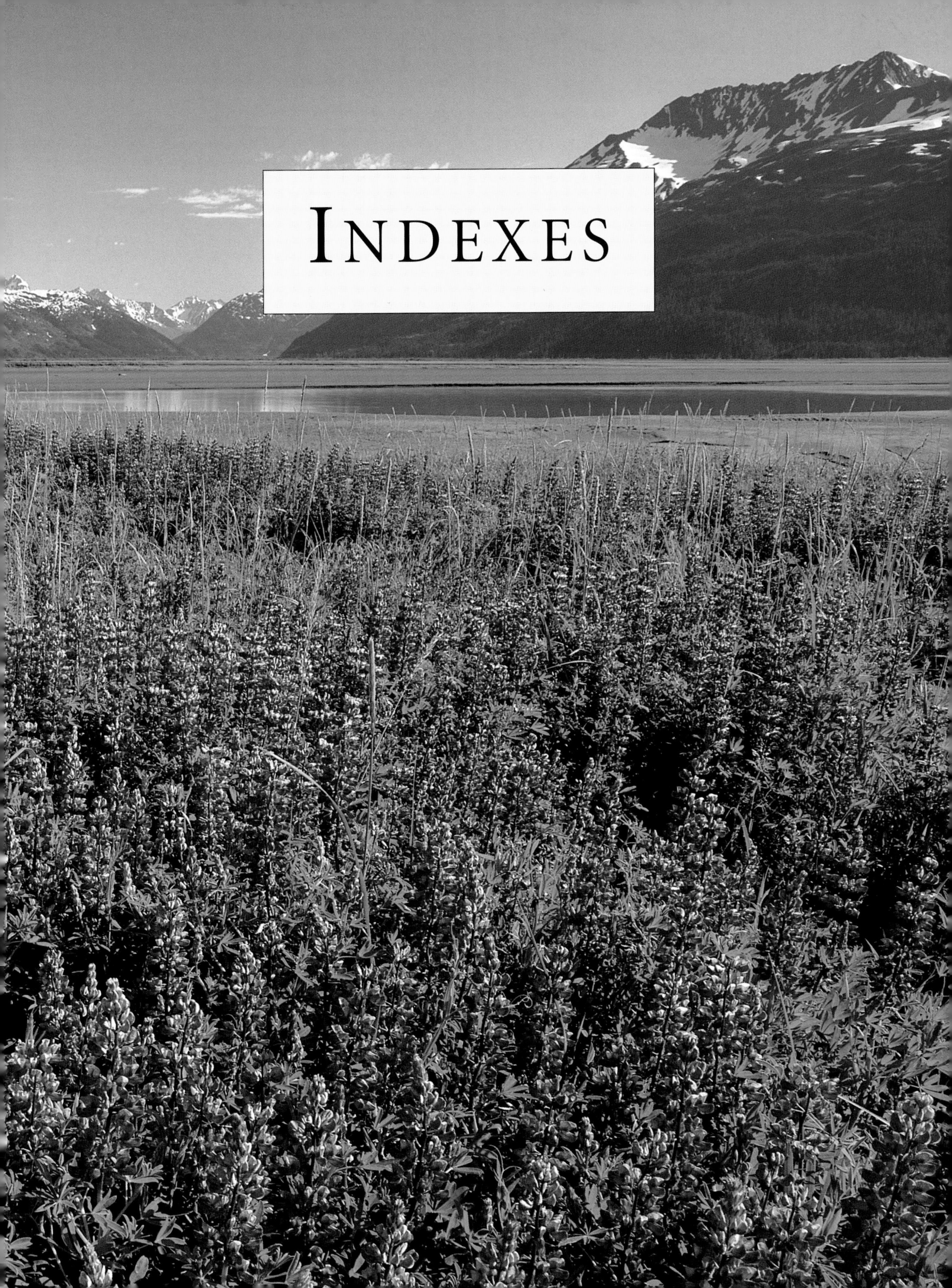

INDEXES

Index to Common Names

Index of Scientific Names

Picture Credits

All photograph are courtesy of Oxford Scientific Films and Animals Animals.

Abronia villosa Stan Osolinski *Achillea millefolium* Geoff Kidd *Achyls triphylla* Osf *Acorus Calamus* Harry Fox *Actea pachypoda* Deni Bown *Actea spicata* Deni Bown *Actonitum columbianum* Patti Murray/ AA *Agrostemma githago* Peter Clark/SAL *Aletris aurea (aletris farinosa)* C.C. Lockwood/AA *Alisma plantago-aquatica* Deni Bown *Alisma plantago-aquatica* Terry Heathcote *Allium Canadensis* Bill Beaty/AA *Allium Cernuum* John Lemker/AA *Allium Tricroccum* Ken Cole /AA *Amsonia tabernentana* Deni Bown *Anagallis arvensis* (inside and back cover) Bob Gibbons *Anaphalis margaritacea* David Fox *Anemonella thalictictrodes* Michael Gadomski/AA *Anemopsis californica* Stephen Ingram/ AA *Apocynum cannabinum* Deni Bown *Aquilegia Canadensis* Richard Kolar/AA *Aquilegia chrysantha* Mills Tandy *Aquilegia coerulea* Breck P. Kent/AA *Aquilegia flavenscens* Breck P. Kent/AA *Aquilegia Formosa* Mills Tandy *Aralia nudicaulis* Deni Bown *Aralia racemosa* Deni Bown *Arbronia villosa* (scene) Adam Jones *Arisaema triphyllum* Perry D. Slocum/AA *Armeria maritime* Richard Shiell/AA *Arnica cordifolia* Patti Murray/ AA Aruncus Sylvester. Gordon Maclean Asarum canadense Richard Kolar/AA *Asarum caudatum* osf *Asclepia Speciosa* Perry D. Slocum/AA *Asclepias incarnata* Deni Bown *Asclepias syriaca* (seedhead) Richard Kolar/AA *Asclepias syrlaca* John Gerlach/AA *Asclepias tuberosa* (double page) David M. Dennis *Asclepias tuberosa* Mills Tandy *Aster novae–angliae* Adam Jones *Aster novi-belgii* David Cayless *Baileya multiradiata* Michael Fogden *Balamorhyia sagitta* Daniel Cox *Balsamorhiza sagittara* osf *Baptisia alba* Maressa Pryor/AA *Baptista australis* Richard Shiell/AA *Berlandiera lyrata* Richard Shiell/AA *Brassica nigra* E.R. Degginger/AA *Brodiaea Elegans* Jack Wilburn/AA *C. purpurea & L. Texensis* Mills Tandy *Calachortus Nutallii* (detail) Jack Wilburn/AA *Calachortus Nutallii* (whole plant) David Welling /AA California poppies W. Shattil & Bob Rozinski *Calochortus Macrocarpus* (inside and back cover) Patti Murray/AA *Caltha palustris* osf *Camassia scilloides* Jeffrey Bergdoll/AA Camissonia *cheiranthifolia* Richard Shiell/AA *Campanula rotundifolia* Niall Benvie *Capsella bursa pastoris* Geoff Kidd *Castijella exserta/ Orthocarpus purpuracens* (view) Mickey Gibson/AA *Castijella exserta/ Orthocarpus purpuracens*(detail) Nancy Rotenberg/AA *Castilleja coccinea* Charles Palek/AA *Castilleja exserta* Jim Steinberg/AA *Castilleja indivisa* (pages 174/5) Adam Jones *Castilleja miniata* Stan Osolinski *Castilleja miniata* (view) Tom Leach *Caulophyllum thalictroides* Bill Beaty/AA *Caulophyllum thalictroides* Robert A. Lubeck *Chelone glabra* Richard Kolar/ AA *Chicorium intybus* (inside and front cover) Berndt Fischer *Chimaphila maculata* John Lemker /AA *Chimaphila umbellate* Tom Leach *Chrysanthemum leucanthemum* Mike Hill *Chrysanthemum leucanthemum* C.C. Lockwood/AA *Chrysogonum virginanum* C. C. Lockwood/AA *Cichorium intybus* Anthony Nyssen/SAL *Clarkia concinna* Gordon Maclean *Clarkia omoena* Deni Bown *Claytonia caroliniana* Michael Gadomski/ AA *Clematis hirssutissima* Waina Cheng *serrulata* E. R. Degginger *Clintonia andrewsiana* David Welling /AA *Clintonia borealis* Ted Levin/AA *Clintonia umbellelata* Richard Kolar/AA *Clintonia uniflora* Jack Wilburn/AA Coastal Flowers (pages 304/5) Waina Cheng *Collinisa Heterophylla* Jack Wilburn /AA *Commelina Erecta* John Anderson/AA *Conium maculatum* Gordon Maclean *Convolvulus cneorum (Ipomoea liptophylla)* Richard Shiell *Corallorhiza maculata* Tom Leach *Corallorhiza striata* John Gerlach/AA *Coreopsis lanceolata* Mills Tandy *Coreopsis tinctoria* Bob Gibbons *Cornus Canadensis* John Lemker/AA *Crinum americanum* Jack Wilburn/ AA *Daucus Carota* M.W. Endler *Delphinium Cardinale* Richard Shiell/AA *Delphinium nudicaule* Jack Wilburn /AA *Delphinium nuttallianum* R&E Thane/AA *Delphinium tricorne* Richard Kolar/AA *Dentaria laciniata* Patti Murray/ AA *Dianthus armeria* Richard Kolar/AA *Diathnus armeria* Bob Gibbons *Dicentra Canadensis* David M. Dennis *Dicentra cucullaria* John Mitchell *Dicentra eximia* John Gerlach/AA *Dipsacus fullonum* (inside and front cover) Jack Wilburn/AA *Dipsacus fullonum* osf *Dodecatheon amethystinum* Joe McDonald/AA *Dodecatheon jeffreyi* John Gerlach/AA *Dodecatheon media* Gordon MacLean *Dodecatheon* sp (page 8) John Cooke *Drosera filliformis* Patti Murray *Drosera rotundifolia* osf *Dryas octopetala* Frank Huber *Dudleya Cymosa* Jim Steinberg/AA *Dudleya farinose* Deni Bown *Echinacea purpurea* Deni Bown *Eichhornia crassipes* (single flower) Joyce and Frank Burek/Earth Sciences *Eichhornia crassipes* (three blooms) E.R. Digginger *Eichhornia crassipes* (pages 352/3) C. C. Lockwood/Earth Sciences *Epilobium obcordatum* Jack Wilburn/AA *Erigeron divergens* John Lemker/AA *Erigeron glaucus* Geoff Kidd *Erigeron philadelphicus* Marcia W. Griffen *Erigonum inflatum* Waina Cheng *Eriogonum umbellatum* OSF *Erodium texanum* Mills Tandy *Eryngium yuccifolium* Deni Bown *Erysimum Capitatum* Patti Murray /AA *Erysimum Capitatum* (under rock) George H. H. Huey/ AA *Erythronium albidum* Richard Shiell *Erythronium americanum* Richard Kolar *Erythronium grandiflorum* Stan Osolinski *Eschscholzia californica Adam Jones (page 14)* *Eschscholzia californica* Carroll W. Perkins/AA *Eschscholzia californica* with fiddleneck Wendy Shattil and Bob Rozinski *Eschscholzia mexicana* OSF *Eupatorium fistulosum* Donald Specker/AA *Eupatorium maculatum* John Lemker/AA *Europhorbia Marginata* Richard Shiell/AA *Eustoma grandiflorum* Mills Tandy *Euthamia graminifolia* Patti Murray/Earth Siences *Filipendula rubra* John Lemker/AA *Fraganaria chiloensis* Jack Wilburn/Earth Sciences *Fragaria virginiana* Prof Jack Dermid *Fritillaria camschatcensis* Frank Huber *Fritillaria lancealata* Bruce McDonald/AA *Fritillaria pudica* Harry Engels/AA *Fritillaria recurva* Dr Raymond Parks *Galium noreale* Scott Smith/AA *Gaillardia pulchella* Prof Jack Dermid *Gentian andrewsii* Richard Kolar/AA *Gentian calycosa* Alan Nelson/AA *Gentian saponaria* Perry D. Slocum/AA *Gentiana Clausa* John Gerlach/AA *Gentiana crinita* Richard Kolar/AA *Geranium carolinianum* Richard Shiell *Geranium maculatum* John Cooke *Geranium viscosissimum* Stan Osolinski *Geum triflorum* Stan Osolinski *Glaux maritime* Harry Fox *Grindel squarrosa* Charles Palek/AA *Gutierrezia sarothrae* J&M Monkman/AA *Helenium autumnale* Gordon Maclean *Helianthus* (page 12) Richard Herrmann *Helianthus annuus* Deni Bown *Helianthus giganteus* Robert Lubeck/ AA *Helianthus maximiliana* Ted Levin/AA *Helianthus Tuberasus* Michael Gadomski/AA *Hepatica Acutiloba* Robert Lubeck /AA *Hepatica Americana* Robert Lubeck/AA *Hepatica Americana* Joe McDonald/AA *Hesperocallis undulata* Stan Osolinksi *Hibiscus coultteri* Caroline Brett *Hibiscus moscheutos* Deni Bown *Houstonia caerulea* Bill Beaty/AA *Hydrastis Canadensis* Bill Beaty/AA *Hydrophyllum canadense* John Lemker/AA *Hypericum perforatum* Richard Kolar/AA

Bibliography

William A. Niering & Nancy C. Olmstead, *National Audubon Society Field Guide to Wildflowers Eastern Region*, Revised John W. Thieret (Knopf, New York, revised edition 2001)

Richard Spellenberg, *National Audubon Society Field Guide to Wildflowers Western Region*, (Knopf, New York, revised edition 2001)

Fenton R Vance, James R Jowsey, James S. McLean, Francis A. Switzer, *Wildflowers Across the Prairies* (Greystone Book, Vancouver, 1999)

Frank D, Venning, *Wildflowers of North America* (St. Martin's Press, New York, 1984)

Lawrence Newcomb, *Wildflower Guide* (Little, Brown & Company, New York, 1977)

Thomas S. Elias, Peter A. Dykeman, *Edible Wild Plants - A North American Field Guide* (Sterling, New York, 1990)

Steven Foster, James A. Duke, *A Field Guide to Medicinal Plants and Herbs of Eastern and Central North America* (Houghton Mifflin, New York, 2000)

Roger Tory Peterson, *Wildflowers of Northeastern and North-central North America* (Houghton Mifflin, New York, 1986)

Herbert S. Zim, Alexander C. Martin, *Wildflowers A Guide to Familiar American Flowers* (St. Martin's Press, New York, 2002)

Jack Sanders, *The Secrets of Wildflowers* (Lyons Press, Guilford, 2003)

Acknowledgements

This book would not have been possible without the help of Ruth Blair and all the research staff at Oxford Scientific Films and Animals Animals in New York. Thanks also to Marie Clayton, Judy Linard, Kate Truman, Vicki Harris, Jill Dormon, Joan Clayton and Paul Pang.